W9-CXO-634

Satisfaction *Not* Guaranteed

Satisfaction *Not* Guaranteed

Dilemmas of Progress in Modern Society

Peter N. Stearns

NEW YORK UNIVERSITY PRESS

New York and London

NEW YORK UNIVERSITY PRESS
New York and London
www.nyupress.org

References to Internet websites (URLs) were accurate at the time of writing.
Neither the author nor New York University Press is responsible for URLs
that may have expired or changed since the manuscript was prepared.

Library of Congress Cataloging-in-Publication Data

Stearns, Peter N.
Satisfaction not guaranteed : dilemmas of progress in modern society /
Peter N. Stearns.
p. cm.
Includes bibliographical references and index.
ISBN 978-0-8147-8362-7 (cl : alk. paper)
ISBN 978-0-8147-8363-4 (ebook)
ISBN 978-0-8147-8855-4 (ebook)
1. Civilization, Modern — 21st century. 2. Progress. I. Title.
CB430.S74 2012
909.83 — dc23
2011045365

New York University Press books are printed on acid-free paper,
and their binding materials are chosen for strength and durability.
We strive to use environmentally responsible suppliers and
materials to the greatest extent possible in publishing our books.

Manufactured in the United States of America

10 9 8 7 6 5 4 3 2 1

To Donna, and the happiness we share

Contents

Acknowledgments   ix

1   Introduction: Being Cheerful and Modern   1

PART I.   The Modern and the Happy: A Tenuous Embrace   13

2   The Gap: Happiness Scales and the Edge of Sadness   15

3   Component Parts: Modernity and Ideas of   29
     Happiness and Progress as Historical Forces

PART II.   Maladjustments in Modernity   59

4   Modernity's Deficiencies   61

5   False Starts and Surprises: 69
     Making Modernity More Difficult

6   The Dilemmas of Work in Modernity   111

PART III. Great Expectations   129

7   Death as a Modern Quandary   131

8   Century of the Child?   169
     Childhood, Parenting, and Modernity

9   Born to Shop: Consumerism as the Modern Panacea   213

     Conclusion: Shaping Modernity   255

     Notes   261

     Index   265

     About the Author   270

Acknowledgments

M y gratitude to Sam Asin for indispensable assistance with research. Thanks to Clio Stearns not only for help with research but for valuable readings of the book as well. Gratitude to Deborah Stearns for guidance in the happiness literature along with her constructive readings of the book. Laura Bell went well beyond tending to manuscript preparation. I appreciate the encouragement and guidance from Deborah Gershenowitz at New York University Press; from the anonymous referees; and from Rick Balkin.

⁄⁄ 1 ⁄⁄

Introduction

Being Cheerful and Modern

The vision of what modern society might be emerged more than two centuries ago, as a product of a transformation in Western philosophy and a new belief in the way material progress and human improvability might combine. It was in the 1790s that the French philosopher Nicolas de Condorcet wrote that he had "no doubt as to the certainty of the future improvements we can expect. . . . Everything tells us that we are bordering the period of one of the greatest revolutions of the human race. The present state of enlightenment guarantees that it will be happy."[1]

Students of intellectual history might quickly add, at this point, that Condorcet was unusual in his optimism. They might cynically note that the fact that he could write his *Outlines of an Historical View of the Progress of the Human Mind* while in hiding from French revolutionary radicals who sought to jail him (he later was arrested and committed suicide) suggests a clear problem in facing reality, and they might then turn to more complex Enlightenment theorists or to the surge of greater philosophical pessimism that would arise in later decades.

But the fact is that much of what Condorcet anticipated has actually happened. Agriculture has become vastly more productive, supporting larger populations. Machines have reduced physical labor. Education has spread. More parents are explicitly concerned about making their children happy. Diseases have receded in modern societies, greatly expanding life spans. And it's fair to note that while Condorcet was unusual, he was not alone. In 1788 Benjamin Franklin himself wrote of the "growing Felicity of Mankind" resulting from improvements in technology, science, and medicine, and wished he could have been born two or three centuries later to see how all this progress would turn out.

Again, the vision was surprisingly accurate—save for two points. It did not cover the entire future of modern society, and it anticipated far more satisfaction from the gains that would occur than has turned out to be the case. This book, focusing on the second point, deals with the surprising double-sidedness of modern achievements. It explores the gulf between measurable advances and perceived happiness, and it probes the struggles people still face with many arguably beneficial results of modernity. Of course we'll touch on the obvious misfires of modernity as well—for example, the increasing horror of modern warfare—but the main target is the satisfaction shortfall.

The basic point is straightforward, though underexplored to date. Even the gains modernity generated brought problems in their wake. Gains also prompted a rapid escalation of expectations that masked progress and brought their own dissatisfaction. And the whole process was complicated by modern claims about the new accessibility of happiness itself. The work of adjustment to modernity continues—we're not that far from a number of basic transformations—and the opportunity for more successful adaptations continues as well. Exploring the gaps between hopes and gains, interesting in itself, assumes even greater importance when it can inform a reevaluation process.

Sweeping optimism about modernity's potential has not entirely vanished. American politicians recurrently if vaguely invoke it—"yes we can"—and society at large sometimes manifests startling hopes about what more technology or more medicine might do in the future. And we'll see in a moment how Enlightenment optimism surfaces almost perversely in the modern need to seem cheerful. But even as we continue to enjoy some of modernity's obvious advantages, we fall short of the kind of happiness the visionaries had predicted. (It's worth noting that the other great optimistic vision of modernity, Marxism, has also run aground.) Indeed, we're as likely to project satisfaction backward in time as to ponder how far we have come. Thus the *Good Old Days* magazine, without making a systematic claim about current conditions, offers its readers "warm thoughts of the happy days gone by," looking variously to the late 19th century, the 1920s, or the 1950s. Similarly, the popular slogan "back in the day," though offering various meanings, connotes a simpler life in the past (sometimes in one's own life span, sometimes more historically), despite constituting an incomplete thought with no clear meaning at all.

Often, the whole idea of a cozier past is just a matter of passing rhetoric, or a brief longing for (highly selective) memories of one's own childhood. But nostalgia can pack more serious meaning as well. The current American penchant for big, traditionally designed houses or Martha Stewart "country chic" ware suggests a desire to surround oneself with an aura of the past—often on the part of people who are in fact working too hard to spend much time at home sinking back into their reminiscent trappings. French bookstores note a surge of interest in glamorized accounts of peasant life on the part of resolutely urban Parisians. And for many years, in France, the United States, and elsewhere, the purpose of many a vacation has been to get back (conveniently briefly) to soaking in the countryside or camping in nature, often on the assumption that some respite from modern conditions is periodically essential.

Modernity, in other words, proves double-edged, even as most of us have come to depend on its key achievements. Modern societies dramatically push back rates of mortality in children—allowing most families, for the first time in human history, to avoid the experience of a child's death. Yet instead of enjoying the gain, modern parents often frantically track their children's health and (particularly in the United States) surround them with annoying safety devices, making parenthood more complicated in the process. There are some good reasons for the concern—premodern societies did not have automobiles—but the lack of perspective is noteworthy as well. Indeed, anxieties around children seem to have surged since the 1980s, with growing fears about letting even older children out of sight. And childhood is just one instance of many where objective changes and widespread perceptions do not match. We can learn more about ourselves by exploring why modern advances have not produced a greater sense of ease.

This is a book about the modern condition and about why the gains of living in modern, urban, industrial, affluent societies have not proved more satisfying than they have. We won't belabor the "good old days" theme. But we will examine why real results that parallel earlier anticipations of progress have not generated the ease and contentment that the forecasters assumed. The book explores a rupture between substantial improvements for a majority in modern societies, and the kinds of reactions they evince—a rupture that affects not only our understanding of recent history but also many aspects of the quality of daily life. It's not so much that modernity went wrong—with a couple of obvious and substantial exceptions, there's no reason to bash the trajectory—as that it has not gone as right as might reasonably be expected from the historical record.

I have been studying some of the changes that go into shaping the modern condition for my entire career as a historian. I was initially fascinated by the impact of the industrial revolution and the question of how people going from rural life or urban crafts into factories managed to survive their experience. The subject is still compelling, even when one recognizes that early factories were not nearly as large or mechanically overwhelming as their contemporary counterparts (they were, however, both noisier and less safe). In subsequent years I've tried to deal with some of the less direct results of modern change, in family life or body types or emotions. In all the work, the unifying themes have been how substantial modern change has been, from its 18th-century origins to the present, and how important it is to figure out how people have navigated it—and still navigate it. Happily, beyond my own endeavors, there has been a huge expansion in the range of historical research, which allows analysis of change and resistance in many aspects of the modern human experience.

In many ways, as I have long argued, people have managed to adjust to rapid, extensive modern change supremely well. There were shocks, and some individual collapses. And at points there was fierce protest. In general, however, most recent research, even on immigrants or the industrial working class, has tended to emphasize adaptation and accommodation, with extreme commitments to protest or disorientation being fairly unusual and episodic. While key passages in modernity have roused passionate opposition, the more characteristic patterns involve more complex reactions and more diffuse targets.

Yet I have also been impressed, probably increasingly over time, with some of the less overt costs involved in trying to deal with the advent and maturation of modernity, even among groups less beleaguered than early factory workers. Living in a modern framework is not easy, and even in societies like our own that have been dealing with the process for several generations, there are still areas where definitive standards have yet to be agreed upon. Assessing how some key problems and tensions have emerged, even amid considerable adaptation, contributes to personal understanding and helps free up space to discuss other options.

This book is a commentary on the emergence and evolution of the modern condition. Over two centuries ago a number of societies, initially in the West, began to forge the urban, industrial apparatus that, gradually but inexorably, came to replace the largely rural and agricultural framework that had shaped the human experience for several millennia. The apparatus foregrounded factories and power-driven technology, but it also recast family life, work, leisure, even sexuality—indeed much of the content of daily activity and personal meaning. Modernity would entail huge changes in government policy, the role of science, the nature of war—a variety of macro developments. But this inquiry deals more with the daily, even ordinary aspects of modernity, often on the more private side of life, which is where many of the nagging issues and conundrums nest. Even here, there's no intention to explore all the details or phases of the establishment of modern life, but rather to focus on key directions and the ways in which contemporary challenges flow from the broad process of modern social change.

Modern developments introduced some unanticipated new problems that emerged on the heels of the resolution or partial resolution of older issues. They also provoked some responses that have turned out to be inadequate and open to review. Both the problem generation and the false starts warrant exploration, for they all contribute to the sense of potential unfulfilled.

Another vantage point is crucial here: the effective recency of the whole current of change that so vividly connects contemporary trends— like the latest iterations of discussions over what constitutes a successful modern childhood—to the first signs of disruption to agricultural patterns over two hundred years before. Though a two-century-plus span is a long time, when considered in terms of the magnitude of the changes involved as well as the deep roots of prior agricultural patterns, it's barely the blink of an eye. We're all still adjusting to basic shifts such as the separation between work and family or the decline in the omnipresence of death or the growing dependence on commercial purveyors of leisure for so much of what we see as the fun of life. We're still trying to figure out how to deal with novel problems modernity generates, such as the unprecedented challenge of obesity, or with first responses to modernity (like retirement as the solution to the issues of modern old age) that probably need a second look. We hear a lot about the "postmodern" or postindustrial, and of course new directions arise within a modern framework. But the fact is that we're still in the early stages of a more fundamental social order—the modern—that may (if past precedents are any model) last for many centuries. This is why most of the adjustments in ordinary daily life remain a bit tentative. This is why it is not at all too late to take hold of the reins of modernity, using the analysis of recent history as a partial guide, and shape it in ways that might work better for us than present patterns do.

A final complication demands attention as well, though more in the West, and particularly the United States, than in modern societies generally. While the dominant process of contemporary history centers on the construction of modern social institutions and experiences, a second process, a bit less familiar, highlights a mounting pressure to seem (and, if possible, to actually be) cheerful and happy. This process also began to take shape in the 18th century, and this meant that many of the really difficult adjustments to the modernization of social and personal life were surrounded by an unprecedented tide of secular optimism from a number of persuasive sources. Here, too, clear connections link contemporary patterns with the earlier directions of change, creating an ongoing relationship between the happiness imperative and the outcomes of modern, industrial transformation. Indeed, the cost of measuring up to intensifying demands for cheer, even while dealing with the inherent complexities involved in constructing modern childhoods or death rituals, has almost certainly gone up in recent decades. Here, too, is a revealing history to be explored not for its own sake but for what it shows about the sources and shadows of the present. The burdens of modernity are compounded by the need to keep smiling.

Combining new requirements for cheerful ebullience with the creation of modern social experiences has not always been inherently contradictory, which is why, at various points, the most starry-eyed optimists have been able to skirt the problem altogether. Elements of a progressive vision have not only come true but have indeed, as pundits predicted, removed or reduced age-old burdens in life in ways that can make it easier to be happy. There is far less untimely death to mourn, to take a leading example, than once was the case. But fulfilling happiness demands could itself be a strain, as several insightful scholars have pointed out, and the context encouraged the development of new expectations rather than the enjoyment of older problems resolved. Here is a set of relationships that has not been fully explored and yet is central to the satisfaction gap that so obviously defines key aspects of modern life.

Any prospectus that tosses around the word "modernity" as often as I already have must offer a few other explanations. "Modern" and "modernization" are terms that have been frequently misused, and much criticized. There's no reason, in my judgment, to back off from the proposition that a cluster of changes has occurred—around new technologies, the rise of urban centers, and the relative decline of agriculture and agricultural forms—that can be accurately and efficiently summed up as modern, but there's also no question that some further, if brief, definition is essential.

First: where, geographically, will this book focus? "Modern" is an encompassing term, and the roster of societies moving into the modern orbit is expanding rather rapidly. Many societies now are modern, in terms of basic urban and industrial structures, with life expectancies and educational levels to match. But modern frameworks, though important, can be variously implemented. In this study, the focus is on the United States, but to carry the analysis through properly some comparisons are essential. Figuring out what has been distinctive about American encounters with, for example, a rapidly falling death rate or the regularization of food supply, and what has been a standard part of the process whether in the United States or Japan, sheds light both on the global present and on the national particulars. The unusually heavy demands of American cheerfulness, which foreign observers noted already by the early 19th century and which have multiplied in recent decades, also transpose a widespread modern dilemma onto a distinctive national canvas. There are a few cases, as well, in which experiences elsewhere in handling modernity seem clearly superior to homegrown models, which is where comparison is practically as well as analytically essential despite a considerable national reluctance to admit any need to learn from abroad.

Issues of evaluation loom at least as large as geography in invoking modernity. Too often, in some social science literature, "modern" has been equated with good or desirable; but since much of the purpose of this study involves assessing the quality of the modern, we can surely hope to avoid this trap. It's precisely because traditional arrangements often worked so well in many respects that the modern becomes more problematic than is often realized; and the fact that several modern societies emphasize happiness in new ways must not lead us to assume that premodern people were actually less happy. Indeed, to anticipate, it's virtually certain that for some people less insistence on happiness would permit greater actual happiness. So the problem, *modern=better*, can be addressed without too much anticipatory agony.

Overgeneralization *within* a modern society is another challenge. It is vital to acknowledge a welter of diverse situations and responses. At various key points, and to an extent still today, the two genders have experienced aspects of emerging modernity differently, and the same applies to social class and other common dividers, including extent of religiosity. American responses to modern childhoods, for example, have been hugely contingent on whether traditional ideas about original sin were cast aside or re-embraced. On the class side of things, it has been easier but also more imperative for middle-class folks to try to measure up to happiness demands than for workers or farmers to do so, though by the later 20th century the huge expansion of the self-professed American middle class qualifies this point at least nationally. While on the whole the happiness push has tended to make expressions of outrage or anger more difficult—which was one of the reasons the whole theme gained so much manipulative attention—this doesn't mean that everyone clusters around a ubiquitous smiley face, even in the United States. The complexities of the modern experience amid overt pressures for happiness demand assessment, but accompanied by recognition of varied subgroups and personality styles. Many people make a good thing out of modernity through some commonsense personal adjustments in expectations, many people are angry or resentful about modern standards and pressures; many fare adequately but amid more anxieties than they think they should have to face. The mixture challenges any glib generalizations about modernity.

This book is not intended as an attack on the modern condition—another evaluative posture that would not be helpful. Modern change has brought all sorts of benefits, and where down sides have emerged, they may yet be more successfully addressed.

It is clear as well, even as we turn to the unexpected constraints on modern happiness, that few people would willingly choose to return to a premodern framework. From the early 19th century onward, periodic experiments offered people the chance to go back to a somewhat idealized past, through bucolic, craft-centered communities. The outlet was important to a few individuals, and it did shed light on the pressures of modern change, but the communities always foundered and never posed a serious alternative to modern, industrial reality. The same judgment applies to the commune movement of the 1960s, briefly hailed as a wave of the future. A few small ventures survived, a few people stayed rural and anticonsumerist, but for almost everyone else modernity quickly resumed its forward march, incorporating a few countercultural trinkets mainly as consumer options. Modernity's triumph over traditional values certainly reflects a lack of imagination—with so many people following the modernist herd—and no small amount of brainwashing by corporate culture, but it also builds on the very real advantages of having access, say, to modern birth control or health care.

So there is no reason to indulge in antimodern fantasies or indeed to overglamorize a premodern past when life was often, to parrot Thomas Hobbes, rude, brutish, and short. The challenge is establishing a more

sophisticated balance. If modernity often seems inexorable to most people, at least in the advanced industrial societies, a popular sense of certain
kinds of loss provides the basis for a more rounded evaluation—an evaluation that can grant real progress but also expose the countercurrents.

For the very vigor of modernity's march can obscure any sense of
options, at least within self-styled paragons of progress such as the
United States. Individuals create successful adaptations, and important
minorities like religious evangelicals preserve or construct more elaborate supplements or alternatives. But a larger sense of the way modern
frameworks might be rethought, or of where initial responses to the
whole modern process have proved less than optimal, occurs infre-
quently at best. The effort is all the more desirable in that some modern
responses may not yet have congealed, given the recency of many key
social changes.

By the 21st century, modern life has generated an almost frenzied
sense of compulsions—to keep up with consumer standards, to maintain a vigorous pace of work, to keep track of often overscheduled kids.
Modernity itself tends to distract from contemplation, replacing it with
a barely concealed impatience or fear of boredom (two relatively recent
products—boredom as an identified state is only a bit over two centuries
old—that are not the most attractive products of the modern condition).
Yet a meaningful life, whether modern or not, deserves to be examined,
and an understanding of the historical legacy of modern change and the
pressures of happiness opens a path to this examination. The process is
at the least interesting and revealing, and at best it offers an invitation to
explore some alternatives to contemporary modern extremes.

The assessment of modern life and the happiness gap does not, for
the most part, feed into the most pressing of today's political concerns.
Specific responses, like retirement policies, do come in for comment, but
we are not in the main dealing with problems for which the government
should devise a response or that feed a clearly partisan agenda. The target is a more personal grasp of where modernity has taken us, and where
as individuals, or as guides to our children, we might think about some
adjustments or enrichments in the process.

The following two chapters flesh out key aspects of my argument, by
offering evidence about the surprisingly incomplete correlation between
modernity and professed happiness and by tracing the emergence of the
happiness imperative itself. Three chapters then deal with key problems

that have emerged as modernity unfolded. Chapter 4 sketches measurable deteriorations under modernity's shadow, capable of at least recurrently affecting resultant overall satisfaction. Chapter 5 explores more subtle issues, where modernity generated initial reactions that were off the mark, causing ongoing divisions and adjustment needs that affect social and personal experience alike, from gender disputes to perceptions of one's own body. Chapter 6 tackles the disjunctures between modern work and both traditional standards and progressive forecasts, a persistent contributor to the gap between modernity and happiness. The final section, with its own three chapters, confronts the clearest spoiler, in terms of garden-variety modern tensions: the way new and demanding expectations quickly erased any realization of the gains modernity had brought. The last of the chapters in this section deals with consumerism, where unfulfilled hopes became almost built into the modern process, not only illustrating the satisfaction gap but acquiring much of the spillover from other modern disappointments.

Historical analysis has often shed light on current concerns by exploring past analogies with contemporary patterns or by highlighting revealing contrasts between now and then, or simply by applying perspective to very recent trends. The explosion of historical research on the wider ranges of human behavior expands these opportunities. Increasingly, groups of historians concerned with aging, or emotions, or childhood, though still genuinely interested in developments in the past, work even more explicitly to show what combinations of changes and continuities reveal how the present has emerged from the past. My effort to explore the reaches of modernity sits squarely in this vein: my central concern is to offer a vantage point on current behaviors and attitudes, rather than simply to examine these behaviors and attitudes as static artifacts or to look at past contrasts for their own sake. Too often, history's public service beyond the classroom rests on museums and heritage entertainment, but more can be offered.

More historians—and again, their number has been growing—need to be involved in reaching a wider public by demonstrating that history can be a source of discovery and contemporary insight, not just a way to avoid repeating the past. For their part, more elements of the public need to expect new things from history: not just battles, biographies, and ancestries or lots of engaging anecdotes or familiar boredom. History can now provide not only cautionary tales and good stories, enlightening as well as entertaining, but also a commitment to exploring and explaining change and through this the conditions of modern life. The extensive grasp of modernity, as an accumulation of changes that have taken us from past to present, translates that commitment in particularly relevant fashion. We can move what we expect from history to a higher level.

This book depends on the twin beliefs that tracing the trajectory of significant contemporary patterns is not only possible but revealing and that improved understanding is a good in its own right and a goad to debate and to action. When we can see current behaviors and assumptions as the product of change, we are best positioned to consider further change—or to confirm the status quo with greater assurance. Thinking more systematically about modernity's development and impacts—and this means thinking historically—is the basis for managing modernity better.

Further Reading

Classic statements on modernization include C. E. Black, *The Dynamics of Modernization* (New York: Harper, 1966) and Anthony Giddens, *Modernity and Self-Identity: Self and Society in the Late Modern Age* (Stanford, CA: Stanford University Press, 1991). For more recent efforts, Ronald Inglebart and Christian Welzel, *Modernization, Cultural Change, and Democracy: The Human Development Sequence* (New York: Cambridge University Press, 2005) and Jerome Braun, ed., *Psychological Aspects of Modernity* (Westport, CT: Praeger, 1993). Otto Bettman offers a provocative comment in *The Good Old Days: They Were Terrible* (New York: Random House, 1974). For a recent and revealingly inconclusive discussion of historians' current take on modernity, see the "AHR Roundtable," *American Historical Review* 116 (2001): 631–751.

The range of historical work on various aspects of human behavior is far too vast to cover here: the expansion can be tracked through publications like *The Journal of Social History* or *The Journal of Interdisciplinary History*. Examples include Paula Fass, *Children of a New World: Society, Culture, and Globalization* (New York: New York University Press, 2007); Gary Cross, *An All-Consuming Century* (New York: Columbia University Press, 2000); Joan Jacobs Brumberg, *Fasting Girls: The History of Anorexia Nervosa* (New York: Vintage Books, 2000); Peter N. Stearns, *American Cool: Constructing a Twentieth-Century Emotional Style* (New York: New York University Press, 1994); Mark M. Smith, *Sensing the Past: Seeing, Hearing, Smelling, Tasting, and Touching in History* (Berkeley:

University of California Press, 2008); Alain Corbin, *The Foul and the Fragrant: Odor and the French Social Imagination* (Cambridge, MA: Harvard University Press, 1988); John Kasson, *Rudeness and Civility: Manners in Nineteenth-Century Urban America* (New York: Hill and Wang, 1990); John C. Burnham, *Bad Habits: Drinking, Smoking, Taking Drugs, Gambling, Sexual Misbehavior, and Swearing in American History* (New York: New York University Press, 1994); Scott Sandage, *Born Losers: A History of Failure in America* (Cambridge, MA: Harvard University Press, 2006); and Claude Fischer, *Still Connected: Family and Friends in America since 1970* (New York: Russell Sage Foundation, 2011). And the list goes on.

PART I

The Modern and the Happy

A Tenuous Embrace

Measuring happiness aims at an elusive target. For all the inherent imprecision, however, we really do know that there is no full correlation between modernity and happiness. In Western and particularly American society, the problem is compounded by the insistence on good cheer that emerged with modernity itself. Modernity has inherently demanding aspects; being told to seem happy may make the necessary adjustments to modern change particularly difficult.

%// **2** %//

The Gap

Happiness Scales and
the Edge of Sadness

Modernity lends itself to two related assessments: an evaluation of key modern trends in terms of their actual, and usually complex, impact; and a discussion of relationships between a society's achievement of modernity and the levels of satisfaction or happiness of its members. This book will actually explore both kinds of assessment, but we begin with the second, more dramatic avenue. Modernity has a positive impact on happiness but a surprisingly incomplete one, and it also increases despair. This is the satisfaction gap, and ultimately we need to know more about modernity in order to explain it.

The measures of modernity are familiar enough, at least for starters. Whether we're comparing current modern societies to their own past or to contemporary developing areas of the world, modern people will: live longer, confront less child death, have more access to education, be wealthier on average and maintain higher consumer standards of living and more daily leisure time, and probably have more opportunities (whether within marriage or beyond) for recreational sex. What's not to like?

Yet the international happiness polls suggest a narrower and less consistent relationship between happiness levels and levels of modernity than the basic gains might suggest.[1] Other data strongly indicate higher rates of psychological depression in modern societies as well. The gap between happiness potential—including the rose-colored visions of modernity before it fully arrived—and actual achievement is not uncomplicated, but it is quite real.

Happiness, of course, is notoriously hard to define and measure. Even within a single society, multiple definitions of happiness emerge—fifteen, according to some studies, within the English language alone. Most happiness research seeks to combine current emotional state (which can be quite volatile) with more cognitive assessments of longer-term satisfaction, but still a firm definition remains elusive. Within a given society, for example, younger adults are more likely to say they are happy than older folks, yet they are also less satisfied with their lives: criteria, in other words, change with age. However defined, happiness clearly also varies with individuals. Research suggests that many people are simply born likely to be happy (including some identical twins who are raised separately). This has led some scholars to dismiss the whole effort to promote happiness as the equivalent of urging adults to be taller. Corresponding complexities emerge at the social level. We can't firmly chart happiness over time, save for the last half-century, for polling data are resolutely contemporary. And even current assessments are shaped by massive differences among cultures, for example between Western societies, where people are urged to be happy and therefore likely to respond disproportionately positively to pollsters, and East Asian societies, where individualistic commitments to happiness may be discouraged and where poll results are accordingly more restrained. We should expect higher self-proclaimed happiness scores in the United States or France, where happiness is more measured by individual success and a distinct sense of self (qualities encouraged by modernity) than in Japan, where happiness has more to do with fulfilling social responsibilities and demonstrating self-discipline, qualities that may be less compatible with modernity—while recognizing that the same cultural differences may mean that Japanese people are "in fact" no less happy than their American counterparts.

Caveats abound. Claiming too much about the meanings of happiness differentials would be folly. But dismissing the data altogether would be foolish as well. Three points are quite clear, even before we turn to the down sides of depression. First, modernity does generate more professions of happiness than more traditional societies muster on average—even across big cultural divides like the Western-East Asian. Second, the differential is muddier than the apparent advantages of modernity would predict. And third, reinforcing this last: within the most modern societies themselves, happiness levels have not significantly improved over the past fifty years, despite the fact that the gains of modernity, though not new, have accelerated. Denmark, for reasons no one is sure of, is the lone exception. Surveys of happiness differentials raise many questions, but by the same token they do confirm, if in no sense precisely delineate, the gap, and by so doing they help launch the inquiry into modernity's mixed results.

The Polls

Recurrent efforts to probe global happiness dot the past decade. The results are not congruent in detail, but they mesh in broad outline, almost always highlighting the real but also the incomplete relationship between modernity and happiness.

The good news, for modernity fans, was that an elaborate 2003 national ranking of eighty-two nations, on happiness and life satisfaction scores,[2] showed that sixteen of the top twenty-two nations were in the definably modern category. Puerto Rico and Mexico, surprisingly, headed the list, but then came a batch of smaller, arguably particularly cohesive modern societies, like Denmark. The United States came in fifteenth, clustered with Australia, New Zealand, and Sweden. The medium-high category (the next twenty-one) was decidedly more diverse, with the big Western European nations but also another batch of Latin American entrants—the region did really well, overall—and also several East Asian cases but with Vietnam and the Philippines leading more modern Japan. Low rankers were mostly in the low-modern to developing category, often with deep political troubles to boot (as in parts of Eastern Europe and Africa at the time). In contrast to the modern societies, where only small minorities discuss living without basic necessities, larger groups in the less modern societies report deprivation. Usually this fact correlates with less overall reported happiness, though in Mexico and elsewhere other factors apparently counteract.

Another ambitious poll, which Gallup carried out in 132 countries during 2005–2006, largely confirmed the standard results.[3] While, collectively, people in richer countries clearly expressed more sense of life satisfaction than those in poorer areas, the correlations within the relatively wealthy category were weak. Denmark, fifth in per capita income, was again tops in the world in self-reports of living the best possible life, while the United States, though first in income, ranked sixteenth, about even with Costa Rica, which was forty-first in the average income standings. The survey was, however, distinctive in separating positive feelings from reports of satisfaction: positive feelings had even less to do with income—with Costa Rica fourth highest and the United States twenty-sixth (New Zealand, twenty-second wealthiest, topped this category). Sage sayings about what money can buy are at least partly right: while wealth—and modernity—contribute to some forms of happiness, they do not assure it with any precision.

Both of the key conclusions from the comparative polls were interesting: that modernity does have something to do with happiness or professions thereof, but that its impact is imprecise. Some smaller modern countries, like post-Hamlet Denmark, perhaps less plagued by the woes of the great power world, do particularly well. Latin American cultures seem to generate happiness claims (and possibly actual experience) that push them beyond their increasing but still-incomplete accession to modernity, except in cases of extreme overall poverty, as in parts of Central America and the Andes. At the other end, East Asian cultures that do not value happiness as much as the West does predictably rank in the medium to low-medium range, despite modernity (Japan, South Korea) or rapid strides in that direction (China). Modernity must combine with culture, and even then the relationships are volatile.

At least as striking was the gap between the modern societies and the potential top score of five in the 2003 surveys. Puerto Rico, at 4.67, came closest, but the United States stood at 3.47, Britain at 2.92. So there is a further conclusion: modernity is relevant to happiness, but only loosely. Obviously, other factors can counteract modernity to some degree, whether positively (parts of Latin America) or negatively (East Asia). Equally important is the fact that, with rare exceptions like Denmark at 4.24, modernity does not do the job all that well, though it's a lot better than nothing. From various angles of vision, the polls suggest, there is indeed a measurable divide between modernity and happiness.

Other data can be adduced that are even more challenging for modernity as a source of joy. A 1999 London School of Economics survey was decidedly more topsy-turvy, even defying the notion that deprivation matters much for happiness.[4] India, Ghana, and others—placing well above the United States, at forty-sixth—were headed by first-rank Bangladesh. Bent on showing that modern consumerism doesn't buy happiness, the survey noted that British perceptions of quality of life had not improved in fifty years, despite a doubling of spending money. Here, obviously, there was not just a gap between modernity and happiness, but a yawning chasm. But the obvious ideological shoulder chip of this particular venture argues against placing too much reliance on precise findings, save as they again point to the obvious ability to find happiness outside modernity and the constraints on easily equating happiness with the achievement of modern conditions.

Finally, a 2008 survey, though more limited than the 2003 ratings in many ways, confirms several points.[5] First, happiness polls are notoriously volatile, yielding inconsistent specific results (Mexico, for example, tumbles in this survey to midrange). Second, leading modernizers like the United States, Britain, and certainly Japan (though doing better in the more recent survey, at number nineteen) are always at some distance from top spot—in 2008, the U.K. ranked ninth, with the United States and France tied for thirteenth place; and a few less modern societies always surpass or rival them (in this case, Venezuela, the Philippines, and, close on their heels, Turkey and Bangladesh). There remains a noticeable gap between level of modernity and reported happiness save in a few cases like (here) not only Denmark but Iceland and some other Nordics as well.

Further polling data confirm the more cautious conclusions and offer some additional explanations. Happiness does not usually rise as the trappings of modernity continue to advance. Societies that first sprint into higher consumerism do experience gains in perceived or claimed happiness—this seems to have been a reason for a high 2003 score for Ireland—but these effects do not persist. More consumerism after the first breakthrough does not produce more happiness. Some of the same complexity seems to apply to work. British surveys reveal that women are happier at work than men, despite more confined job categories and lower pay. Family has a great deal to do with happiness, with married people distinctly more happy than others and special categories like single mothers well down the list. To the extent that many modern societies have disrupted family life, with higher divorce rates and more open tensions between spouses or between parents and children, their effects here tend to foul the positive modern nest. Again, the modernity glass seems definitely half full, or maybe even two-thirds, but also definitely partly empty. The gap is particularly interesting in societies like the United States where people have long been urged both to be happy and to expect happiness. The remarkable happiness push surely leads some people to want to please pollsters by claiming satisfactions—Americans have long been taught to be cheerful in public—but it may also lead to expectations that are more easily shattered than would be true in less pleasure-drenched contexts. This is where the additional polling data, which suggest a happiness stagnation in the most modern societies during the past fifty years, are particularly revealing. Despite a doubling of average wealth between 1954 and 2004, for example, for the typical American, with consumer advances to match, not only has happiness not increased but reports of actual deterioration mount. A steady diet of modernity seems to satiate, whether we try to measure happiness over recent time or explain the surprisingly modest comparative scores of places like the United States or Western Europe.

To be sure, the happiness surveys often ask only a question or two, and it's easy to poke holes in any wider judgments that rest on this base. But there is more elaborate expertise to deploy, as in assessing how happiness combines emotion or affect—"feeling happy"—with cognitive beliefs about well-being. People—at least U.S. people—are not always good judges of their own happiness, being particularly likely to expect that a happy event—winning the lottery—will produce far more lasting happiness than it does. People frequently change their minds a lot about happiness, again partly because recent events so condition memory. Americans often claim to want a lot of choices in order to be happy, but then prove to be less happy in fact when confronted by the need to choose. All the experts agree that genetic personality makeup plays a huge role in individual happiness or lack thereof, but this can't explain the national differences or changes over time: one sensible study suggests that genes account for about 50% of the variations in individual happiness levels, with the rest due to choice and situation (including, one could add, elements of modernity). Cultural factors are real but hard to sort out. Thus the measurable happiness difference between Americans and Koreans at least in part, and perhaps almost entirely, reflects the fact that Americans have been told that it's bad form to express unhappiness, while Korean culture does not instill a high expectation of individual happiness. Yet this factor arguably makes it all the more surprising that American scores are not higher than they are—which returns us to the gap.

For all the disclaimers about the elusive qualities of happiness and the constraints of polling in this area, especially in comparing times and places, it remains possible to define the complexities in the relationship between modernity and happiness without claiming quantitative precision. While the Americans are not a measurable 23.8% lower on the happiness scale than they should be if degrees of modernity correlated more fully with happiness, it is still meaningful to show that big modern societies like the United States have not done as well on happiness as they have in achieving modernity. They have benefited—only the clearly agenda-driven anticonsumerist polls would contest this—but they have not won through. The ongoing complexities of modern social changes surface blatantly here. Modern Western pressures to report happiness clearly show up in polling along with modernity itself, but the incomplete correlations in places like the United States suggest again that some of the pressures have become counterproductive, leading to willingness to evince disappointments along with some impulses to try to keep smiling when the pollster shows up. There is a clear—if incompletely quantifiable—analytic issue to chase down, where modernity, happiness, and American conditions are concerned.

The Dark Side

The complexity of the modern experience shows up from another general angle as well: the rise of certain kinds of mental illness seemingly directly associated with modernity to some degree. Another set of caveats looms immediately: this is a really tough subject, far trickier than the opinion polls. It's very hard to measure rates of mental illness either over time or from place to place. We cannot be sure that mental illness "really" increases with modernity: the premodern West expected many people to be slightly depressed, and premodern societies are much more tolerant of certain kinds of aberrant behaviors than modern societies are in any event, which means they did or do not quantify or label certain manifestations clearly at all. And even if modernity does expand the psychological pressures on a minority, this does not necessarily reflect on majority happiness: it's quite possible that modernity improves happiness for most people, as the polls suggest, and only damages 10-15%, which might be viewed as an acceptable bargain overall. We briefly enter another field with lots of empirical disputes and lots of room for analytical disagreements—but a field that, as well, both illustrates and explains part of the modernity-happiness gap.

For there is a considerable probability that modernity increases psychological depression (we'll not be dealing with all mental illness, though some other facets emerge in later chapters). The result is another modern dilemma that needs fuller exploration and that surely contributes at least a mite to the larger polling disparities.

We can begin in a safety zone, with a little history that, unlike the larger patterns of modernity, has not only a beginning but an end. Late in the 18th century, in Western Europe and the new United States, doctors began to note a rise in hysterical paralysis, that is, people (mainly but not exclusively younger women) who were paralyzed for no physical reason. The disease gained ground through the 19th century, affecting some famous individuals like Alice James (sister to William and Henry) though not sparing the lower classes, but then by the 1920s largely disappeared. What seems to have happened was as follows: some people, faced with growing social changes like commercialization and early industrialization, mentally decided to opt out, "choosing" a disease that would spare them from functioning in public. Women, encountering growing gender constraints, could also "use" the illness as an exaggerated though actually rebellious statement of women's weakness. Acceptance of the disease category by doctors provided a kind of legitimization, as is common in medical history, which actually helped more people "choose" the illness as modernity advanced. Over time, however, as modern public life became more familiar and as women gained more opportunities, the disease lost function and, intriguingly, largely died out—perhaps to be replaced in part by psychological depression.

We cannot be sure that hysterical paralytics would not have found some other disease path before modernity—that's where the history of mental illness incidence always can break down. We can substantially prove that modernity channeled expressions of mental illness, but not conclusively demonstrate that it increased basic mental disturbance that might previously have taken other forms. But even the channeling suggests the gulf that some people have faced between modern conditions and semblance of happiness—which turns it into the still more modern problem of depression.

Depression surely existed in premodern times in Western society, even if it was not always or even usually recognized as disease. Contemporary studies, like those used by Kleinman and Good,[6] for example, in discussing Indian villages, suggest that strong, premodern community and extended family ties reduce the incidence of depression (but without preventing it entirely), but we cannot be sure that this applies to the more melancholic premodern West. We do know that a modern type of depression began first to be identified in the West early in the 19th century by Esquirol, a French researcher who coined the term "lypemania" in 1820 to describe a delusional state and a "sadness which is often debilitating and overwhelming." Use of the term "depression" occurred first around 1856, and gradually won out, though there was always (and still is) imprecision about boundaries between sadness and the newly identified illness.

Reports of depression began to push up in the middle of the 20th century. Some researchers continue to claim that there's been no change, but the balance of evidence—though impossible to pin down too precisely— is against them. The same evidentiary balance suggests that while the increase has affected many societies, both modern and less modern, it's been particularly severe in the United States.

Two phenomena have interacted. Many reports suggest that, from the generations born right before and during World War II onward (1935-1945), rates of depression began to mount—some claims go as high as doubling over a 50-60-year span. Second, doctors and, even as important, pharmaceutical companies began to promote the idea of depression, arguing that it too often went undiagnosed and untreated and that, now that drugs like lithium were becoming available, there should be much wider awareness of the disease among the public and among primary caregivers alike. The combination was familiar enough in medical history; professional awareness unquestionably increased identification, while (though less certainly) the "real" rates of illness went up as well. From the 1960s onward, advertisements, conferences, and popular articles trumpeted the importance of identifying the illness and seeking treatment. In 1987 the federal government mounted its own awareness campaign. New classifications in the Diagnostic and Statistical Manual (DSM) III newly highlighted "major" depression in 1980, urging doctors to see it as a serious debility and not simply distress.[7] Here, then, was a surefire formula for getting more reports of the disease and more people believing they experienced the disease alike—as with hysterical paralysis in the 19th century.

By the 1980s and 1990s, 7.5% to 15% of all Americans were reporting at least one depressive episode sometime in their lives.[8] Virtually all groups—whatever the age, race, or gender—were involved except, intriguingly, Hispanic Americans. International comparisons also mark a general change, particularly in other modern societies like Sweden, Canada, and Germany. High rates in less modern societies like Lebanon spiked more around political crises, unlike the more sustained patterns in the United States.

A modern Western/depression correlation would be stressing the data, but there were some suggestive pointers. Rural areas, revealingly, including one strikingly stable Canadian county with a 5% incidence rate, lagged well behind urban, even amid overall modernity. And, granting all the admitted complexity and conflicting reports, the United States did stand out, with rates of depression twice as high as Mexico and 50% higher than in oft-troubled Argentina, and with similar 50% margins over Western Europe. (Asian rates generally were far lower than those in the West or Latin America, again suggesting different approaches to happiness and sadness alike that culturally loosened any clear relationship to modernity.)

By the early 21st century 16-20% of all Americans claimed to suffer from depression sometime in life, with almost 7% experiencing the condition in any given year. Explicit treatments for depression obviously reflected the increasing awareness of the disease (by ordinary folk and professional diagnosticians alike) as well as a growing willingness to seek help, with rates rising in the United States from .7% of the population in 1987 to 2.3% in 1997 and with the use of antidepressant medicines increasing apace. Age of onset of depression also began to drop, into adolescence instead of some stage of adulthood.

Critics of the larger surveys abounded, as with the happiness polls and sometimes for similar reasons. They noted that reports of depression depended on memory, which was often fallible. But even if American memories often played false—suggesting less a really disproportionate American disease problem than a particular national self-perception issue—the fact that so many people were willing to make the claim, in a happiness culture, was in itself very revealing.

As with the happiness polls as well, explanations abounded: many authorities cited excessive consumerism and the decline of welfare protections to explain late-20th century increases, particularly in the United States and Britain. Others pointed to the decline of family stability and community support more broadly linked to modernity. In the early 21st century psychologist Randolph Nesse advanced an intriguing explanation especially for the United States, reminiscent of de Tocqueville's comments on American happiness frustrations in the mid-19th century: Americans are particularly eager to set ambitious personal goals but unusually unwilling to admit they're not going to reach the goals—in the culturally encouraged quest for happiness, "persistence is part of the American way of life."[9] Hence, the unusual wave of depression.

It's vital to remember, finally, that depression is only the most recent and obvious manifestation of modernity's promotion of a psychological backlash, affecting an important minority in close relationship to new professional diagnoses. The neatly encapsulated story of hysterical paralysis reminds us that something began to go awry early on.

Roughly similar findings, finally, apply to suicide rates, where modernity seems to have a predictable impact though one that can happily be modified by intervention. Historically, suicide rates have varied regionally, in large part by climate. Suicide causes even in modern societies are both complex and numerous, with modernity providing at most a context, not a precise spur. This said, it's widely agreed that rates increase with the impact of modernity (the only real question is whether willingness to report shifts as well). Thus Mexico's and Poland's rates more than doubled, per capita, between 1960 and 2008, while levels in South Korea rose by 250%.[10] In most modernizing regions, increases were particularly great among men and among younger adults. At some point, however—in the United States by the 1950s, in France by the 1990s—per capita rates stabilize and even drop a bit, though never to premodern levels. The break in trends results primarily from more psychological service, new drugs, and more active prevention programs like hot lines. In modern societies where acceptance of help continues to be seen as shameful—South Korea is the leading example—rates keep rising (affecting thirty-five individuals a day in contemporary Korea). Here, as with depression more generally, modernity exacts a severe toll, though a new branch of medicine/social service can compensate in part.

Most modern people report themselves as happy or pretty happy, except perhaps in Asian cultures. But the incomplete correlation of modernity and happiness finds its echo in rising rates of, or beliefs in, some kind of restricting mental disorder, most recently psychological depression. The stresses of modernity but also the not-so-subtle pressures of the happiness imperative combine to produce this Western and particularly American result. More people judged themselves ill when happiness did not pan out for them, all the more as doctors conscientiously touted this disease route. If they did not self-report at the time—there was still a huge gap between recalled illness and annual quests for treatment—at least they were willing to identify problems in the past, which was perhaps a more legitimate way of saying that happiness had not worked out adequately even in a culture that still urged happy presentations in most public settings. Finally, in the same happiness culture, doctors found themselves becoming increasingly eager to see even normal sadness as a sign of disease. A 2008 study suggested that by this point up to 25% of all American depression cases at the clinical level were simply normal sadness that doctors, families, and affected individuals alike could accept only if defined as illness. The happiness imperative, in various ways, risked distorting modern American responses.

Claiming exact findings, in a single brief chapter, from two areas of substantial controversy—about comparative happiness and comparative depression alike—is the height of temerity. Yet so long as claims of intricate precision are not pressed too far, overall conclusions are highly plausible. The happiness gap in modern Western society is confirmed and its significance extended, with the important additional note that certain cultures—Latin American in one direction, East Asian in another—add another variable to the equation. Shadows on the impact of modernity in the United States and Western Europe have darkened in the past half-century, as stagnant polls and depression rates both suggest.

For most Westerners, Americans included, modern social changes and the ongoing happiness culture simply don't fully mesh; for an apparently growing minority, in their own eyes and those of a society intolerant of sadness, they clash outright, sometimes with tragic personal results. A fuller exploration of the partial discords between modernity and overall happiness more fully assesses the complexities that underlie both aspects of the happiness gap.

Further Reading

On happiness: World Values Survey 2008, www.worldvaluessurvey.org; Derek Bok, *The Politics of Happiness* (Princeton, NJ: Princeton University Press, 2010); L. Bruni et al., *Capabilities and Happiness* (Oxford: Oxford University Press, 2009); and Todd Kashdan, *Curious? Discover the Missing Ingredient to a Fulfilling Life* (New York: William Morrow, 2009). Carol Graham, *Happiness around the World: The Paradox of Happy Peasants and Miserable Millionaires* (Oxford: Oxford University Press, 2010) offers a recent statement—even stronger than the common polls indicate—of the basic modernity-happiness gap theme. See also Frank Fujita and Ed Diener, "Life Satisfaction Set Point: Stability and Change," *Journal of Personality and Social Psychology* 88, no. 1 (2005): 158-64.

On depression, see Neal Conan and Joanne Silberner, "History of Treating Depression," *Talk of the Nation*, National Public Radio, March 25, 2004; Arthur Kleinman and Byron Good, eds., *Culture and Depression: Studies in the Anthropology and Cross-Cultural Psychiatry of Affect* (Berkeley: University of California Press, 1985). Carl Nightingale's *On the Edge: A History of Poor Black Children and Their American Dreams* (New York: Basic Books, 1993) shows an extension of the happiness-consumerism links: African American families by the 1970s that could not afford this system, but whose children were fully aware of the rules thanks to watching happy consumer kids on television, found their offspring increasingly alienated through the realization that their parents had let them down in the happiness category.

On suicide, see Peter Stearns, *Revolutions in Sorrow: The American Experience of Death in Global Perspective* (Boulder, CO: Paradigm Press, 2007); Howard Kusher, *Self-Destruction in the Promised Land: A Psychocultural Biology of American Suicide* (New Brunswick, NJ: Rutgers University Press, 1989); and Emile Durkheim, *Suicide: A Study in Sociology* (New York: Free Press, 1997).

Component Parts

Modernity and Ideas of Happiness and
Progress as Historical Forces

The basic framework of modernity began to emerge from the late 18th century onward, initially in the West. Not only obvious trappings, like new steam-driven factories, but also more personal signs, like a new commitment to comfort, mark the inception of trends that still, broadly speaking, continue. The novel interest in happiness emerged at the same point, and has actively—though as we have seen, not fully successfully—intertwined with modernity ever since. Optimistic proclamations of progress long sought to marry the advance of modernity and the hopes for happiness, but this matchmaker glue has dissolved a bit in recent decades.

This chapter emphasizes the tight connections between contemporary modern frameworks and processes that date back over two hundred years, and the similar links between injunctions toward cheerfulness and their recent past. Only a grasp of the chronological sweep of both phenomena allows accurate assessment. Their long mutual relationship also feeds the present, helping to explain why we sometimes expect more from modernity than we find. Seeing modernity as a long though still-recent process and sketching the stubborn simultaneity of the happiness claims both contribute to an understanding of what has—partially—gone wrong.

We're dealing with historical puzzle pieces, tantalizingly shaped but, ultimately, not quite fitting together. Modernity and expectations of happiness were both huge departures from the traditional past. They launched at the same time and place—the 18th-century West. They reinforced each other in many ways, and their impact, though evolving, has in each case continued to the present day.

But the two developments were distinct. Modernity, and its ongoing unfolding, involved problems as well as opportunities—hardly a formula for consistent cheer. Efforts to blend modernity and happiness, through formal ideas of progress, glossed over distinctions for many articulate optimists into the early 20th century. Ultimately, however, the combination could not survive the onslaughts of the 20th century or the persistent complexities of modernity itself. Modernity did not roll back as a result, nor did the happiness injunctions disappear. But the links became more tenuous, and in some cases more obviously counterproductive. The puzzle had not been assembled, as the gap between modernity and happiness, and the fraying of progress claims, both revealed.

Modernity as an Ongoing Process

The list of changes is breathtaking, as a host of characteristics modern people take for granted began to emerge for the first time. Not everyone was involved, of course; modern change drew in propertied groups— some of which would ultimately be called the middle classes—more than the poor, urban elements more than rural. But change was no mere elitist monopoly, as the ranks of middling wealth began to expand and as urban influences began to touch the countryside even apart from outright city growth.

We begin with some unproblematic examples, to establish the 18th-century credentials for the origins of deeply rooted modern patterns within which most of us still live and that we still embellish. Except in the area of sexuality, where changes were upsetting to many, the examples were not for the most part disruptive save to ardent lifestyle conservatives: most people adjusted to them fairly easily as soon as they had the means to do so, and the adoption process continues in modernizing societies like China and India even now.

For instance, new ideas of comfort developed around the middle of the 18th century, and arguably the whole idea of being as comfortable as possible took root in Europe for the first time, or at least for the first time since the Romans, quickly spreading to the American colonies as well. The French and, soon, the English began, for example, to use umbrellas. These devices had been known in Rome (they were of Middle Eastern origin) and were common in parts of Asia, but seem to have been forgotten in the Western world for many centuries. Now they emerged with a vengeance and with them the idea that there were desirable alternatives simply to getting wet when it rained. A few English stalwarts, to be sure, briefly worried about what this kind of nicety would do to English character, forged amid sodden clothing, but for most people (where resources permitted) using umbrellas simply made good sense. Obviously, most modern people fully agree—just as they benefit from new ideas about keeping houses warm that also began to gain favor in the 18th century. Comfort was in, and while achievements were not yet at contemporary levels—air conditioning, for example, was still to come—the basic idea that this was an acceptable goal around which further improvements would always be welcome was firmly established. A modern framework, quite obviously.

On another front—though some people's comfort might be involved here as well—the biting of other humans seems to have declined. As recently as the 17th century, in England, of all bites reported to doctors, those by other people constituted half. This percentage dropped off considerably after 1700, suggesting among other things some serious changes in the socialization of young children. Obviously, success here remains incomplete even in the present day, as witness the famous ear-biting by a leading American boxer, but most of us don't spend a lot of time worrying about getting chewed on by other adults. A corollary shift: kissing, which once involved quite a bit of biting, by the later 18th century seems to have tamed into gentler practices, as well as becoming a more private act.

Naming began to change. In some rural areas, traditionally, many people had not bothered naming kids at all before age two, presumably on the grounds that they were so likely to die that the effort was a waste of time. More generally, lots of people had reused names of older children who had died and had shown a marked preference, beyond this, for old family names or biblical names. Some of this now changed entirely: almost all children were promptly named and names were not reused by parents, both suggesting new attitudes toward children's death and a new sense of children's individuality. Less completely, growing interest began to apply to selecting new and catchy names, rather than family or religious heirlooms.

The validity of love as the primary basis for marriage began to gain ground. A hundred years earlier, if a young man or woman objected to a mate parents had selected—usually relying on economic criteria in seeking to set up a household that was appropriately endowed with property or property prospects—he or she would normally be out of luck. By the

THE MODERN AND THE HAPPY

middle of the 18th century, however, if a youth stated that she or he simply could not imagine falling in love with a selectee, the parents might well cancel the match. And in a few places the young person could even go to court, and expect a sympathetic hearing for a plea for lovability. Obviously, this change cannot be pressed too far: surely all sorts of people were pushed into loveless matches, and it remained true (as is still the case today) that most people conveniently fell in love with a partner in the same socioeconomic bracket, which means that economic considerations have hardly abandoned marriage. But there was a significant change in rhetoric and expectations alike.

On a related front: the later 18th century saw the first modern sexual revolution, though some social groups were more involved than others. The importance of sex in a relationship, apart from simply conceiving children, and the acknowledgment of pleasure as a goal in sex began, haltingly and amid great dispute, to gain ground. We have two kinds of evidence for this claim, beyond the bitter lamentations of contemporary moralists who began to see young people as fonts of lechery. First and most important, increasing numbers of people began to have illegitimate children, suggesting strongly that the links between sex and marriage were fraying, at least among certain categories of youth. As commercial relationships expanded in an increasingly market economy, opportunities to meet people of the opposite sex expanded as well, which was one explanation for the new behaviors. Historians have, to be sure, vigorously debated how much pleasure seeking was involved, as opposed to coercion. Family controls over sexual behavior were clearly weakening in some cases, but this could lead to more cases where men misled or bullied women rather than a mutual embrace of carnal joy. Interestingly, there's also evidence that sexual activity in marriage was increasing in the same period. What's called the conception cycle was evening out through the year. Historically, in northern-hemisphere agricultural societies, people conceived babies disproportionately in May and June, partially perhaps because of better weather but also because resultant babies born in February and March minimally interfered with their mothers' work capacity. Now, however, the conception cycle began to level off (though there are still some modest fluctuations even today), reflecting less dependence on agriculture but also fewer accepted seasonal constraints on sex. This first modern sexual revolution has not made it into most of the textbooks— partly because there is real debate over many aspects of it but also because we're still not supposed to talk about sex too much with students—but it seems to have been quite real. Beyond this, many historians of the phenomenon, despite important mutual debates, would also argue that there is at least a zigzag connection between this first opening to recreational sexual interest and the more famous sexual revolutions of the later 20th century, which pushed the age of first sexual activity back still further and even more obviously loosened the link between sex and marriage.

One of the great discoveries by social historians involves the effective origins of modern consumerism. Consumerism—the acquisition of goods one clearly does not need, as a measure of personal identity and success in life—was once considered a product of industrialization. Once factories really began cranking out product, by the later 19th century, people began finally to have enough time and money to expand their material horizons, and companies had every reason to push them to buy. Plausible, but wrong—though there was a further jump in consumerism at that point and for those reasons. But considerable consumerism had developed far earlier in parts of Asia and Western Europe, followed closely by North America, which climbed on the bandwagon in even bigger ways by the 18th century. There is debate over causes: shopkeepers unquestionably increased their wiles, using new advertising and gimmicks like loss leaders to draw people in. New love interests may have spurred buying, particularly of items like fashionable and colorful clothing. Changes in older status markers, such as landed inheritance, probably caused many people to think of consumerism as a more egalitarian substitute, and groups, including many women, suppressed in lots of ways, found opportunities for expression in the new behaviors. Products in global trade, like sugar, coffee, and tea, attracted buyer interest, and along with this came new kinds of servers and tableware. Whatever the mix, consumer interests gained ground rapidly save among the very poor. Thefts of clothing went up, for example, a sure sign that people's perceived needs were changing (and this behavior persists today, as witness stolen high-end running shoes in American high schools).

And a final example, in what could be a far longer list of modern innovations: sometime between 1750 and the early 19th century, perceptions of age hierarchy began not just to change but to turn upside down—and here North America may have taken a lead. In 1750, an American lying about his age would move upward, claiming to be older than he actually was. Presumably this reflected the respect given to age, and positive perquisites (at least in the middling classes and above) in serving on town councils, getting preferred seating in churches, and the like. Elements of costume also favored the older man, particularly the gray wigs. By the early 19th century, this was shifting dramatically, and someone lying about age would move it downward, wishing to seem younger than he or she actually was. Wigs had been abandoned and elements of dress style began to emphasize a more youthful look. Youthfulness was now associated with energy and being up-to-date—and the less fortunate implications for the elderly continue to haunt us even today. Indeed, the whole point, again, is that a major change occurred that reversed many traditional emphases while setting up a new framework *and* that we continue to operate within this framework.

All the caveats labels that cautious historians usually attach to claims of major change clearly apply here:

- Not everything shifted. In their initial excitement at discovering modern-traditional contrasts, some historians exaggerated the differences, arguing, for example, that love was absent from premodern families. We know better now, for the species is still the species: but this does not wipe away the fact of some major transformations.
- Not all change was for the good. Child abuse (as opposed to strict discipline) may have been less common in premodern settings, in part because of more extensive community monitoring of individual families. Greater impersonality and privacy, particularly in urban life, may have created a largely new problem. In the United States, periodic "crises" of child abuse began as a result to gain attention from the 1860s onward.
- Even changes ultimately largely accepted, like power-driven machinery, initially provoked extensive resistance. Resistance to modernity seldom prevailed, though compromises and rear-guard action might continue. But it is important not to claim uniform agreement.
- Finally, the beginnings of modernity hardly meant that the full transformation was rapid or evenly distributed. Biting, for example, remained a standard aspect of fighting in the American South into the later 19th century. We're bypassing undeniable complexities in this book, arguing that the main point is that modern seeds did sprout, with results that continue to define many aspects of life in the United States and elsewhere.

Most Americans have long since adjusted to key aspects of modernity. We take comfort for granted, except for some much newer concerns about potential environmental impacts. We no longer even think about naming a child for a dead sibling. We usually have considerable success in training our kids not to bite. Much of the modern has become so routine, so unproblematic that, while it still defines our behaviors, it hardly calls forth complex responses.

Yet it should already be obvious that some of the initial modern pushes continue to inform some clearly unresolved issues. The idealization of youth, for instance, while it continues to define many fashions, always raised some tensions around the qualities of other age groups and today—even as this modern trend persists in large measure—generates obvious problems around the growing segment of the elderly population. Worries about sexual change or consumerism, mounted initially in opposition to stark innovations, take on new contours today, but they maintain some of the original themes as well, clearly demonstrating that a now two-centuries-old innovation has yet to be fully assimilated. Eighteenth-century attacks on lower-class efforts to emulate the dress of their betters, through the first installment of modern consumerism, echo still in comments about how "they" should know better than to buy showy second-hand cars or fancy sneakers. Understanding how we remain connected to the evolving innovations of modernity allows us to explain dilemmas over time, to see how major disruptions continue to reverberate if only because we have only a few generations' worth of experience in adapting to them. The way we interpret issues in our lives can change—and potentially improve—when we see some of them as results of a transformative process in which we are still engaged.

Take for example the whole modern idea of time itself. Western people began to carry watches in the 18th century, or the early 19th at the latest, unless they were quite poor. Some historians have argued that the initial impulse for many was consumerism, not time-keeping at all. Watches were worn for show, a sign that one could afford this kind of decoration (and the showy aspect of watches has hardly gone away, though the particulars have changed a lot from the gold chain stretched across a vest to the modern capacity to check the season on Mars). But even if this is true, the larger point is that in this same period the need to know the precise time of day became more important than ever before, which was in turn a huge change in the ways people actually lived. Premodern people knew seasons, and they might have had public clocks or other signals to designate prayer times; but otherwise they did not organize daily life around time very closely. This now began to change. The most striking initiation came for factory workers, from the early 19th century onward, compelled by fines and goaded by whistles to show up within fifteen minutes of a designated time, increasingly gaining legitimate breaks only at specified intervals, released from often-locked workplaces at yet another point on the clock. Trite to say, but profoundly true: the result was an unnatural human experience, and one we still live with.

From the time clocks in early factories, the new compulsions of clock time began to spread to leisure activities by the later 19th century: events were organized by the clock, so people had to plan entertainment almost as precisely as they planned work. Even more revealingly, key modern sports began to keep time records or otherwise undergo regulation by the clock, blurring the line between recreation and labor in this regard. Schools operated by the clock as well, and some cynical historians have argued that one of the (few) successful purposes of early schools was to instill a sense of clock time into hapless students, the workers of the future. By the later 19th century as well, clock regulation spread increasingly to office work; one German office manager even installed a steam jet in toilets, designed to go off if an employee sat on the john for more than two minutes. The early 20th century was the age of the industrial efficiency engineer, using his stop watch to time workers and devise systems to make sure that all workers were forced to the pace of the most efficient, through time and motion studies. Elements of the computer framework, particularly when enhanced by devices like Blackberries and laptops, for many people push time compulsions further into home life and vacation experience than ever before—it becomes ever more difficult to stop glancing at the watch or its equivalent. The discipline of the clock, launched in the late 18th century, increasingly ramifies into the clearly contemporary period.

Obviously, contemporary people in industrial societies such as the United States are well past the first jolts of the introduction of clock time. We wonder, indeed, at societies where people are congenitally late, drifting into scheduled meetings twenty or thirty minutes after the assigned hour, seemingly at random and governed by a clearly distinctive sense of what time is all about. So there's no reason to argue that Americans are still trying to figure out how to react to clock time, though it's worth remembering that for many women, pulled into the formal labor market only in the 1950s and 1960s after a long period of domesticity where clock time played a lesser role, the full discipline of clock time is a fairly recent innovation. (College students are another group whose habits remind us that clock time, even when pushed in the schools, is not easily assimilated until the full compulsions of the world of work.) But to the extent that clock time is both still fairly novel and clearly unnatural, we're still in an adjustment mode to a significant degree. And when we turn to the topic of stress—first identified in the later 19th century and clearly a product of the timed pace of modern life—we realize that for many people the question of how to adjust to clocked time remains quite vivid.

Here's another ongoing adjustment area, though taking us less into the unnatural and simply more into the profoundly difficult: one of the simplest but most basic changes in human life that have become central to modernity involves the separation of work from home and family. This did not, I hasten to add, begin in the late 18th century, save in a limited fashion, but became dominant in urban settings from the early 19th century onward as more and more societies began to industrialize. To be sure, a few types of workers had faced a work and home division even earlier, including slaves enmeshed in certain kinds of production systems. But for most people, home or near-home had been the key production center for millennia, whether the output was manufacturing or agricultural, and most sales activities had occurred in or around the home as well. Even unrelated workers, like craft apprentices and journeymen, had been pulled into a domestic system and treated, though sometimes harshly, as part of the family in terms of eating arrangements and other matters.

Industrialization brutally disrupted these arrangements—to the extent that even craft workers who could have maintained older domestic arrangements began to abandon them in favor of stricter divisions between employer and worker, the latter now responsible for his own board and room. Work and home no longer mixed, which meant—and this is obviously the main point—that work and family became increasingly difficult to combine successfully. And this difficulty persists big time into the present day. As a subset of this problem, as we all know, separating work from home also involved the initially novel phenomenon of commuting, which added to the burdens of finding enough time to accomplish both job and family responsibilities adequately.

The first response to this modern dilemma, in the Western world and, by the 20th century, in Japan, was the famous and novel division of gender spheres into (ideally) work male, home female. Some groups simply couldn't afford this division: urban African Americans, for example, had to assume wives and mothers would work, separate from their households. And of course the many women who increasingly stayed home after they were married, in both working and middle classes, did work hard on domestic matters and sometimes a certain amount of home-based paid labor as well (like taking in boarders or laundry). But the ideal of men serving as breadwinners, women as mothers, shoppers, and domestic arrangers, spread widely, because it so obviously seemed to resolve the work-home separation dilemma. While individuals could not have it all, families still could.

There were huge costs to this, as modern people increasingly discovered by the 20th century. Women were cut off from key sources of power and interest, leading sometimes to an inchoate sense of boredom or frustration. Men actually had it worse in many ways, because amid jobs away from home and often long hours, they simply lost active connections with their families. There were compensations. Husbands and fathers could solace themselves that they were expressing their family feelings by bringing home a wage. They could turn bossy when they did get home, as if they still had a dominant family role; the disciplinary tag, "wait till your father gets home," was a silly pretense that distant men might still have some special authority in the family. (By the 20th century, in most American families, women dropped this game, and clearly exercised more active disciplinary power over children than men did.) Other men developed a culture of male camaraderie that distanced family presence even further, as they stopped in bars or insisted on boys' nights out, but that might offer its own pleasures. For a brief time, some men also tried to compensate a bit by bringing sons or nephews on the job with them; this did not repair the home-work divide, but it did continue some family involvements. But this recourse, though never disappearing, became increasingly difficult when child labor declined and schooling demands mounted. Finally, by the later 19th and earlier 20th centuries, some dedicated workers, including a growing number of professional women, sought to solve the problem by not forming families at all, or not having children if they did marry.

As we all know, the first basic adjustment to the cruel demands of modernity in this area did not survive. Women rejoined the formal labor force even when married, even when mothers, despite the modern fact that this meant they now had to leave home and family. They did this increasingly in the United States and Western Europe from the 1950s onward, they did this increasingly in Japan from the 1990s onward—and they'd never had any wide opportunity for the domesticity experiment in Russia at all, for they'd stayed in the labor force all along. Several factors conjoined to undo the initial response: new labor force needs, particularly in the clerical area, cried out for a female response; rising levels of education for women were incompatible with purely domestic roles, particularly when birth rate reductions also lightened domestic labor; some men began to indicate at least a limited interest in increasing family involvements, now that their own work hours were somewhat more restrained.

The result, over the past several decades, has been a new and dramatic encounter with the work-home/family divisions. Large numbers of women have had to juggle serious work obligations with primary domestic commitments. Many men have moved in to fill part of the domestic gap, but often in ways that leave women feeling that equity has not been achieved. In the United States, it turns out that as men have begun to do more around the house, children have done less, leaving wives with the legitimate sense that their work has not diminished though sometimes unaware that the gap is not just their husbands' fault. A certain amount of frenzy can surround the whole process: in some communities, "soccer moms," rushing from work to a kids' commitment, have become the most likely drivers to run red lights, as they try in their own ways to reduce the tensions posed by the separate locations of home and work.

Some families have tried to reduce the dilemma by having stay-at-home fathers, though this is an approach taken by only a small minority. More women have decided to retain or return to the domestic option, or to adopt a deliberately low-key "mommy-track" approach to careers—to the outrage of many feminists. Technology may yet bail us out to an extent, creating more opportunities for telework that recombines work with household (though not, any more, with kids, who can't rejoin the family work group in any serious way). To date, however, the tension persists for many families, creating undeniable pressures and guilts about a genuine modern problem—a problem that people have been trying to solve now for almost two centuries with no fully satisfactory result.

Another important, though less familiar, connection between current issues and the earlier advent of modernity involves the death of children. We have seen some stirrings of change in the late 18th century, as in the decision not to reuse the names of dead children. Child mortality remained high, but certain kinds of discomfort with children's deaths were increasing. When families began reducing birth rates, a pattern emerging in some quarters by the 1790s, this could heighten attachments to children born, making death harder to accept. Poignant and elaborate funeral memorials to children marked Victorian cemeteries by the mid-19th century, among the middle classes in the Western world, again suggesting new levels of anguish. Equally important was a marked tendency in the new genre of women's magazines to imply some special parental (particularly maternal) inadequacy when young children did die. Mothers were not feeding kids correctly, not keeping them warm enough or keeping them too warm, whatever. The message was clear, if frankly unfair: in a proper, respectable household, children would not die, which meant that to grief, often, was added a keen sense of guilt.

In this area, the onward march of modernity did provide a substantial solution: between 1880 and 1920, again in the Western world, young children stopped dying in such considerable numbers. From about 25% of all children born perishing by age two in 1880, the figure had dropped to 5% four decades later. This was a huge, and obviously welcome, change in the human experience. But while it removed the guilt and sorrow problem for most households, it almost inevitably upped the ante for that small number of households in which young children did still, tragically, die, and it created anxieties even in other households lest something go wrong now that, clearly, the resultant death would not be part of a standard experience. For families where children do still die, the result is, frequently, a collapse of marriage, as partners simply cannot live with the new levels of blame and guilt involved. For other families, concern about children's safety and health, including the discovery of new diseases like Sudden Infant Death Syndrome, or crib death, cuts significantly into the experience of parenting. Here is a case, then, where modernity early on generates a new attachment to individual children and a new sense that, in a properly organized society, children should not die. This basic change was significantly refined when children were at last removed as one of the prime death groups, but the modern tension was not obliterated, living on in continuing concerns and responses that differ from those characteristic in premodern societies.

Much of this book will involve exploring the complex emergence of the modern problems that have accompanied modern patterns over what is by now an extended period of time. At this juncture, the point is to repeat the vital role of historically informed understanding—not necessarily a lot of data or detail, but a sense of direction—in dealing with the issues involved. Many of the reasons modern progress has not generated a greater sense of satisfaction in modern people—apart from the inherently disputable definitions of progress itself—involve the tensions that social adjustments have created even amid many positive gains. The fact that the tensions are often themselves deeply embedded in the modernity process itself, and not simply recent contemporary artifacts, improves our grasp of modernity and also our capacity to see how and why the tensions began to emerge in the first place. The magnitude of change explains why, even two hundred years into the experience, neither solutions nor fully agreed upon responses have yet to emerge. Modernity seems inescapable, largely desirable, but it's a tough process. Exploring how tough it is, though, is essential in understanding ourselves and our society.

Happiness as Modern Companion

The complexities of modern social change—not so much the initial disruptions as the ongoing dilemmas such as work-family separation—already explain much about the partial gap between levels of modernity and levels of satisfaction. The second element of the equation, also dating back to the 18th century, involves a new insistence on happiness and cheerfulness that sometimes, measurably, makes it more difficult to acknowledge and work through the down sides of adjusting to social change.

The push toward happiness, a major change in Western culture, stemmed in part from new intellectual impulses—including a greater philosophical acceptance of material progress—but it seemed to nestle compatibly enough with the first phases of modernity. In contrast to centuries in which people had been urged to humility before God, amid considerable valuation of a slightly melancholic personal presentation, a new chorus of advice urged not only the validity but the social importance of cheerfulness. The idea caught on rapidly enough that upstart Americans even included a right to happiness in their revolutionary documentation. It's not that people had never been happy in premodern conditions—contemporary polls suggest the continuing possibilities in comparable traditional societies even today; it's just that, until the advent of the Enlightenment, they'd not lived in a culture that highlighted the goal. In the West (both Europe and colonial America), overt happiness might even occasion apology. Images of God suggested a figure who "allowed of no joy or pleasure, but of a kind of melancholic demeanor and austerity." A diarist like Ebenezer Parkman, a Puritan New England minister, correspondingly, "grievously and sadly reflected" on a moment of laughter, "I think I might have spent more time with the graver people."

All of this makes the new tone that began to emerge toward the middle of the 18th century all the more striking. Thus Alexander Pope declaimed, "Oh happiness, our being's end and aim! / Good, Pleasure, ease content! Whate'r thy name." Or John Byrom, in 1728: "It was the best thing one could do to be always cheerful . . . and not suffer any sullenness . . . a cheerful disposition and frame of mind being the best way of showing our thankfulness to God." Two changes actually combined in this new approach: first, the idea that people could and should exercise control over their emotions, and not assume that emotions were simply conditions that washed over the individual from outside forces; and second, obviously, the increasing sense that it was not just desirable, but really a positive obligation, to present oneself as happy. Up-to-date Protestant ministers began urging their charges to think well of themselves, as a means of promoting the "Happiness of the World."[1]

Laymen, in this new context, began to be more candid about their interest in pursuing wealth "as a means of enjoying happiness and independence." But good cheer was not simply a recommendation for the upper classes. A Boston writer in 1758 described how "[t]he cheerful Labourer shall sing over his daily Task. . . . A general Satisfaction shall run through all Ranks of Men." Emotional self-control, including the projection of happiness, was certainly essential if a person wanted to advance in the world, but really constituted a moral duty for everyone. Even disasters, like a brutal yellow fever epidemic in Philadelphia in 1793, produced recommendations to the survivors to keep up their spirits and not be bowed down by grief. A cheerful countenance was taken as a sign of an active, competent personality, capable of solving problems and moving on with life.

The new push toward cheerfulness affected popular presentations on both sides of the Atlantic, but they seemed stronger in what would become the United States. British journalist William Cobbett commented in 1792 on the "good humor of Americans." Another British traveler in 1837 revealingly claimed that an American rarely complained, "Because the sympathy he might create in his friends would rather injure than benefit him." Frontiersmen, similarly, were described as "always ready to encounter dangers and hardships with a degree of cheerfulness, which is easily perceived as the effect of moral courage and consciousness of power." Harriet Martineau, often cited as the first female sociologist, was almost taken aback at how often people she met for the first time immediately tried to make her laugh: one stranger "dropped some drolleries so new to me, and so intense, that I was perplexed what to do with my laughter." She found "cheerfulness" subsequently in all sorts of American settings, including an asylum for the deaf, and in individuals like the lexicographer Noah Webster, who struck her as "serious but cheerful." A final example: another traveler, visiting the United States for the first time in 1818, used the word "cheerfulness" eleven times in the first eleven letters she sent back home, also adding descriptions like "good-humored," "gay-hearted," and "smiling." The smiling American became a virtual stereotype, even for less favorable observers who attack American boastfulness, exaggeration, and superficiality.[2]

Again, there is no claim that Americans were always and uniformly interested in projecting cheerfulness. We will see that 19th-century American culture included high esteem for grief. Even here, however, there might be a cheerful twist. It was the United States, in the early 19th century, that pioneered a new kind of garden cemetery, where people might contemplate departed loved ones amid trees and the beauties of nature, a setting not without a potential for sadness but certainly designed to mask the worst realities of death.

What was going on with this emotional revamping, this reversal of the more conventional Christian esteem for humble melancholy? One historian has noted that it was in the 18th century that dental care began to be available in Western society, saving more teeth in decent condition (for those who could afford the service) and therefore making more people comfortable with their smiles. He argues, intriguingly, that earlier, more restrained self-presentations, like the famous mien of Mona Lisa, can be attributed to a desire not to show too much oral interior. But there was more. Cheerfulness obviously translated the growing interest in happiness into personal guidelines, sometimes blurring the boundary between goal and requirement in the process. For some—and perhaps particularly for some Americans—actual improvements in life conditions backstopped this new intellectual context. When more comforts were available, when political changes produced new opportunities for self-expression, it might be easier not just to show happiness but to expect others to do so, for there was arguably less to complain about. The European observers—though frequently biased by wanting to use a real or imaged American setting to push for reforms back home—often claimed that American good humor owed much to social egalitarianism, to the lack of firm boundary lines among social classes. (Slaves, women, and many immigrants, obviously, need not apply.) A final factor may have entered in, though it is important not to read back too much contemporary currency into a past time: as more and more people, particularly men (to whom the cheerfulness recommendations particularly applied, at least for several decades), became involved in commercial transactions, they may have found that projecting cheerfulness was a good way to approach both customers and competitors, in a situation where rivalries might otherwise get out of hand.

Were people really getting happier? It's actually possible up to a point that they were, at least for those who were enjoying some improvements in living standards broadly construed. But the main point is not the degree of reality of the new valuation of cheerfulness but the new standards this valuation placed on people in social interactions and, sometimes, self-evaluations as well.

And from this significant change, two other vital points emerge. First, the turn to cheerfulness, like the larger embrace of happiness, not only persisted but also strengthened in the 20th century, with the United States again in the forefront. The connection between 18th-century innovation and ongoing standards was both real and intense. Second, the cheerfulness standard was not merely projected as a general point but also began to infuse various facets of social life, from work to childhood to death itself. It interconnected with some of the key areas of social change, often complicating what was already an inherently complicated process. The first point, on recent acceleration, completes the commentary in this chapter; the second, on diffusion, will be picked up in the chapters that follow.

Even as World War I and other contemporary setbacks began to shadow a more general belief in progress (without, however, eliminating it, particularly in the United States), a new breed of popularizer began to drive home the importance of cheerfulness with enhanced vigor from the 1920s onward. The theme was inherited, part of the Enlightenment legacy broadly construed, but the enthusiasm was unprecedented. To be sure, there were some new signs of doubt at the level of high culture. Sigmund Freud's theories, though they did not erase a goal of getting close to happiness, suggested strong psychological impediments to being really happy. Contemporary art, whether in literature or painting or music, hardly emphasized themes of happiness, as works explored either internal demons or the chaos of the external, contemporary world. And there can be little question that these outpourings both reflected and caused some popular misgivings. But they also generated new campaigns at the popular level to emphasize and seek happiness regardless.

Signs and stimuli abounded, as the earlier happiness theme joined more openly commercial interests in selling people on the happiness goal. From the 1920s onward, but with renewed vigor in the 1950s even amid the new tensions of the Cold War, a new kind of literature emerged not only promoting happiness as a goal but also, in the best how-to fashion, suggesting that individuals could achieve the goal through their own concerted effort. The corollary, sometimes unspoken, was that individuals who were not happy had only themselves to blame: they could have arranged things differently. The characteristic titles, and their sheer volume, were revealing. A simple list can suffice: *14,000 Things to Be Happy About; 33 Moments of Happiness; 30-Day Plan: 101 Ways to Happiness; One Thousand Paths to Happiness* (claiming to be an "emerging science"); an eating manual called *The Book of Macrobiotics: The Universal Way of Health, Happiness, and Peace* (arguing that it is a "proven fact" that happiness can be found in astrology, love, and the power of dianetics). It goes on: *Baby Steps to Happiness; Infinite Happiness; Absolute Happiness; Everlasting Happiness; Happiness That Lasts; Happiness Is a Choice; Happiness Is a Choice for Teens; Happiness Is Your Destiny; Happiness Lives within You; Happiness Is No Secret; Happiness Is a Serious Problem; Happiness without Death; Happiness without Sex; Compulsory Happiness.* Targeted programs included happiness for *Black Women Only* and *Gay Happiness.* Billy Graham got Christianity into the act with *The Secret of Happiness* (and a host of positive-thinking books worked in the same vein), and this was matched by R. L. Kremnizer's *The Ladder Up: Secret Steps to Jewish Happiness.* For the optimistic, perhaps the most satisfying title was *Find Happiness in Everything You Do.*

The Walt Disney empire, building from the 1920s onward, played an intriguing role in the latter-day happiness movement, both capitalizing on public interest and promoting an expansion of the goals involved. The current mission statement of the corporation is quite simply "to make people happy," but the theme easily predates the popularity of one-line summaries. At least by the 1930s, Disney animators began to specialize in feel-good, remove-the-pain versions of classic children's stories, as in making Cinderella's triumph over her evil stepsisters an occasion for laughs at their modest humiliation rather than sadistic enjoyment of their torture or death. The advent of Disney theme parks after World War II provided occasions for piped-in commercials, delivered for example over transit systems from parking lots to admission gates, about how happy the visitors already were and how much happier they would become during the day. Disney stores, another later-20th-century phenomenon, featured training for sales clerks designed to teach them not only how to persuade customers that products would make them happy but also how to convince them that they already were, simply as a result of being in the stores. Constant smiles were to combine with various verbal cues to create this sense of shared delight. Here, clearly, was a case in which a corporate genius identified the mood or at least the hopes of a large swath of the American public (and later, an international public) and sought to build it into the whole atmosphere, from constantly smiling cartoon characters to light and cheerful music, as well as the specific messages that tried to convince people that they were succeeding in their happiness goals simply by turning to Disney.

Disney was not alone in promoting and capitalizing on this cultural theme. In 1963—not a good American year in the wake of the Kennedy assassination and the mounting involvement in Vietnam—an advertising executive named Harvey Ball created the first copy of a modern icon, the yellow smiley face, which became one of the great global symbols of all time. Corporate executives commissioned the figure as they tried to soothe employee anxiety over the merger of two insurance companies. But the device quickly gained far wider popularity. By 1971 annual sales of smiley-face buttons were exceeding fifty million, and the image spread widely to tee-shirts, bumper stickers, and many other venues, including imagery available ultimately on emails. While Harvey Ball never copyrighted his brainchild, a clever outfit named the World Smile Corporation has now done the honors. And currently a website offers over five hundred smiling logos for those seeking variety within the common culture, while the Smiley Section on e-bay runs for over forty-five pages. New York City offered a number of smiley-face skywriting products after 9/11, suggesting the need for cheer even amid disaster.

Advertisers and advertising manuals picked up the message more generally, again from the 1920s onward. Business textbooks taught that smiles were essential to show the pleasure and success of a consumer item—"the man smiles as he puffs his cigar," despite the fact that smiling and puffing simultaneously constitute an impossible combination. Radio and then television introduced the laugh track, a revealingly American invention, to try to induce cheer where none might otherwise be found, trying to make people think they were enjoying the show without requiring them to complicate their emotional response through evaluation or thought.

Smiles spread well beyond commercial usage. Photographs, from the 1920s onward, routinely emphasized the importance of smiling, in contrast to the dour faces that greeted most 19th-century photographic efforts (compounded, to be sure, by the length of time people had to sit or stand for the early camera technology, increasingly simplified in ensuing decades). Politicians, beginning with American prototypes like Franklin Roosevelt, began to campaign with an almost constant grin, demonstrating the cheerful demeanor that people clearly expected from leaders and acquaintances alike.

By the middle decades of the 20th century onward, the happiness theme was gaining momentum both because of its secure place in modern culture and because of the new forces defining contemporary economic life. Companies, obviously, discovered that smiles and cheerfulness boosted sales, and that products and advertisements that could link to the happiness theme might prove particularly successful. Accelerating consumerism thus helps explain why, even in a more complex environment when objective evaluations might point away from joyous confidence, happiness signals became more ubiquitous than ever before. The rise of corporate managerial structures created another push. In a context in which happiness was already highly valued at least in principle, it was not surprising that experts and managers alike concluded that the new and complex hierarchies would work best if participants were expected to be normally cheerful.

The results spilled over into concurrent efforts to urge a cheerful demeanor, another important if unsurprising continuity. Even by the later 19th century, cheerfulness began to be added to advice to women—an important shift from the largely male orientation of the original push. Cheerfulness, according to the prescriptive popularizers, was part of the duties a good wife owed her husband; some family manuals included a whole chapter under the cheerfulness rubric. A husband should be able to rely on his spouse's "never-tiring" good humor, and a wife should "always wear a smile." And this should not be a matter of artifice: good wives should be genuinely happy, their feelings not just displayed but inwardly felt. Women had already been identified, in the Victorian ideal, as responsible for a successful family environment; the cheerfulness theme simply upped the ante. Sulkiness, here, became a sign of domestic and personal inadequacy. Not surprisingly, the happy housewife theme persisted strongly into the 20th century, the often-amusing accompaniment to advertisements for products from foods to toilet bowl cleaners.

The 1920s placed cheerfulness in the center of the expectations of the growing force of salespeople, male and female alike; it was essential to recruit and train (and monitor) "cheerful salespeople careful to avoid provocation of vital customers." In the 1930s, railroad corporations introduced "smile schools" to train conductors and ticket clerks. Dale Carnegie's massively best-selling book on *How to Win Friends and Influence People*—first issued in 1936 and ultimately generating over fifteen million copies—put cheerfulness at the center of his advice. Carnegie wrote explicitly about his ability to maintain a smile even when being berated by an angry customer, ultimately embarrassing her by his ability to live up to contemporary expectations and defusing her whole complaint. Like happiness, the cheerful imperative began to generate a growing popular literature, with manuals entitled *Cheerfulness as a Life Sunshine, Be Merry,* or *The Influence of Joy.* At yet another level: cheerfulness became one of the twelve requirements in American Boy Scout law.

The impulse could run deep, suggesting an imperative that went well beyond advice and symbols. At the famous World War II conferences, including Yalta, Franklin Roosevelt spent a fair amount of time trying to get the notoriously dour Joseph Stalin to crack a smile. An American need to be surrounded by good cheer, lest it reflect badly on the individual, might even have diplomatic consequences; Stalin took some quiet and possibly meaningful delight in rebuffing the American leader's appeals. (Russians *still* mock our smiling habits—there's a phrase that means "a smile is the sign of a fool, or an American.") The phenomenon was ubiquitous, as an 18th-century innovation was translated into a key contemporary response—in consumerism, politics, work, and beyond.

The idea of happiness embraced some imperious qualities even amid its 18th-century origins, when it already began to correlate with incipient developments in consumerism or the valuation of youth. It was often uncertain whether happy people won more open approval, or whether people in general were under new obligations toward happiness display. Obviously, the happiness theme persisted and even accelerated, just as modern social changes such as time consciousness did. The evolution highlighted the complexities. Unhappy people or situations were not easily tolerated: the obligatory qualities of happiness became more apparent with the abundance of self-help literature on how to acquire the state. Injunctions to keep smiling might well make encounters with nuanced social change more difficult to face honestly, while expectations of happiness right around the corner easily increased disappointment amid modern realities. The persistent happiness imperative, in other words, both fueled and complicated modernity itself, particularly in the United States.

The Progress Claim

One final 18th-century innovation sought a direct relationship between unfolding modernity and the embrace of happiness: the idea of progress. Here was an explicit link between actual social and economic change, on the one hand, and commitments to happiness on the other. If conditions were improving, as the optimists now contended, then there was no disjuncture in expecting people to be happy. Belief in progress provided connective tissue.

And the combination worked pretty well, in many persuasive quarters throughout the Western world, at least into the 20th century. Only in the early 20th century did the faith begin to falter, among some of the very segments that had sustained it. And by the 21st century the progressive vision, though still available, had dimmed considerably—a function of the complexities and inadequacies of modernity that increasingly separated actual perceptions from the continued injunctions toward cheerfulness. Here, a long-standing link to the 18th-century origins of modernity has been compromised.

Of course, the progressive faith was never universal. In the 18th century itself, a number of conservatives, dismayed by change, would have dissented, and the majority of people, whether buffeted by innovations or not, were largely unaware of the new faith. Even some apparent advocates could be of two minds. One of my favorite quotations, from French industrial leader François de Wendel, around 1830, runs, "If progress were not inevitable, it might be better to do without it altogether." In other words, the magnitude of modern change might unnerve even partisans and beneficiaries.

But in leading middle-class and, increasingly, official circles, a vision of progress, linking modernity with rising satisfaction, continued to win favor for many decades. The process started with the Enlightenment, building in turn on the growing excitement around the expansion of scientific knowledge. I opened this book with the expansive optimism of people like Condorcet and Ben Franklin. Both not only preached progress, but anticipated that its scope would apply to virtually every aspect of human endeavor. Thus Franklin again, in another letter: "We may perhaps learn to deprive large Masses of their Gravity & give them absolute Levity, for the sake of easy Transport. Agriculture may diminish its Labour & double its Produce. All Diseases may by sure means be prevented or cured, not excepting even that of Old Age, and our Lives lengthened at pleasure."

This kind of sweeping optimism was a crucial legacy, long allowing many and diverse spokespeople to urge (happy) acceptance of modernity in the name of progress. Many were sincere, some manipulative as they sought to persuade people that new work regimes or more dismissive approaches to death were part of the modern march forward. A whole breed of Whiggish historians emerged in the 19th century, in various parts of the West, arguing that the whole of the human past could be seen as a staging ground for the progressive achievements of the modern middle class—a viewpoint that American school history has not entirely abandoned even today.

One of the easiest confirmations of the persistence of the belief in progress, even amid new challenges, comes in the editorials that hailed the advent of a new, 20th century, as they emerged in popular newspapers in the year 1900. Particularly in the United States but also in many parts of Europe (despite some anxieties in Britain about growing competition for world power), popularizers looked back on the century past as a time of impressive gains and assumed that there was more to come. Condorcet's criteria were largely maintained, but some other points were added as well.

Thus the *New York Times* intoned, citing a Catholic preacher, "There was perhaps some danger of exaggerating the amount of progress that had been accomplished in the nineteenth century; danger of over-exalting what we had done ourselves. But it was not too much to say that the nineteenth century was the most remarkable century in the history of the world. The material progress that had been made was astounding, but the spiritual progress was equally remarkable." A song pointed more clearly to the future, echoing but expanding Enlightenment enthusiasms a hundred years before: schools would grow further, war would decline, the huge achievement of abolishing slavery would be extended into greater harmony among all peoples.

The criteria for confidence were predictable enough, though with an enlarged range. Education had gained ground, with most people in industrial societies now literate. Science had continued to push forward. Medical and public health advances translated Enlightenment hopes into growing conquest of disease and pain. Standards of living were on the upswing. A few commentators noted growing advances for women, for example, in education and the professions. Parliamentary political systems with at least extensive voting privileges and constitutional protections for individual rights were becoming more common. Major wars, at least for the previous thirty years, had receded. There were no clear dark spots on the contemporary horizon. As even a labor leader noted, the "march of progress will continue until triumphant."

To be sure, there was an additional note amid these turn-of-the-20th-century hymns of self-satisfaction, as Western observers noted the massive progress of Western empires and the justifiable dominance of the white race over lesser peoples. Advancement was not just Enlightenment-style but also nationalist and racist. Americans, particularly, trumpeted that "we shall soon be . . . citizens of a Nation recognized throughout the world as the greatest," another morsel from the *New York Times*. But in the terms of the time—still visible today—this merely added to a more general conviction that recent history confirmed the dominance of progress in ways that should lead to still further advance.

A *Los Angeles Times* editorial, again greeting the new century in 1900 and picking up comments from a variety of "distinguished scientists," embellished the basic progress theme particularly elaborately, without depending on the Western superiority claims. The long column included expert predictions that people would increasingly cluster around the equator, since the earth was cooling rapidly, and a worry that since people were increasingly choosing spouses on the basis of intelligence, human beauty might deteriorate. More to the point, the long columns embraced an interesting mixture of Enlightenment themes and more recent signs of progress, but pushed to unusual extremes. Thus the extensive commentary anticipated that the death of an infant would become a rarity, while anticipating that "chemically pure drinking water" would eliminate poisons from the human body and thus allow longevity to the age of Methuselah or at least 150 years with possibilities of further improvement. Mental faculties would improve, and intellectual capacities would increasingly reign over brute force. Humans would rid themselves of all depressing and evil emotions, and would no longer "commit crimes or indulge in warfare." Airplanes would form a major improvement in transportation, but they would not be a factor in military operations since these would cease. Increasing protection from storms would be another key gain (an interesting theme). Punishment would naturally become obsolete, and, in a strange aside, children would have to study less for they will "learn spontaneously and will be encouraged to do what their minds naturally lead them to prefer," thus eliminating any worry that the growing obligations of schooling would qualify the basic improvement of childhood and children's happiness—another theme to be addressed more soberly in a later chapter. And for sheer but fascinating hyperbole: "Man will develop more in the 20th century than he has for the past 1000 years."

Admittedly, the Los Angeles effort pushed the turn-of-the-century envelope, as befitted the frequently buoyant contributions of California to modern life. But the fact that this kind of enthusiasm was possible, unqualified by any particular concerns about the future, is a testimony to the power of basic Enlightenment conviction and the kind of reading of the 19th century that this conviction enabled.

Things had changed, as we all know, by the time the 21st century rolled around. Here, the connection between present and modern past has severely frayed. Again, anticipations of the century (and in this case millennium) to come, issuing from the late 1990s onward, provide a convenient if superficial comparison. In 1999, the *New York Times* noted that

> many people were looking to the future with as much dread as joy. . . . It now looks as if human nature, which includes both good and evil, does not change as humans learn more. Technology doesn't necessarily make people better or worse—it just makes people more powerful. It doesn't change the music, it just turns up the volume.

And the editorial explicitly looked back to prior optimism: "A hundred years ago, our ancestors looked into the future and thought they saw 100 years of progress and peace. Today, as we look ahead, we don't have a clue what the world, or our descendants, will look like in another 100 years." The *Los Angeles Times*, though in this case only implicitly, also tucked tail: it noted improvements in medicine that had doubled life expectancy, and dramatically enhanced technology and education. "But it's hard to say if we're happier. . . . The optimism of early 20th-century Americans would be taken today as either Pollyannaish or simply as boosterism. It's far more fashionable now to be knowingly cynical or simply coolly indifferent." And of course there was no more fitting symbolic contrast between the atmospheres of 1900 and 2000 than the fears of computer collapse associated with Y2K; instead of trumpeting progress, all sorts of people hovered nervously around keyboards, investing vast sums in security systems that proved entirely unnecessary.

To be sure, a strain of progressive aspiration survived. Another anticipatory *New York Times* piece, again in 1999, while acknowledging that bloodshed, disease, poverty, and ethnic violence all persisted and that great anxieties showed how "heavily" the world's problems weighed on people, still felt that

> it behooves us to imagine the future with a sense of optimism, something that eluded our ancestors as they struggled just to survive. We have the humane vision and technological means to lift the world family to new levels of liberty, affluence, health, and happiness. Forging that possibility into reality is the task that greets us in the morning of the new millennium.

Famous for unintentionally embarrassing quotations, former vice president Dan Quayle perhaps caught the mixed spirit of the times when he opined, "The future will be better tomorrow." More to the point, individual experts and popularizers showed an intriguing capacity to seize on recent developments as a reason to slide back not just into greater hopefulness but into soaring confidence. Thus Frank Fukuyama converted the cessation of the Cold War and the advance of democracy into the "end of history": as open political systems spread globally, he argued, reasons for conflict would cease and the whole dynamic of the human past would change course. Thomas Friedman harbored similar hopes on the strength of globalization. The spread of consumer opportunities, he contended, would turn people away from war: no two societies with a McDonald's restaurant, he claimed, had ever clashed, McDonald's here serving as a symbol of new opportunities for personal pleasure that would wean humanity from outdated aggressions. The urge to hope big, around themes of world peace and political advance that the Enlightenment had first sketched out, clearly had lifelines still.

But the facile outbursts of sweeping optimism had declined considerably. Several major factors contributed to this important shift. The first involved alterations in memory. In the West at least, the ability to refer back to premodern conditions faded. Even though significant gains continued in the 20th century, like the doubling of life expectancy through both the end of high infant mortality and improvements in adult longevity, some of the biggest breakthroughs were simply not recognized as such. It seemed normal for children to be in school rather than at work, as this historic battleground receded, and even continued longevity gains began to fall into the ho-hum category rather than contrasting with premodern constraints.

Added to this change in memory was the sense of positive nostalgia for the often indeterminate "good old days" that at least vaguely measured the present in less than progressive terms. Several historians have deplored the inaccurate sense that families really worked better before recent times, but the positive image of premodern family life has gained ground, glossing over the tensions of poverty, occasional abandonment, or frequent deaths of partners. Similar nostalgia often infuses the area of crime and violence, with people assuming, often inaccurately, that conditions were better before the advent of more complex urban structures. From the 1920s onward, when the so-called Chicago School of sociology began positing a direct correlation between cities and crime, many Americans came to believe that crime was constantly on the ascendant, since cities obviously were; the fact that rates in fact oscillated rather than steadily increased, and that on a per capita basis some particularly striking crimes like murders had actually declined since the premodern era, was ignored in favor a declensionist vision that proved very resistant to data.

More important still, in dampening the heritage of the Enlightenment, was the fact that huge swaths of the 20th century had been simply dreadful, almost impossible to reconcile with any idea of progress. For many Europeans, World War I was itself a crushing blow to optimism, already somewhat less firmly established than in the United States. The unprecedented loss of life at the front, along with additional maiming and civilian suffering, flew in the face of any sense of progress—including the jaunty cheerfulness with which many citizens and soldiers had greeted the onset of the war, convinced that it would be a brief but exciting episode after some of the humdrum qualities of industrial, consumerist existence. The United States, less deeply involved, undoubtedly suffered less damage to morale, and from American inspiration in part came such intriguing gestures during the 1920s as the Kellogg-Briand pact, which purported to establish enduring peace among nations, based on the conviction "that the time has come when a frank renunciation of war as an instrument of national policy should be made to the end that the peaceful and friendly relations now existing between their peoples may be perpetuated." But pacts of this sort obviously did not work—the 1931 Japanese attack on Manchuria just two years after ratification was an immediate slap—and each failure may have made Enlightenment optimism harder to come by. The fact was that the 20th century was the bloodiest on human record, with outright deaths in war compounded by genocides from the Holocaust onward and the often atrocious results of internal strife, like the Spanish Civil War or, more recently, the many bloody conflicts in Africa.

From war also came the new capacity humankind developed to destroy itself. The somber tones sounded at the end of the 20th century frequently referred to the advent of nuclear weaponry, with the fate of humanity itself now depending on conscious restraint from a species that had shown scant recent capacity in that area.

Other complexities entered in. It was harder to argue for the benefits of economic and technological advance when, by the later 20th century, the adverse environmental results were increasingly difficult—though not, for some enthusiasts, impossible—to ignore.

There's room for some interesting comparisons here. The 19th century, which so many optimists rendered into a showcase for human progress, had all sorts of warts, even aside from brutal Western imperialism. Exploitation of workers, new kinds of subordination of women, the advent of modern warfare with the North-South conflict in the United States—it would not have been hard to present a factual record to dispute the progressive view, and a few voices offered precisely that. Was the 20th century so much worse (or simply worse in different ways?), or had observers begun to find the complexity of the human record increasingly difficult to simplify, hence loosening the hold of optimism? A bit of both, as we have seen, but it's hard to avoid the conclusion, with deliberate mass killings of other human beings in the forefront, that key behaviors did deteriorate, creating a new gap between reality and optimism that was harder to bridge than before.

A few other developments compounded the change. Obviously, that important element in the complacency of 1900, a delight in the global triumph of the West, vanished increasingly during the 20th century. None of the editorials anticipating the 21st century mentioned this point, as open advocacy of empire became less fashionable—indeed, the whole point could be stood on its head, with hymns to the reduction of imperialism—but the shifts of power balance clearly helped to shake Western confidence.

Even within Western societies themselves, it may have become somewhat more difficult to blame blots on the progressive record on the faults of inferior beings like the working class. There were still people ready to say that continuing poverty must be the result of personal laziness or immorality, which had been a common way to dismiss this complexity a century before, but the argument now stretched thin. And one positive aspect of the later 20th century ironically also constrained optimism. Thanks in part to greater media coverage and the tireless efforts of many NGOs, thanks in part to greater humanitarian empathy, disasters or suffering in one part of the world drew more sympathetic attention from other regions than ever before. The result was not always effective action, but at least the combination prompted a new level of charitable giving on reports of famine in Africa or an Indian Ocean or Japanese tsunami. The kind of painful awareness even Enlightenment leaders had experienced on hearing of a major earthquake now became possible on a global scale, and for larger numbers of at least occasionally empathetic people than sensitive intellectuals alone.

Surrounded by evidence of unalleviated or even worsening suffering, less mindful of premodern yardsticks as a basis for measuring progress, many people loosened their grip on beliefs in a systematically better future. A century and a half of steady drumbeats of confidence gave way to greater uncertainty and more mixed evaluations. In this respect, the contemporary present began to move away from the modern past.

Linkages Disconnect

The decline in easy claims of progress obviously parallels the earlier findings about happiness in the most modern societies, where for the past half-century levels of professed satisfaction have stagnated, except in societies with particular cultural supports (like parts of Latin America) or those newly entering modernity. Most people have long known that modernity was more complicated than full-blown publicists' optimism could capture, but now their mixed feelings emerged more strongly; now there was less rhetorical confidence in a simpler progressive vision.

But with the measurable decline in commitments to progress, the connections between continuing adjustments to modernity and happiness claims began quite obviously to fray. At the personal level, injunctions to be cheerful and happy hardly diminished, as the plethora of how-to books and psychological advice attested. Lacking the glue of confident progressivism, however, it became harder to link the insistence on smiles with actual, ongoing modern change.

Elements of the combination, to be sure, continue to work smoothly enough. Modernity components like a commitment to comfort or more individualistic naming for children have been assimilated long since. Even where additional changes are involved, adjustment in some cases in simple enough. Most moderns continue to believe that extensions of life expectancy are a Good Thing, and so far these extensions persist. Most modern people believe that science can help us, even if the most sweeping faith has dimmed a bit: thus, confronted with a new problem like AIDS, we assume that raising money for scientific research is a response that will be successful. Advances in education continue in the main to be cherished, and for many people consumer gains still constitute a vital measure of personal and social success. Modernity has not failed, and it is not being rejected.

But nor is it a consistent success. Reductions in a confident belief in progress both reflect and promote new levels of uncertainty. Promptings toward happiness may gloss over problems in some areas, but they cannot cover the whole modernity front and in some cases, either by promoting excessive expectations or reducing a capacity for honest confrontation with real problems, they clearly make things worse. While cheerfulness advocates have added good health to the many reasons to keep smiling (also noting that smiles use fewer muscles than frowns do), the compulsion to seem happy can be a real strain. The primary issue, however, is the complexity of modernity itself, and the status of some of the adjustments to it that have developed over the span of a century or more. Here's the real analytical challenge in unpacking the gap between modernity and satisfaction.

Further Reading

Helpful guides on modernization history, in addition to books listed with the introduction, include Peter N. Stearns, *The Industrial Revolution in World History*, 3rd ed. (Boulder, CO: Westview Press, 2007) and Gilbert Rozman, *The Modernization of China* (Florence, MA: Free Press, 1982). On the history of happiness, see Darrin McMahon, *Happiness: A History* (New York: Grove/Atlantic, 2005); Bertrand Russell, *The Conquest of Happiness* (New York: Norton, 1996); and Nicholas P. White, *A Brief*

History of Happiness (Malden, MA: Blackwell, 2006). See also Christina Kotchemidova, "From Good Cheer to 'Drive By Smiling': A Social History of Cheerfulness," *Journal of Social History* 39 (2005): 5-38. An important older study, reminding of the premodern/modern divide but also the gradualness of change, is Peter Laslett, *The World We Have Lost* (London: Methuen Young Books, 1971) and the more recent *The World We Have Lost: Further Explored,* 4th ed. (New York: Routledge, 2004).

On the complex topic of family modernization, see John Gillis, *A World of Their Own Making: Myth, Ritual, and the Quest for Family Values* (Cambridge, MA: Harvard University Press, 1996) and *For Better, for Worse: British Marriages, 1600 to the Present* (New York: Oxford University Press, 1985); and Stephanie Coontz, *The Way We Never Were: American Families and the Nostalgia Trap* (New York: Basic Books, 2000). Also see John Weaver and David Wright, *Histories of Suicide: International Perspectives on Self-Destruction in the Modern World* (Toronto: University of Toronto Press, 2009). On time, see E. P. Thompson, *The Making of the English Working Class* (New York: Vintage, 1966). On consumerism, see John Brewer and Roy Porter, eds., *Consumption and the World of Goods* (London: Routledge, 1994). On progress, refer to Peter N. Stearns, *Millenium III, Century XXI: A Retrospective on the Future* (Boulder, CO: Westview, 1998) and Francis Fukayama, *The End of History and the Last Man* (New York: Avon, 1992).

PART II

Maladjustments in Modernity

Several factors, not surprisingly, contribute to the gaps between modernity and satisfaction, and to the retreat of large progressive visions. The first chapter in this section deals with the easiest—and undeniably important—explanations, in a (modern?) impatience with undue gratitude for past gains and with the clear failures of modernity, where deterioration is unmistakable. The second chapter focuses on misleading initial reactions to emerging modern patterns, for example with gender relations, which have complicated ongoing adjustments. The third chapter takes up the modern experience of work as a special case, both significant and complex, where clear initial deterioration has yielded only incomplete remedies and, indeed, only incomplete recognition: major issues still attach to this one.

At the points where modernity has simply misfired, worsening important aspects of life, but also where it has generated confusing responses that require further adjustment, the linkages between modern patterns and satisfaction inevitably loosen. Work, still a vital component of modern life, involves a striking mixture of change amid injunctions to happiness that challenges analysts and modern workers alike.

Modernity's Deficiencies

We've touched already on some of the key reasons modernity can go a bit stale after initial enthusiasms. Ingratitude and what-are-you-doing-for-me-today expectations are high on the list, but the small but pressing agenda of modern missteps looms even larger. Major historical change always has down sides. In the case of modernity, though they can be briefly stated, the minuses can be agonizing.

Two centuries into the modernization process, it's hardly surprising that most people have only a dim sense of how much better modern societies are than their premodern predecessors, in areas like longevity, and therefore retain no active sense of gratitude. To be sure, the initial shock of modernity has ended, which cushions ongoing response, but awareness of contrast has faded by the same token. More inclusive historical training, that would explore a wider range of human experiences before modernity, might help a bit, and we've seen that there is real reason to work on some areas of unwarranted nostalgia. Comparison with contemporary "developing" societies might generate more active appreciation as well, but happily it's become less politically fashionable to bash non-Western settings. It's also obviously true that, as more and more societies move toward the modern, finding comforting contrasts with nonmodern neighbors is becoming more challenging. Politicians still try to assure us that the United States is the best in the world, but probably few native-born Americans experience more than a brief surge in their happiness thermometers as a result of this dated rhetoric. The fact is that a waning of active gratitude for modern achievements is a given in the historical process.

Understandable lack of historical gratitude couples with another modern human impulse: to want more, and to focus on goals not yet achieved rather than stressing existing accomplishments. Rising expectations—a sense that modernity is not only taken for granted but quickly seems inadequate in light of hopes for further gain—will enter our exploration of a number of more specific facets, like death or childhood. They obviously color reactions to material achievements. Gregg Easterbrook calls the sense that many affluent Americans have, that they are somehow not yet wealthy enough, "abundance denial," which is not a bad phrase.[1] A more nuanced study by Richard Morin identifies four segments of the American middle class,[2] even before the 2008 economic collapse: a full sixth, though calling themselves middle class in the best national tradition, actually are poor by modern standards; about half are in fact satisfied, either because they are incontestably successful or because they value less material aspects of their lives; but a full quarter, though well off by any reasonable global measure, just can't get over a nagging anxiety that they are falling far short of their own aspirations. This intriguing group, more likely to be married than most Americans (thus not, at least overtly, suffering family instability), rates their current standing as medium to low (against objective evidence) and their futures even bleaker. Overall: in the modern context, where vestiges of a belief in progress still linger and people are still urged to become more uniformly happy, it's particularly easy to find even a fairly full glass a bit empty—another reason for a satisfaction gap.

Even more important are the more systematically adverse trends that form part of the modern record to date. There are at least three obvious candidates here (and an active debate on others would be quite appropriate).

We've already noted the decline of community cohesion in this passage from premodern to modern societies. While some historians properly warn that this should not be overdone, noting that many accounts have communities implausibly deteriorating every twenty years or so, the overall trend is probably real. Less cohesive and supportive communities probably contribute to higher rates of psychological depression, possibly to more child abuse, certainly to the increase in divorce. The decline in community-based leisure, replaced in part either by privatized enjoyment or by larger, anonymous crowds, is another fascinating aspect of modernity that may factor a reduction in quality of life. It's not all bad, of course; the same trend of looser community ties promotes greater tolerance, at least in certain respects: traditional community monitoring can be quite repressive. A similar argument about a weakening of extended families is more complicated, at least in Western history, because intergenerational links were shaky before the advent of modernity. There is some change even here. In comparison to 19th-century patterns, older people in the 20th century became less likely to live with younger kin, and this undoubtedly meant less multigenerational input into child rearing (hence, among other things, the new need for lots of child-rearing manuals). On the other hand, the same trend often reduced tensions and allowed friendlier grandparenting and less friction with younger adults. This change, even more than the weakening of community in general, is not necessarily in the loss category.

On a more sweeping canvas, it's hard to argue against the proposition that war becomes more vicious with modernity, beginning with the killing fields of the American Civil War. Technology is the key villain here: it has become increasingly easy to decimate large groups of people from a distance. But organization enters in as well: beginning with World War I, governments learned how to mobilize resources, labor, even opinion in new ways, increasing the kind of involvement, hardship, and passion that war entailed. Then, developments between the wars, initially spearheaded by Italy, Japan, and Germany, began to reduce the boundary between civilians and the military in combat—as witness the famous bombings of towns during the Spanish Civil War immortalized in Picasso's *Guernica*. This was carried further by all parties in World War II, as one civilian bombardment led to another in retaliation, with no apparent restraint. It was Winston Churchill, watching a film about the British attack on Hamburg, with forty-five thousand largely civilian casualties, who properly wondered, "Are we animals? Are we taking this too far?" Lessons learned in the big wars were not lost on others. Conflicts later in the 20th century, including civil strife, where advanced technology was not always involved, and also new forms of terrorism, continued to show a rare bloodthirstiness in attacks on civilians.

Many of the visionaries of modernity, back when optimism was more current, argued that war itself would disappear with greater human enlightenment. Even sober business leaders during the early phases of the industrial revolution contended that business competition and middle-class rationality would replace military conflict in building a better society. Echoes of these hopes still linger, as in some globalists' belief that the spread of consumerism will displace the motives for aggression—as in Thomas Friedman's famous dictum about mutual peace among societies that have McDonald's restaurants. To date, however, these comforts have not systematically materialized: the most modern of all centuries to date has also seen the most wanton attacks on other human beings. It's hard to slot this in anything but the minus column.

Then, of course, there's the environment. From the outset, the industrial revolution led to environmental degradation through new levels of smoke and water pollution. It also encouraged planters and mine owners in other societies, eager to export more copper or cotton to the industrial giants, to damage their environments as well. Cotton planted in Mozambique under the spur of the Portuguese, or rubber plantations in Brazil were two examples of rapid crop expansion in areas not fully suited, with resultant water pollution and soil erosion. Then, in the later 20th century, the sheer magnitude of global industrialization and automobile use began to generate environmental changes well beyond the regional level, with damage to ozone layers, acid rain, and global warming leading to potentially worldwide changes in climate and species survival. To be sure, advanced stages of industrialization also produce opportunities to remedy the worst regional damage: smoke levels abate in key centers in Japan or the United States, fish return to the Thames in London. And there's always that hope that concerted international action can reverse problems on a larger scale. To date, however, environmental impact is another low grade on modernity's report card—and, like war, a subject of immense importance to the human experience now and in the future.

Add war and environment together and the picture may become even darker. Human beings have developed the capacity to destroy themselves and the planet, and some would argue that they are busily doing so already. No wonder that happiness and modernity correlate so badly. It's easy to look at modern life racing out of control in favor of faceless global factors, whether in government or corporate guise.

In fact, there are complications. In the first place, there are plenty of people around who would dispute the negative vision. War, after all, was often horrible in the premodern past, and it's impossible to say for sure that, on a per capita basis, 20th-century bloodshed is necessarily worse than the earlier tactics of, say, Chinggis Khan when he besieged Chinese cities. And debates aplenty flourish around the question of environmental trends and responsibilities.

At least as important for our purposes is the question of how much ordinary people, in the most modern societies, include war and environment in their calculus of satisfactions. To be sure, one poll in Britain did mention environmental concerns as one of the two top reasons people were hesitant about happiness. But most Americans, notoriously less collectively passionate about environmental issues, don't call the subject up at all when responding to happiness surveys. And local environments, for example in the United Kingdom, have in fact improved, which surely complicates the relationship.

As to war, there's no question that huge conflicts—most notably World War I—played a great role, at least for a generation, in countering previous optimistic expectations of progress. But some time has passed since the most extensive Western involvements with modern war, and it's not clear how much judgments are swayed by the larger historical trends. Efforts to calculate fears of nuclear confrontations, from the early atomic arms race onward, have been inconclusive. People get scared around specific incidents, like the Cuban missile crisis, but overall Americans proved capable, from the mid-1950s onward, after just a few years of adjustment, of putting nuclear anxieties in the back of their minds, in ways that did not directly affect judgments of current satisfaction. Since Vietnam, furthermore, American policymakers and military leaders have become fairly clever about minimizing war's impact back home. Tactics designed to cut American losses (sometimes at the expense of killing other nations' civilians, through aerial bombardments intended to limit the need for ground-based action), conciliation of the news media through "embeddedness" programs that prevent too much independent exploration of war's seamier sides, even limitations on public awareness of the arrival of flag-draped soldiers' coffins, all tend to remove even active engagement in war from most people's evaluations of their lives. Explicit opinion management—and the same applies to corporate obfuscation of environmental issues—helps limit public reaction to some of modernity's worst features.

To be sure, Americans, with high expectations for personal security but a long series of wars or near-wars since 1941, may have become particularly prone to fears that color overall outlook. Reactions to the terrorist attacks of 9/11 revealed considerable and persistent unease, arguably surpassing the provocation involved. On a larger scale, historians who have tried to figure out how much reasonable anxiety over possible nuclear conflict actually affected satisfaction offer a mixed report card (once initial shocks passed and distractions such as consumerism regained their lure). Many modern people actually shrug off these new challenges or keep them tucked away as they pursue consumerist and other personal goals. War and weaponry have worsened, in other words, but many modern people manage to downplay these criteria.

As people think about happiness amid modernity—unless in the midst of a war or environmental disaster—the decline of community, though a more complex topic, may loom larger in guiding responses. It's also a more obvious source of potentially exaggerated nostalgia, and it will certainly inform a number of our specific explorations of modernity—around childhood, for example, or even work.

For while modernity has a number of measurable down sides, its more complicated impacts may in fact be the more interesting and decisive contributors to the happiness gap. Arguably, the processes that require adjustment in daily behaviors, particularly when they mix advantages and disadvantages, induce the most nuanced reactions to modernity as a whole. Many passionate critics would contend that it's precisely the environment or, perhaps less commonly, the deterioration of war that should command prime attention, and in principle they may be correct. But the worst aspects of modernity—at least on my list—do not greatly advance our understanding of the inconsistency of satisfaction, for they are either sporadic or at least thus far somewhat remote from normal concerns. Human nature may contribute more directly, in terms of selective memory and disquieting expectations, but here too the connections show through more directly in relation to specific facets of the modern human experience. There's still a terrain to explore, in terms of adjustments and false starts that continue to dog modernity's impact on our daily routines and personal evaluations.

Further Reading

Gregg Easterbrook, *The Progress Paradox: How Life Gets Better While People Feel Worse* (New York: Random House, 2004) castigates middle-class Americans for lack of gratitude—here's the source of the term "abundance denial"—and for too much attention to minor problems. On the important topic of ignoring contrasts between modernity and the past, see Paul Connerton, *How Modernity Forgets* (New York: Cambridge University Press, 2009). Richard Morin, "America's Four Middle Classes," retrieved July 29, 2008, from www.pewsocialtrends.org, reviews the way in which individuals rate their quality of life. On the environment, see John McNeill, *Something New under the Sun: An Environmental History of the Twentieth-Century World* (New York: Norton, 2000); and Stephen Mosley, *The Environment in World History* (New York: Routledge, 2010). On modern war, Paul Boyer, *By the Bomb's Early Light: American Thought and Culture at the Dawn of the Atomic Age* (New York: Pantheon, 1985) and Jeremy Black, *War and the World: Military Power and the Fate of Continents, 1450—2000* (New Haven, CT: Yale University Press, 2000). See also Peter N. Stearns, *American Fear: The Causes and Consequences of High Anxiety* (New York: Routledge, 2006). On the knotty topic of community decline, Thomas Bender, *Community and Social Change in America*, 2nd ed. (Baltimore, MD: Johns Hopkins University Press, 1982).

5

False Starts and Surprises

Making Modernity More Difficult

This chapter deals with four aspects of modernity—gender, sexuality, aging, and eating—that incorporate immensely promising changes away from traditional patterns. In contrast to the trends of war or environmental degradation, we're not discussing measurably "bad" outcomes. Nor, however, are we focusing on unproblematic results, like the rise of comfort, which most people have assimilated (where available) without major difficulty.

Prospects for food and longevity were highlighted in Enlightenment optimism, seen as sources of happiness and progress. Gender and sexuality had their heralds as well, though they were less mainstream. All four areas have in fact registered changes that many people today would clearly regard as desirable, even actively conducive to happiness. But all four areas turned out to involve deeply rooted cultural assumptions that were at some variance with modernity and proved hard to change; many of these assumptions indeed initially intensified in response to the magnitude of modernity's transformations. All of the changes in these areas, as well, involved some immediate problems and opportunities that could distract from objective or longer-range assessment.

As a result, all four areas generated false starts that complicated reactions to change and created divisions and diversions that still bedevil responses today. The result is often polarizing debate, prompting discomfort or uncertainty about modernity for various groups and generating new sources of guilt even for people who embrace the more modern behaviors. There's a direct link, in other words, between the inability to identify modern potential fully at the outset, and the constraints on happiness in modern societies today. Where sometimes bitter arguments still cloud gender adjustments, or where it remains impossible to advance successful tactics to handle modern eating problems, modernity has clearly roused hesitations that the heralds of progress simply could not foresee.

For gender and sexuality, false starts—that is, the inability at first to see or accept the implications of the modern context—surfaced early, and more recent decades have seen important readjustments. Here is in fact a hopeful sign, showing that innovation can address modern complexities even after the process of change is well underway. But the earlier false starts have left no small legacy, and they help explain some of the discontents modernity still inspires. Modern issues of aging and eating emerged clearly only by the later 19th century, making it less surprising that uncertainties continue to shape both policy and personal satisfaction.

None of the four false starts is free from controversy. Even labeling reactions as mistakes risks offending certain groups, and indeed each of the false starts was quite understandable at the time. It's contemporary hindsight that provides a clearer vision. But this claim too—that we now have a firmer sense of what the modern path should be—involves evaluations that could and should be discussed. Even modern obesity generates a surprising amount of dispute.

Still, the realization that modernity produced responses we can now regret should be no surprise. Any change in historical direction—and modernity was certainly that—carries these risks. Some problematic first responses were realized fairly early on, and have long since been resolved. For example, the initial stages of industrialization almost everywhere generated an impulse to attack traditional forms and levels of leisure, on grounds that more assiduous work was essential. Moralists and officials alike reproved many leisure customs on this basis, and some, like the community festival, have really never recovered. But within a few decades it was clear that systematic opposition to popular leisure was a mistake. Workers pressed for new recreational opportunities, and employers themselves realized that a bit more leisure might improve job performance and also provide more opportunities to sell goods. Modern leisure was different from premodern forms, involving for example more commercial provision and more spectatorship, but its abundance has clearly reversed the early industrial impulse.

Other false starts, however, have not been so easily fixed, and the legacy is accordingly more complex. With gender and sexuality, there has been enough time for considerable review, though amid ongoing tension. With eating habits and old age, we are much less far along in identifying and revising the initial responses today. In all four cases, confusions surrounding missteps directly affect ongoing responses to modernity.

Gender

From early on, the logic of modernity argued for a substantial reduction in differentiations between men and women. There were, and are, two basic reasons for this. First, a new array of jobs, many supported by technologies that reduced strength requirements, made it more possible than ever before for men and women to do the same work. Second, the reductions in birth rates that became essential when children stopped being economic assets and turned into cost centers, as they moved from work to schooling, meant that women would spend less of their lives in pregnancy and early child care than had been the case either in agricultural societies or even in hunting and gathering economies. These two basic reasons could be supplemented by new educational gains among women, which turn out to happen in all modernizing societies, no matter how patriarchal to begin with; and by ideological movements among some groups of women: it was no accident that the first clear intellectual stirrings of feminism began to emerge, in Western Europe and the United States, with modernity itself.

Gender differentials in agricultural societies had varied. When men were not available, women could and did do virtually all types of work; strength requirements were not prohibitive. Women could also do craft tasks, and certainly worked alongside men in family-based craft shops. Formal differentiations between men and women were much greater in the upper classes, which had enough money to pretend that women were primarily child bearers and decorative items, than in society at large. But all agricultural societies were essentially patriarchal, assuming that men and women were very different and that men were clearly superior. The fact that on average women had to prepare and care for six to eight children during early to middle adulthood was the core practical differentiator between the two genders' roles; based on this, men normally did perform the more important economic functions, in farming and the urban economy alike, which added to the gender gap. But fundamental practical distinctions were normally reinforced and extended by all sorts of additional symbolism and legal differentiations.

Western societies had not introduced the harshest forms of patriarchy; they could adduce nothing so striking, for example, as Chinese foot binding. But they provided a firmly patriarchal framework as modernity began to take shape, and one that in some ways had been getting worse in the immediately preceding centuries. In contrast to Islam, for example, many Western regions made it difficult or impossible for women to own property separate from male stewardship. After the Middle Ages, Western European women were chased away from most manufacturing crafts, which helped associate urban production with male dominance as the early factories first emerged. Some versions of Protestantism, including American Puritanism, also gave men a special role as moral guides and Bible readers within the family. Only a few straws in the wind, before modernity's advent, even vaguely qualified the separation between the genders and the conviction of male superiority.

And this helps explain why, in initial reactions to modernity, gender differentiation was not only perpetuated but in many ways enhanced—even though this would turn out to misread the basic thrust of modernity in the gender arena and would require remediation. At a time when people—particularly male people, but many women as well—were experiencing so much change in other respects, fully redoing gender assumptions was simply asking too much, except for the few brave pioneers who, for example, translated some of the Enlightenment assumptions about progress into gender terms and produced the first statements of women's rights.

More than simple maintenance was involved, for more extreme formulations of gender took shape as well. We have seen that as work increasingly moved out of the home, with the rise of factories and early offices, there was a huge question about who could take care of children and discharge other domestic functions. It would have been radical indeed to assume that, given the fact that someone had to be home, that someone should not be female. To be sure, a few women worked on after marriage and childbirth, usually because of financial pressures but in some cases because they were too bored with the alternative. But there was a real dilemma for most people, which pulled the vast majority of women from the formal labor force, at least in adulthood. The result was a reduction of women's independent economic contribution and power, which made many of them more dependent on family, and therefore on men, than ever before. And the result fed into the (largely male) notion that women were incapable of providing for themselves, requiring male support and protection. The idea that women were weak was not new, but it gained new vigor in part because, in economic terms, it became truer than ever before. It also quickly came to involve some self-fulfilling prophecies. On the basis of women's weakness (as well as special domestic responsibilities), well-meaning reformers began to argue that women should not work the same hours as men—which in fact made women less suitable for many jobs, ironically reinforcing the impression of dependent vulnerability.

Economic marginalization and a more vivid emphasis on feminine weakness showed how agricultural assumptions persisted even as a new kind of economy was being formed, which is hardly surprising given the deep roots of the earlier system. Some compensation for new tensions men faced in the workplace also fed revised gender formulas. The John Henrys of the world might lose when their prowess was confronted by machines, but they could derive some comfort from the extent to which their women were more dependent on them than ever before.

Another kind of adjustment occurred as well, however, and this one gave women new authority within the family and actually contradicted some of the fundamental tenets of patriarchy. Here was a first sign that modernity was going to undercut the agricultural system of gender relationships, despite the brief enhancement of inequality.

As more and more people became involved in competitive commercial relationships, as businessmen and professionals, a need to project home and family as a moral alternative gained ground rapidly. Men might enjoy the pursuit of the dollar and the rough and tumble of business rivalries, but they liked to think they were serving a higher purpose—the idealized family—and also that they had a refuge to repair to after work was done. "Haven in a heartless world" is the way historian Christopher Lasch termed the new sense of family. The imagery involved required that someone be responsible for the family who was not tainted by trade and money, and this someone, of course, was the wife and mother. Rather suddenly (the process began in the 18th century), women became regarded as more moral than men, a huge reversal of the traditional view. Women were to serve as "presiding spirit" in the home, "removed from the arena of pecuniary excitement and ambitious competition," "unmixed with hate or the cunning of deceit." A leading woman editor, Sarah Josepha Hale, put it this way: "Our men are sufficiently money-making. . . . Let us keep our women and children from the contagion as long as possible." Though moral superiority did not fully compensate for economic vulnerability, it did allow women to criticize men (for example, through temperance movements that stressed the evils of male drinking habits) and also to take on various charitable initiatives.

The Western gender response was not the only approach possible as industrial modernity took shape. In Russia and later the Soviet Union, women were not withdrawn from the labor force as was widely done in the West, and a special imagery of female virtues emerged less strongly as well. After an initial period of heavy reliance on women's work, Japan began to pull women out of the labor force, giving them primary family responsibility much as in the Western model, but without quite so much moral window dressing and amid somewhat starker emphasis on male superiority. In no case—though the Soviet pattern came closest, at least in principle—were the full, longer-run gender implications of modernity immediately brought into play. The jolt of this level of innovation pre-cluded a full review of gender alignments, as people adjusted to other changes and as men arrogated to themselves a new degree of separation in part to compensate for challenges modernity posed to their work roles and other badges of male identity.

In the West, at least, the gender patterns that first responded to modernity became wrapped up in the concomitant happiness equation, which made them more difficult to assess objectively. Many men became accustomed to thinking of the idealized family as their source of satisfac-tion, whatever might be happening on the job (or, on occasion, in military life). Women were urged to remain cheerful as part of their ministering roles as wives and mothers. Assessing gendered assignments, or even complaining about them, faced additional constraints as well.

The failure more seriously to rethink gender roles during modernity's first decades did, however, constitute a significant false start. Admittedly, this became clearer over time, when birth rates began to drop more rap-idly and all the energy devoted to women's maternal qualities began to count for less, and as schools began to take over more of the care of chil-dren after infancy. Even if, as seems probable, more maternal energy was devoted to each individual toddler, the reduction in numbers clearly lim-ited investment in child rearing, particularly as a definition of a woman's whole life.

By the late 19th century also, refinements in technology and the matu-ration of industrial economies made the initial overemphasis on women as weak and domestic more evident. New machinery opened jobs in print-ing or shipbuilding to women. To be sure, discrimination, including now labor union pressure, limited the impact, except in special circumstances like wars, but the separation between women and the modern labor force began gradually to ease even so. More important still was the blossoming of white collar jobs, with women actually seen as particularly appropri-ate for roles in clothing sales (better sense of fashion) or school teaching (better with children) or clerical work (no particular reason except they were much cheaper than men). As is well known, the full revolution of women's reentry into the economy would await the 1950s and 1960s throughout the Western world, held back by older gender assumptions, but change was happening around the edges well before this.

Growing involvement of females as well as males in modern education was a fundamental development. The spread of schooling as part of modernity hardly quelled gender quarrels. In the mid-19th century there were serious arguments that schooling would damage women's reproductive capacity, given their distinctive weakness. Well into the 20th century schools maintained quite separate curricula for the two genders, with females trained in readings that would prepare them for family life and motherhood, increasingly complemented by classes in home economics that would teach even the most benighted lower-class girl how to maintain a proper home. And when subject matter increasingly failed adequately to differentiate, as women showed up in all sorts of classes and increased their entry into law and medical schools, though initially as suspect minorities, separate extracurricular activity patterns reminded everyone that schooling had not erased gender.

But education did weaken gender barriers steadily from the mid-19th century onward. The fact was that females could excel in school, and even though a few disputes linger about differences in subject matter skills, the idea of some huge gap between the genders has been exploded by educational results. Gender itself provided one initial argument: if mothers had new responsibilities in raising kids, and society needed kids to be attuned to modern economic and political needs, it was imperative that mothers themselves be literate and numerate, if only to incubate successful sons. Gender-specific education was fine in this rationale, but no formal education at all (which had been the dominant temptation in premodern societies, when males had vastly disproportionate access to what schooling there was) no longer made any sense. Once this concession was granted, other factors amplified the opening: girls' own school success whetted appetites for more, as greater numbers of women pressed into high schools and colleges. New needs for teachers and clerical workers took advantage of women's new educational levels but justified still more. Once launched, the momentum could not be stopped.

Here, in fact, even amid lingering gender divisions in curriculum and activities, was the first clear demonstration that modernity meant less gender specificity, not more. It was an indication that became increasingly global, despite wide differences in cultural traditions concerning women and women's public roles. Japan in 1872, in what was still a famously patriarchal society, launched universal primary education for both genders—partly because this was what the West was now doing, partly because of the felt need for educated mothers in the modern world. Communist countries embraced both genders in educational expansion. By the early 21st century, key Middle Eastern countries, like Iran, not only educated both genders but found women dominating higher education by a sixty-forty margin.

With less gender distinction in education, other changes accelerated. Women now had new bases for entering the labor force, in terms both of skills and of motivation. Everywhere, educational gains would correlate with reductions in birth rates, as women gained new expectations and were open to new sources of information about both goals and methods. Generally as well, advances in education would soon be echoed by new political rights, including the vote. Amid considerable furor and ongoing dispute over precise limits, the classic gender structures of agricultural societies, as well as the initial responses of modernity, were being supplanted. Women's rights enthusiasts might continue to thunder against patriarchy as they fought large remnants of inequality, but in point of fact literal patriarchy was dead or dying. The functions and rights of women and men were becoming less different than ever before in human history.

By the early 20th century in the West, by the later 20th century in urban settings virtually everywhere, the decline in gender distinctions in roles and characteristics became an inescapable component of modernity. Initial, gender-enhancing reactions to modern conditions slowed and gradually reversed, and the initial mistake in using gender to respond to modernity was increasingly corrected.

Earlier patterns did not, however, die away entirely, which is why the initial false start, though amply adjusted in recent times, plays a role in complicating satisfactions with modernity. It was during the 20th century, for example, and particularly after World War II, that American sales operations and adults began to accept a clear color differentiation for girl and boy babies, with the familiar pink and blue division. The distinction was largely harmless, in all probability, but it was on the surface strange: precisely when gender divisions were fading, Americans were persuaded into clearer color coding than ever before. Symbols had to be reinforced when reality was changing. The same applied more generally to children's clothing, at least until the end of the 20th century; where young boys and girls had been similarly clad in dresses in the 19th century, trousers now became increasingly common even for the youngest boys. It was going to take time for all aspects of gender presentation to catch up with basic modern requirements.

The same applies even more significantly to ongoing confusions in expectations. Polls taken in the 1960s, when the percentage of mothers of young children in the labor force was rising rapidly, indicated that a growing majority of women (mothers included) believed that women should not work at least until their children reached school age. At least for a time, if the soundings could be taken literally, a number of women were committing in fact to life patterns of which they disapproved—never an easy combination. Even today, a minority of men and women in Western societies argue firmly against the idea of greater equality of gender roles, often with clear throwbacks to the gender imagery that was first created to respond to modernity. None of this is surprising: gender is a difficult topic in most societies in times of change, which means that disagreement is inevitable. But the false start that enhanced the idea of women as both weak and blissfully domestic greatly exacerbates modern disputes. Most important, it contributes strongly to frequent feelings of guilt and confusion when modern realities, including participation in the labor force, are edged with a sense that somehow this definition is incorrect, that the all-encompassing wife and mother should reemerge.

The full ending of the essential gender revolution that modernity imposes has not yet occurred. We can't predict how different cultures will separately define or constrain a modern gender arrangement. Even in the United States, we don't know how much inequality will remain, despite significant recent reductions in wage gaps and other distinctions. It remains remarkable that, in a nation that has led in many of the gender adjustments required by modernity, women's advancement in political careers lags behind the experience of many other societies, and while we may assume that this anomaly will be corrected, we cannot be sure. Practical problems, such as who will care for even the smaller number of children most modern families venture and with what impact on work roles, are not easy to resolve, quite apart from cultural remnants of the past. What we do know is that modernity requires radical readjustments of customary gender assumptions and arrangements and that the readjustments have been complicated by misleading but potent first responses. The result impinges, finally, on satisfaction, when adaptations fuel a sense of guilt or when larger societies face the distraction of debates over the roles and imagery that complicate the reception of latter-day modernity.

Sexuality

If the dramatic changes ultimately required in gender relations posed challenges in the larger process of building modernity, it is not surprising that redefinitions of sexuality raised issues as well. Indeed, there was some link in the adjustment issues in the two areas, particularly where women's behavior was involved. But sexuality had its own contours. Like gender, some pressing if temporary practical problems combined with larger cultural responses to produce an understandable but untenable initial modern statement of sexual norms that used traditional ingredients but added innovation as well. As with gender, the result would not last, but it would continue to complicate and divide later reactions, producing confusions easily visible in many modern societies—and here, perhaps particularly in the United States—today. Initial missteps in modern sexuality, even though substantially redressed, continue to generate confusion and constrain satisfaction.

Stating what "modern" sexuality is, and how it contrasts with agricultural patterns, entails more risks than the comparable endeavor with gender, because there are even more contemporary disputes and because past patterns are harder to uncover, without the tidy framework of agricultural patriarchalism to guide generalizations about premodern traditions.

Granting the risks of controversy and oversimplification, it seems clear that for most people in premodern society, sexual activity was strongly conditioned by an emphasis on procreation and the related lack of reliable contraception, while surrounded as well by potent community and religious norms. Sex for pleasure surely occurred, sometimes combined with procreative efforts, sometimes separately. The availability of prostitutes in premodern urban centers, plus mistresses for some members of the upper classes, confirms the interest in pleasure seeking. But the impact of frequent pregnancy combined with the need to avoid too many children imposed some obvious constraints for most people. The average premodern family normally sought to have between six and eight children, which meant that a great deal of a woman's adult life, in monogamous marriage, was spent carrying a child or recovering from childbirth, which would condition male sexual opportunity as well. But this birth rate, though high by modern standards, was only about half the number of children a couple would have if they had attempted maximum fertility, from puberty to menopause; and this gap imposed the need for various kinds of sexual restraint (along with some use of uncertain herbal contraceptions), not only before marriage but often during marriage as well. Finally, patriarchal traditions consistently added much more rigorous attention to women's sexual activities than to men's, creating an obvious context for double-standard behavior.

Sexual modernity emphasizes the importance and validity of recreational sex, with procreative sex becoming a minor element in the larger sexual equation. The movement toward sexual modernity can include (depending of course on prior norms) greater tolerance of sexual activity at relatively early ages and before marriage, greater tolerance of multiple sexual partners for women at least before marriage (sexual and gender changes here intersect), growing openness of sexual references and images in popular culture, growing interest in diverse sexual methods and positions, and growing commitment to sexual activity even in later age. Sex for fun, and the role of sex in providing fun in life, both gain ground as part of modernity.

The premodern-modern contrast in sexuality offers no big surprises, as was the case with gender, since most of us have been living through some of the later stages of the transformation. Stating the substantial change, if not revolution, in emphasis is relatively easy. Working it out in practice has been hugely difficult, which is where the next example of a modern false start comes in.

Western society provided a particularly challenging context for a sexual revolution. Compared to religions like Hinduism and Islam, Christianity was notoriously reticent about sexual pleasure. Its Catholic version clearly stated that celibacy was preferable to sexual activity, and while this priority drew only minority interest, it stood as a deterrent to too much open zeal. Christian family advice contained none of the explicit promptings toward providing sexual pleasure to a spouse that Islam enjoyed. To be sure, Protestantism, attacking celibate institutions, did haltingly countenance a bit more attention to sexual satisfactions within marriage, but this was hardly a robust premodern embrace. Furthermore, premodern European family patterns, for ordinary folks, emphasized late marriage age, imposing additional sexual constraints on youth. Here was another reason why acceptance of sexual change could prove difficult.

Sexual modernity arrived with a vengeance during the late 18th century. We have seen that many young people in the lower classes began to indulge more freely in premarital sex, as evidenced by the rising illegitimate birth rate. As more people moved away from village community and parental supervision, opportunities for abusive sex almost certainly increased. But some greater quest for earlier and more ample fun in sex was surely involved in some of the key signs of sexual changes among young people. Sexual activity in marriage also increased, though we have more trouble figuring out if pleasure was a clear goal or result. On yet another front: thanks in part to improved printing and literacy, new forms of pornography began to emerge, a first if still illicit move toward changing public sexual culture. Though their behaviors were by definition atypical, it was no accident that individuals with open claims to elaborate sexual adventures (Casanova) or to bizarre appetites (the Marquis de Sade) starred in the 18th century. Arguably, despite or because of its prudish past, Western society seemed launched on a decisive early turn to sexual modernity.

But it did not last, or at least it was vigorously and successfully counterattacked, which is where the sexual false start took decisive shape. The sexual implications of modernity were not only downplayed but positively resisted. After all, one person's sexual liberation was—perhaps particularly in the Western traditional context—another person's moral panic. A German official made this clear around 1800, though with predictable exaggeration, in claiming that "both sexes are so inclined to debauchery that you scarcely find a girl of twenty who's not already a mother," while another observer claimed that virgins were completely disappearing from view.

Traditional moralism aside, there were several problems in the first stirrings of modern sexuality. The most obvious challenge was the potential increase in the birth rate, at a time when the middle classes, particularly, were beginning to make the transition to smaller family size. Work opportunities for middle-class kids declined and schooling requirements increased, the combination that invariably produced a recalculation of the numbers of children families could afford. It became terribly important for "respectable" people to make sure that their own offspring did not complicate their lives by having children early, and then even in marriage to try to keep procreation under control. Popular cautionary literature for the middle classes filled with stories about daughters cast out from the home because of a pregnancy out of wedlock, and the disgrace that attached to the offended family.

The situation seemed to demand innovation, and not just an insistence on older standards of behavior. After all, new levels of birth limitation were essential, just as the larger society seemed to be indulging in higher levels of sexual interest. The obvious response should have been, and ultimately would be, new devices for birth control, that would simultaneously permit both more sex and fewer children. Unfortunately, however—and this was an ironic little tragedy of history—truly reliable new devices began to be available only after the 1830s-1840s (when the vulcanization of rubber produced opportunities to mass produce both condoms and diaphragms). By that point, the guardians of respectability had already responded to the crisis—and it was a crisis, in the terms of the time—by introducing new levels of hostility to sexual activity and new disciplinary measures as well. For in the absence of reliable contraceptive tools, the only recourse was a variety of unprecedented insistences on sexual restraint and the positive undesirability of sexuality in many circumstances. And this prudery train, which involved far more than simple insistence on Christian traditions, once it left the station, took a long time to slow down. It was further accelerated by new social-class divisions that had respectable people worrying about the irresponsibility and potential menace of their inferiors, which novel birth rate differentials now ominously demonstrated (for in premodern societies, the poor had normally maintained lower birth rates than the well-to-do, a ratio that modernity has reversed).

The result was what is conveniently labeled Victorian morality (alas, the rumors that Queen Victoria had a less-than-fully-Victorian private life are probably not true). And this morality proved to be an understandable but powerful and durable false start to the interplay between sexuality and modernity. For, far from embracing recreational sexuality, the most rigorous Victorians tended to argue that sex was both bad and dangerous. And while some debate continued in various social groups, the basic Victorian message proved hard to shake off.

Under the Victorian umbrella, popularizers and medical authorities alike added a host of health issues to justify sexual restrictions. Nervous middle-class people now learned that having sex too often, possibly more than once a week, could induce premature death or insanity. Warnings about venereal disease also (more realistically) increased, but so did dramatic accounts of the risks of heart attacks if one slept with someone other than one's spouse. (Some French doctors took the next step, urging marriage precisely because sex would be boring and therefore safe.)

Young people and women took extra hits. For the young, given the concerns about premarital sex, huge new warnings about morality and health combined. Masturbation came in for great anxiety. Although it was always a biblical sin, there is no particular indication that masturbation drew much active attention until the 19th century. Then, however, it became the source of a later life of sexual perversion, mental problems, premature aging, sterility, blindness, and acne, a list guaranteed to frighten both responsible parents and young people alike. And for women of all ages, ideal typologies now posited a low level of sexual interest, which was a great blessing because it allowed women to be arbiters of activity in ways that would impel restraint; sexual control was a centerpiece of the new beliefs in women's superior morality. Good girls should not want, much less engage in, sex before marriage, and in marriage they should guide control of passion as well. In an extreme British example (again, there were varying degrees of rigor in advice), wives were urged to shut their eyes against an experience they could not as good women enjoy and to "think of England"—that is, recognize their patriotic duty for at least as much sexual activity as would be needed for procreation.

All of this was accompanied by increasingly rigorous efforts to control pornography, as a long battle was engaged against the steadily expanding developments in print technology and photography that encouraged production at low cost.

Most important, and the point at which the Victorian story becomes a quietly tragic one, the attacks on sexuality not only persisted long after effective artificial birth control devices became available but also long discouraged knowledge or use of the devices themselves.

Here's how a straightforward history might have worked: new signs of interest in sexual pleasure inevitably troubled moralists, parents, and those who monitored the lower classes, who invoked traditional values to urge greater restraint. By the 1820s, however, a growing number of middle-class families found that they could achieve the limits on birth rate they desired without depending on abstinence or attacks on sexuality, by buying condoms or diaphragms. Reformers were also able to disseminate these devices to the lower classes, particularly as new production methods lowered cost, which reduced birth rates here as well and gradually allayed middle-class concerns about the excessive natality of the poor. Traditionalists still worried, and adjustments did not occur overnight, but a brief clash between modernity and morality was increasingly smoothed over.

Lots of unhappiness would have been avoided had this described reality, but it did not. Quite possibly, the hold of premodern and Christian tradition was too strong to permit this streamlined adjustment to modernity; the tensions sexuality is currently causing in the Islamic world, in a religious culture much less nervous about sexuality in principle than was Christianity, may support this argument as well. What is certain is the fact that the additional concerns about sexuality—the new elements forged in the early 19th century as the first official response to modernity—made easy adaptation impossible.

For birth control and related issues now became matters of deep contention, rather than practical developments to integrate into modern behavior. Products to facilitate contraception were widely seen, instead, as devices that would promote rampant sexuality and encourage the worst impulses of young people and the lower classes, as goals shifted from legitimate birth control needs in a society that had to redefine family size to restraint of sexuality altogether. Victorian prudery began to outlive its purpose, but the resulting tensions would reverberate for a very long time. A variety of people, some in high office, had concluded that abstention or great restraint were crucial goals in their own right, independent of birth control save to the extent that the threat of unwanted children was a useful goad.

Great effort was devoted to maintaining ignorance about the new devices. American states and other governments tried to ban sales and advertisements alike. Anthony Comstock, a zealous postmaster general in the 1870s, sponsored legislation banning use of the mails either for sales or for notices, and the Comstock Laws had impressive longevity in the United States. Other laws attacked abortion, now made a crime. Religious authorities had long frowned on abortion, but even in Puritan times popular beliefs that souls did not form until a fetus was at least three months old limited actual restrictions. In the 19th century improved surgical methods made abortion a wider and more effective possibility than had been the case in premodern centuries, and interest in the procedure expanded rapidly given the new interest in sexuality and the new need to limit family size. In some European cities substantial percentages of working-class women, including many wives, had at least one abortion by the latter part of the century. But the new illegality was a considerable deterrent, despite oscillations in enforcement; many doctors and even more midwives were jailed for their involvement. Large numbers of women and girls had to seek recourse to back-alley procedures that could be very destructive.

At least as important were the efforts supported both by moralists and by many parents to convince children of the evils of sex, in ways that could promote lifelong guilt about sexual expression even within marriage. Extreme cases showed how far the new campaign could go: a French girl in the 1870s becomes hysterical when she had to sit on a train seat just vacated by an adult male, convinced that she might become pregnant or diseased. From France as well, a wife filed a divorce suit against a husband who apparently just showed a good bit of sexual interest, on grounds that he subjected her to "unnatural caresses." New American food products, like the Graham cracker or Kellogg's corn flakes, were introduced with claims that their nutritional purity would help keep children on the straight and narrow, whereas more savory foods might lead toward perdition. A substantial middle-class youth culture emerged, quite clearly in the United States, that tried to reconcile modern beliefs in love and a surging quest for romantic happiness with the widespread constraints on sex. Intense courtships, complete with passionate love letters, were predicated on a conviction that a religious-like devotion could unite couples and serve as the emotional basis for engagement and marriage, while also helping to keep them free from fleshly involvements, a kind of Victorian effort to have one's cake while not eating it too. Thus the American Eliza Duffey warned men that "[p]assion must be accompanied by the tender graces of kindness and self-denial, or women are quickly disgusted." Here a cooler and more cynical youth culture would arise in the 20th century that increasingly defused this particular Victorian construct. Still, the effort was intriguing as a brief attempt to create a modern relationship without sex, and well into the 20th century many women, particularly, would continue to delay sexual activity or evaluate it in terms of romantic content.

For ultimately the main points about the Victorian sexual false start are, first, and obviously, that it began to erode, but, second, that key elements survived amid change, greatly complicating adjustments to modernity in this crucial arena. The erosion process—to an extent, a resumption but also a spread of the earlier sexual revolution—began clearly by the later 19th century in the West. The implications of modernity—toward less procreative sex, contraceptive assistance to recreational sex, and a growing interest in new sources of pleasure—gained ground fairly steadily from that point onward. For example, the Mosher Survey, a poll of upper-middle-class American women, showed significant gains in the experience and awareness of orgasm for respondents born after 1870, compared to their older counterparts. Use of birth control devices became increasingly standard for middle-class couples by the 1930s. The new institution of dating in the United States, though it maintained rules against "going all the way," facilitated an increasingly sexual element in what had once been called courtship. Pornography expanded—a key development was the inexpensive postcard, available before 1900.

These new or renewed modern trends, clearly reversing the Victorian response to modern sexuality, obviously gained broader momentum later in the 20th century. Availability of birth control devices widened further. A public culture that encouraged the pursuit of sexual pleasure did develop: this included access to a growing array of pornographic materials but also expert recommendations about the desirability of sexual enjoyment so long as it was consensual and sexual explicitness even in normal media fare. Age of first sexual activity dropped, gender gaps in access to recreational sex lessened (though they did not disappear), and even older people began to participate more widely in the quest for sexual pleasure. Somewhat unexpectedly, given their prior history, Western societies began to take a lead in redefining sexual standards even on a global level (along with other participants such as Brazil and Japan).

But the carryover from Victorian sexuality remained strong as well— the false start was significantly modified, but not eliminated. Debates about abortion and birth control, particularly durable in the United States (as against more successful European compromises), reveal ongoing beliefs that recreational sex must not be unduly encouraged. Hostility to signs of lower-class sexual indulgence continue to run strong, and the medical authorization needed for the more effective birth control devices acts as a class-based constraint on the full conversion to recreational sex.

Victorian survivals show vividly, even after the assaults of the 1960s and indeed partly in atavistic response to them, in the enthusiastic endorsement of "just say no" campaigns in the 1980s and again after 2000. The 1960s, though less dramatically novel than enthusiasts proclaimed at the time as in fact the decade merely continued the momentum of sexual modernity, did see a reduction in the first age of sexual experience and a related increase in premarital sex, particularly striking among women. The result was a marked increase in teenage pregnancy. Many affected societies, headed by Japan and Western Europe, quickly responded by facilitating adolescent access to birth control devices, and pregnancy rates began to tumble as a result. But in the United States, participant in the same modern trends, many authorities hesitated, on the classic grounds that while births might be discouraged, sexuality would actually be endorsed instead: and young people—particularly young people in certain social and economic groups—must still be taught restraint. Thus sex education courses, where available, continued for the most part to emphasize the problems and dangers associated with sex, and while most young people clearly either ignored these messages or shrugged them off, there could be some ongoing impact that might cloud a search for pleasure in recreational sex. A distinctive New Jersey approach in the 1970s—"And you can give yourself pleasure, too, and that's okay. When you touch your own genitals it's called masturbating"—was easily surpassed by emphases like a 1980s program in Atlanta whose main goals were "to help boys and girls resist pressures to engage in sex" by graphic representations of venereal disease as well as unwanted pregnancies. Certainly, a fair amount of ignorance about the range of meanings in modern sexuality, if not outright distaste for sex, could be perpetuated by programs of this sort. Most interesting of all were the more novel attempts to discourage sex directly. Considerable American government funding poured into abstinence campaigns, and many teenagers, loving the spotlight, loudly signed up for not-before-marriage pledges. And some doubtless lived up to the pledge. But the most obvious result of this anomalous American approach was a teenage illegitimacy rate well above European or Japanese levels and, by the early 21st century, a striking increase in oral sex among adolescents. For better or worse, for lots of people, modernity and just-say-no did not mix, and by this point modernity was clearly winning out.

Victorian survivals were most striking on the conservative side, where they promoted policies that could seriously complicate modern sexual behaviors. But they showed up in other quarters as well. Feminists, for example, recurrently agreed with certain Victorian strictures. Many feminists, of course, advocated attention to women's capacity for pleasure, and at first the culture of the 1960s was widely embraced. But the notion of women as purity regulators had appeal as well, both around 1900 and again by the 1970s. A number of leading feminists worried that women might be harmed by elements of modern sexual culture, particularly the exploitation of the female body both in imagery and in bedroom reality, and they were concerned as well that sexual opportunities might divert some of their colleagues away from the more serious purposes of feminist endeavor.[1]

Finally, even as some Victorian bastions crumbled, many societies, including the United States, began to identify other kinds of sexual behaviors for new levels of reproof. Most obviously after a 19th century in which the subject was not widely singled out, homosexuality began to be redefined and increasingly attacked as deviant and avoidable. Middle-class parents and adolescents, a bit less anxious now about masturbation, had a new subject to worry about, and children might be carefully monitored for indications of homosocial impulses. Same-sex contacts, including embraces, standard in the 19th century, now drew nervous prohibitions, especially among males. It was hard to avoid some identification of sexuality as a danger zone, even as the turn to recreational sex, overall, continued to advance.

Assessing sexual modernity is a truly complicated task. Many will judge that the continued remnants of Victorianism are quite appropriate, and some will argue that we should have more of them, that the impulses of modernity are tasteless and dangerous. Certainly there are many societies elsewhere in the world that remain hesitant about Western sexuality, despite its wide influence. The happiness imperative itself could be a huge distraction. As experts and popularizers began to turn away from Victorian shibboleths, from the 1920s onward but particularly in the 1960s, they clearly established the legitimacy of consensual pleasure. Marie Stopes, the British interwar commentator who was spurred by the "terrible price for sex-ignorance" she had paid in a first marriage, roused women throughout the English-speaking world to believe that they had a right to sexual enjoyment and deserved both the knowledge and the male consideration to realize this right.[2] Common recommendations in the 1960s, under titles like *The Joy of Sex* or *The Pleasure Bond*, pushed even farther in urging that anything was permissible so long as agreed to by participants. Clearly, in principle, the components of modern sexuality were at last coming together, with a clear embrace of recreational sex as the main point of sexual activity and an explicit junction with the happiness principle as well. Yet the more open quest for sexual satisfaction had its own snares, as many sexual gurus had to admit. Some reports suggested that a majority of American women were dissatisfied in part because of ongoing problems of male haste and inattention, but also in part because their own expectations had risen so considerably. Even apart from the Victorian false start, modern sex was a complicated business.

The reconciliation between sex and modernity has clearly gained ground. Sex has become a more important, or at least more openly important, ingredient of happiness, with many specific changes in behavior and popular culture to match. The initial impulse to reject modernity in this area has largely been abandoned in most modern cultures. But lingering elements from the rejection campaigns continue to constrain or confuse sexual behaviors for some, and to create divisions and disputes that complicate adjustments to modernity—with the United States presenting a particularly nuanced case. Moving into modern sexuality from traditional values and behaviors would have been challenging enough, but there is no question that the difficulties have been exacerbated by the Victorian misstep and its continuing, though weakening, hold.

Gender and sexuality both elicited initial modern responses that, however understandable, were misguided, and whose effects continue to bedevil the modern transformation, despite now over a century of emendation. The categories also, however, illustrate the encouraging possibility of rethinking first adjustments with the aim of advancing midcourse corrections.

Modern Old Age

Two other false starts that constrain satisfaction with modernity, involving old age and food consumption, developed only from the end of the 19th century onward—not, as with sex and gender, a hundred years earlier. Improvement both in old age and in agriculture/nutrition were more clearly part of the optimistic 18th-century preview of modernity than sex and gender were. It took longer, however, for actual changes to become clear, and when they did emerge the context was ripe for another set of misguided responses. But with old age and nutrition, the need to reconsider first reactions emerged clearly only recently, so modern societies are in the midst of the dilemma, not merely sorting out the remnants of earlier mistakes. The paths of an appropriate modern solution are still incompletely charted. The result is another set of significant modern transformations that in turn generate social issues and personal tensions greatly affecting daily life and the contemplation of happiness in modernity.

At the most basic level, the modern history of old age is an unalloyed success story: more people are living into later age than ever before, virtually worldwide, and in the advanced industrial societies adult longevity pushes up steadily: on a percentage basis people in their eighties are the most rapidly growing demographic segment in American society, and longevity gains in some other modern countries are even more striking. Also unprecedented—though with this change there are clear minuses as well as pluses—is the increase of the "senior" population as a percentage of the total. With more people living longer and at the same time the birth rate modest or dropping, a dramatic shift in the age pyramid of industrial societies, compared to agricultural patterns, was inevitable.

There are to be sure a few misconceptions to clarify. The low life expectancy in agricultural settings was due primarily to the high rate of infant and child deaths. If one made it into early adulthood, there was in fact a reasonable chance of lasting into one's fifties or sixties, and occasionally beyond. The experience of old age, and the existence of a definable population sector in later age, is not a brand-new modern phenomenon. Still, the improvement in expectancy at age fifty or sixty, due to better standards of living and improved medical care, is unprecedented. And whereas in pre-industrial societies the elderly (age sixty and beyond) constituted at most about 4% of the population, they were already up to 8% by the early 20th century and they press toward 25% in contemporary settings.[3]

These huge changes were a fulfillment of Enlightenment progressive dreams. We have seen how expectations of greatly increased longevity played a prominent role in calculations of a better future. Enlightenment scientists and popularizers were fascinated with the probability of extending human life, mainly through somewhat unspecified reductions in disease. Though some of the most ambitious projections have not yet materialized—though there remain some neo-Enlightenment prognosticators around who recurrently claim that life spans of well over a century will soon be within reach—and though even more modest hopes took a bit longer to realize than the 18th-century progressives had anticipated, there's no question that in broad outline this aspect of the Enlightenment vision has borne fruit. The huge improvements in the chances of living into one's seventies or eighties, in many parts of the world, are a legitimate cause for historically informed happiness, a case where social change and Enlightenment bombast arguably coincide.

There was of course one problem: the Enlightenment forecasters assumed that massive extensions of later age were such obvious gains that there was no particular need to worry about the actual results, either for individuals or for societies at large. Their hopes provided an incomplete road map for what turned out to be a very complicated aspect of modernity, one that is still a work in progress in the early 21st century.

For it quickly turned out that many aspects of modernity were inimical to the quality of life of older people, producing a deeply ironic tension given the longevity gains. The movement away from pretending to be older than one actually was—the mid-18th-century phenomenon—to pretending to be younger (by the 1850s) symbolized a very real preference for youth and the real or imagined qualities of youth associated with the rise of industrial society. The increasing number of old people clashed with a growing sense that the elderly were antiquated nuisances in a modernizing context, and the dilemma has yet to be fully resolved, though it would generate one tantalizing false start that continues to complicate the situation.

Traditional Western culture, it must quickly be noted, had not itself been uniformly friendly to old people, even old men. When, in the 1970s, historians began to craft a history of old age—belatedly, for like most modern people historians long neglected the elderly—they quickly realized that there were some important myths to debunk about the good old days. In some popular visions and even amid some less than historically informed gerontologists, a notion had taken root that modernity's slams against old age, which have been quite real, could be contrasted with a "golden age of age" back in the day. Not so. There were, unquestionably, some bright-spot contrasts with contemporary conditions—else why would people have wanted to seem older than they were? In a less literate society, older people could be turned to as sources of memory and therefore wisdom. Protestant churches, for example, often highlighted "elders" as sources of governance, and older people gained preferential seating as an extension of this esteem. On the civil side, older age and judicial wisdom might also be associated, and this is one aspect of traditional thinking the United States has preserved, for better or worse, by not requiring retirements for older top judges and legislators. Arguably, in a setting in which longevity was undeniably rarer than it is now, simply making it to later age drew more favorable attention.

But the down sides in Western custom were also huge, in contrast for example to East Asia where the Confucian tradition was at least in principle far kinder and more consistently respectful of people in later age. From the Greeks onward, Western culture had offered abundant nasty commentary on old folks. The classical Greeks, after all, though not modern, had their own preferences for youthful bodies, so characterizations like those of Aristophanes—"a disgusting old fellow, all bent and wrinkled, with a most pitiful appearance, bald and toothless"—were hardly surprising. Many laments highlighted the sufferings attached to physical aging. More interesting still were the gibes at mental competence. The propensity of old men to lust after young women, and often make fools of themselves in the process, was a common theme. Greed and avarice drew frequent notice, obviously vastly qualifying any general belief that old age brought superior wisdom and freedom from passion. Small wonder that, even in the 18th century, Samuel Johnson could complain that "life protracted is protracted woe." And the contradictions applied to old age were not cultural alone. In the Western family system as it had developed by the 17th century, young adults were unusually constrained by the continued survival of their parents: full adulthood could not occur before the death or retreat of older parents freed up property. Huge generational clashes attached to the inheritance system. In some cases, bitter fights and feuds resulted, and it was no accident that in premodern France older men formed the largest category of murder victims. Older people had to negotiate furiously, when their work capacities began to decline, to receive adequate support from their adult offspring, and the results were not always pretty given the tensions over property.

In the Western context, then, the elderly had possibilities for a gain in modernity beyond simply living longer, and arguably they have indeed advanced in some additional respects in fact. It remains true that, with the advent of modernity, those aspects of traditional culture that emphasized wisdom and the importance of respect did decline, while earlier concerns about the disgusting aspects of appearance and foolish behavior persisted strongly. The result was not, overall, clear progress. For it became apparent, as industrialization and modern culture jointly gained ground, that modernity and old age did not readily mix, beyond the achievement of greater longevity, whether traditional values had been supportive or not.

There were two related problems. First, as factory machinery and urban settings took hold, greatly increasing per-worker productivity, some labor-force sectors retreated toward a more optional category, in a situation in which unemployment loomed as a constant threat. Women, as we have seen, entered this category for many decades, and so, more quietly, did the elderly, for an even longer time. There were some genuine problems with maintaining old age involvement with industrial labor during the 19th century—as in the other false start arenas, some empirical issues help explain the mistake. But the unavoidable glitches were compounded by the larger cultural turn—the second clear problem: as modernity became disproportionately tied to an imagined view of youth and youth abilities, it turned geria-phobic in the process. The youth blinders did not necessarily do actual young people much good, but they definitely and durably affected the evaluation of the place of older people in a modern society.

Older people had always faced potential problems when their work was physical, when and if their own capacities began to diminish. This was one reason they tried to negotiate deals with younger relatives. Rarely did older people retire outright, because their resources would not permit this, but often they would scale back—or, unable to readjust, face increasing misery. The advent of modern society did not fundamentally change this difficult combination, but it may have extended the vulnerability of many older people, and it certainly made their dilemmas more visible. Factory and other urban jobs continued to require considerable physical strength, and as a result many workers found it hard to retain steady employment as they aged. At various times and in various places, as a result, old people crowded into poor relief centers or even the new mental hospitals, because they had no other alternatives for support.

And this in turn fed, though it hardly entirely accounted for, the more decisive change in culture. To many partisans, the advent of modernity seemed to call for a vigor and openness to new learning that the elderly—particularly given traditional biases in the West—simply did not seem to have. The call for the qualities of youth was irresistible, and since the birth rate had not yet declined significantly, there were lots of youth around to answer (and to agree wholeheartedly). The shift became obvious by the second half of the 19th century, when pejorative terms like "geezer" began to enter the language in the United States, providing new specificity for a perception that the elderly, whatever their numbers, did not fit in. A variety of observers—employers, doctors, popular commentators—formed an increasingly hostile chorus after 1850 as well. In addition to the real or imagined demands of industrial work, and the general notion that in a period of rapid change the elderly by definition could not keep up, medical discoveries increasingly reinforced the belief that the elderly were unfit. Pathological research revealed apparently inevitable changes in key organs as a person aged, creating a sense of deterioration and decay that were out of keeping with the qualities now associated with modern life. A French doctor went so far as to say that old age was itself a disease –the "last, sad revolution in life that leaves only ruins behind"—and who wanted a diseased person around? Attention to senility and some sense that senility was a virtually invariant condition in the elderly, put paid to any sense that old people had relevant mental attributes to contribute to society at large. While a few tributes survived to the idea of special wisdom and experience, they paled (in a society increasingly dependent on the written word) before the sense of the irrelevance and decrepitude of the elderly.

Here was the clear false start: as modern progress improved at least survival rates in old age, culture actually, and unnecessarily, turned more hostile. The confusion was compounded as, during the later part of the 19th century, increasing mechanization and the rise of more office work created occupations where physical strength played less of a role than ever before. But the elderly, because of increasingly fixed prejudice, including the sense that keeping up with change or the demands for new learning were incompatible with the stage of life, were not encouraged to apply. The perception of disjuncture with modernity simply deepened.

While the most obvious victim in all of this was any appreciation of the functionality of older people, the clash with hopes for happiness was vital as well. As against the earlier eager anticipations of expanding life expectancy, the new image of the elderly amid modernity emphasized decline—"old age is a mosaic of deterioration"—and many older people themselves, even when not particularly afflicted, could easily accept this view. A middle-class magazine in France stated the case simply: "One cannot hope to become old. It should be easier to die with some hope left." Or as an American doctor, J. M. French, put it in 1892, "The old man's bank is already overdrawn. He is living from hand to mouth." By the later 19th century, it seemed that what had been a progressive dream of a growing population in later age had turned into a modernist nightmare.

There was of course a solution, and it began to be explored precisely around the turn of the century, though rather tentatively still: systematic retirement. Discussions of facilitating retirement for older workers began to heat up from the 1870s onward. A few private companies, like American Express, founded small pension programs, and by the 1880s, headed by Bismarck's Germany, some governments started to do the same. The initial plans were modest, and most workers still had to make individual arrangements, often having to remain on the job whenever possible, despite employer tendencies to cut pay and increase layoffs for older personnel.

Retirement options did gain support from unlikely allies. Many businesses were favorable, costs permitting. After all, executives largely agreed with the common wisdom that older workers were less productive and distinctly less desirable; a means of getting rid of them with a decent conscience could be just the ticket. Burgeoning trade unions increasingly agreed, by the early 20th century. They could play up retirement plans as a favor they did for older workers, again on the assumption that modern work and later age did not mix well. More to the point, getting rid of older workers helped assure jobs for younger, dues-paying members, and retirement could be used as a tradeoff for a seniority system that would increase pay with experience on the assumption that there would be a retirement cutoff point. The arrival of the Great Depression gave new vigor to the retirement push, as unions, businesses, and governments were eager to reduce the labor force and make room for new blood, while groups of older workers began to campaign directly for a state-run plan. The result in the United States was the Social Security system. Designed initially to aid older workers in need, and not to support a generalized retirement pattern, Social Security quickly turned into the basis for widespread mandatory retirement—just what business and labor had been looking for.

Here was a real, and clearly modern, innovation in human history. Individuals had always retired when means permitted and needs required, but as we have seen there had never been a generalized pattern, in part because no agricultural society could have afforded one and in part because in some of the wealthier professions (government service, clergy) old age was often considered a positive asset. The sense of asset, now, was largely a thing of the past. Virtually no one was loudly defending the desirability of older people in the labor force. Retirement plans could meet genuine needs of those older workers who found it hard to keep a job, whether because of employer bias or personal infirmities. They also addressed the larger sense that the elderly were (perhaps after children) the least useful potential workforce segment. Retirement requirements could excuse employers from having to make painful individual decisions about efficiency. As societies gained enough wealth to improve support, retirement seemed to be a universally desirable solution to the problem of old age in modern society. It was revealing that, while Western countries led the way as first industrializers, other societies joined in when they could, including Japan, which turned to widespread retirement, based on a lump-sum payment at age fifty-five, with obvious enthusiasm.

As many observers, including many older people, have pointed out, the retirement innovation, despite its broad adoption, was in many ways a strange and possibly inappropriate overall response to later age amid modernity. While there were some good and humane reasons to support retirement plans, particularly amid economic crises like the Depression, for the most part the innovation was backed for reasons that had little to do with sincere concern for older workers. It fit corporate thinking about bureaucratizing the approach to the labor force, and it fit union and government hopes to appeal to young workers. Above all, it was based on a wide but not really tested belief that older workers were damaged goods. Retirement, in other words, whatever its merits in practice, depended on accepting the false start where modern old age was concerned.

For the tensions were clear. At a time when the numbers of older people were growing, retirement increasingly removed them from the labor force. In societies like the United States, where power and validity depended heavily on work capacity and earnings, retirement told older people that their productive period was over and they should step quietly to the social sidelines. At a point—the early 20th century—at which not only the numbers but the health of many older people was improving, retirement requirements largely ignored these gains in favor of blanket assumptions that traditionally defined old age—usually between fifty-five and sixty-five—could be written off as useless. Modern retirement, at least at Western welfare state levels, also assumed, as against more traditional ideas, that families should not have to expect to support older members: the advent of American Social Security had exactly that effect, as both older people and younger adults shifted expectations from family to state. This shift may have been entirely consistent with modernity and its narrowing redefinition of what families were all about, but it created some additional confusion in the process.

Not surprisingly, many older people found the arrival of retirement as the modern solution to the treatment of old age disconcerting and objectionable, for while some older voices had been involved in the construction of the systems, they had hardly been dominant. As mandatory retirement spread in the United States, in the 1950s, many people reported real disorientation as they faced a life with no clear work routines and inadequate social contacts outside the job. Marital tensions could increase in older couples, when living patterns shifted so abruptly. For some, disruption and loss of function could lead to physical deterioration, even death, though there were authorities who pointed out that mortality rates increased for people at that age anyway, so sorting out the retirement impact was not easy. Depression and other mental health issues surfaced, though again a chicken-and-egg causation issue lurked beneath the figures. And while pension improvements gradually reduced poverty among older people, retirement could still bring active material concerns as well as other burdens. Most gerontological experts agreed that forced retirement, particularly for the increasingly healthy age group between sixty-five and seventy-five, was a truly bad idea.

But many older people themselves, especially after the new retirement system was established and expected, made a positive adjustment. Modern retirement, though based on a clear false start in terms of assumptions about older people, gained wide acceptance, adding yet another complexity to the reevaluation of assumptions about modern old age. By the 1970s, most American retirees were reporting reasonably positive adjustments, and nervousness about the imminence of retirement decreased as well. The fact was that large numbers of people began retiring earlier than the mandatory requirements—by the 1970s the average age of a retiree from General Motors was fifty-eight, and only 20% of all men were working after age sixty-five—which suggests that, however misbegotten the mandatory requirement concept, quite positive adjustments were occurring within its framework.

Two developments combined to create this unexpected pattern. First, older people themselves, particularly from the 1920s onward, were beginning to introduce positive innovations in their lives, rather than assuming they were at the mercy of the whims of family or larger society. As health improved in later age, and as retirement support became more adequate, a more abundant leisure life developed. By the 1950s advertisements in what had been a very modest magazine, *Retirement Living*, blossomed into full consumerism, complete with world travel opportunities, golf resorts, the works. Remarriage rates and sexual activity among older people were also on the upswing. Political voice improved, with immensely successful organizations like the American Association of Retired Persons, at least modifying any impression that modern old people were by definition out of power.

At the same time, retirement as a means of escaping work drudgery clearly gained growing appeal. Not surprisingly, eagerness to retire correlated closely with type of job: unskilled workers were most interested in early retirement (even though in all likelihood their material circumstances would be particularly constrained), followed by other blue collar categories. White collar workers were interestingly close behind, even though employers had often tried to persuade them that their work was far more prestigious than that of manual labor. Businessmen followed, but at some distance; interest in retirement varied more substantially. And professionals were very divided, with many people eager to continue working. The point is that the acceptance of retirement probably owed more to distaste for work than to a positive attraction to the retirement state. Interestingly, and unfortunately, the workers who retired best, with greatest satisfaction, were people like professionals who could sustain interests off the job, whereas the unskilled had the least favorable reaction once retirement actually hit. Retirement, in other words, continued to serve purposes only partially related to later age, in this case reflecting an inability to confront modern work issues more directly. The growing acceptance of retirement masked some serious issues in the interaction between old age and modernity: the false start on which massive retirement itself was based—the overgeneralization about elderly debility—had not been entirely overcome.

Old age brings potential problems regardless of social system, with great individual variety depending on health, family structure, and sheer temperament. But the lack of adequate accommodation between modern conditions and later age plays a measurable role in constraining the experience of later age for many people and in complicating preparation and support for that stage of life.

Dramatic differences among national policies provided one sign of ongoing modern confusion. From the later 20th century onward, several countries continued to use retirement as a tool to deal with unemployment. France thus lowered its retirement age to fifty-five, while Sweden, long more exemplary in maintaining a mandatory age of seventy, dropped its age target as well. Many workers, in these settings, had to retire whether they wanted to or not, and though Western Europe for the most part maintained strong welfare structures, pensions were not always sufficient. Japan, with a less adequate welfare system, experienced growing old age poverty; many older people, though forced to retire from their lifetime jobs, actually took other work after sixty-five, which compensated for the official system to some extent but hardly assured adequate job choice.

The United States took another tack, widely hailed as a more appropriate modern response. The flush of civil rights activities in the 1960s allowed old age advocates and friendly experts to push through the Age Discrimination in Employment Act (1967), which banned mandatory retirement save for a few job categories. The idea, obviously, was that many older people wanted to work and had abundant health and talent to continue service. False-start ideas about the incompatibility of old people and modern work were increasingly countered with stories about the importance of experience and reliability, as against the fecklessness of modern youth. Notions of inevitable mental deterioration were also resisted. Activist groups, like the retired-teacher-dominated Gray Panthers, played a strong role in this important redefinition of modern policy. It was relevant to note that Americans in general felt less comfortable with leisure-based definitions of life than contemporary Europeans were, so that maintaining work opportunities made good cultural sense. Sheer economics also entered in, as policymakers realized the implications of the growth of the old age sector and gradually pushed the full-benefit retirement age for Social Security up from sixty-five to sixty-seven. But the recognition that the elderly should not be uniformly marginalized was important, and many authorities urged that the policy would ultimately have to be extended to other advanced industrial societies around the world. In fact, the new policies did not lead to massive increases in work participation by older Americans; the taste for retirement and distaste for ongoing work trumped the new options, with some occasional employer pressure despite the new law tossed in. But the existence of new flexibility was arguably important even so.

Amid obvious and intriguing variety, the complex history of old age in modern societies leaves one question definitely unanswered, and a second related issue at least somewhat obscured. The gorilla in the room was the basic modern achievement itself: the huge increase in life expectancy and in the percentage of older people in the population. Could societies continue to afford the common modern retirement options as the old age percentage kept climbing? When, in the American case, by 2020 there would be only two adult workers for every retiree, instead of the current three, would the burdens of Social Security not become impossibly expensive? And societies with earlier retirement ages, or larger elderly percentages as in the Japanese case, were going to face the unresolved modern dilemma even sooner. And in this case—as many individual older workers or job reentrants were already realizing—the most sweeping modern response to date, widespread retirement, would have to be rethought, whatever the extent to which older people had managed to adjust to it. The elderly were not alone involved: society at large, accustomed to questioning the competence of older people and willing to embrace the elderly mainly in peripheral social roles—great to see the grandparents, but keep them out of my way at work—might have to reconsider core assumptions. Modern demographics almost assured that the initial approaches to modern old age, false starts and positive adaptations both included, could not endure. Was new thinking about elderly capacity, rather like the more advanced rethinking about women's capacity, going to prove essential to successful modern societies, and perhaps to more general life satisfaction as well? Whatever the ultimate definition of modern old age turns out to be, it must be informed by a clear grasp of the initial false starts as well as the successful adjustments many older people themselves have forged to the initial impacts of modernity.

Old age and modernity is still, clearly, a work in progress. There have been real advances, some of them unquestionably conducive to greater happiness both for older people and for family members who cherish them. At the other extreme, some tensions seem built into modern patterns: the growth in numbers of the quite old bring issues, like the increase of diseases like Alzheimer's, that are quite real. But in between there is the problem of some unnecessary and partly modern assumptions about the elderly—various polls for example show a great deal of nasty bias against older people as a category—and a response through widespread retirement that is almost surely unsustainable. People approaching later age face a mixture of measurable gains, very realistic worries, and a number of misconceptions and barriers that in principle can and should be rethought. The burdens on satisfaction are arguably greater than modernity need require.

Food and Obesity: Happy Meals

Historical hindsight is a marvelous instrument, and it's quite reasonable at this point to recall our indulgence in this chapter. It would have been better, in terms of long-run adjustments and considerable human happiness, if the gender, sexual, and age implications of modernity had been accurately realized earlier in time than they actually were. Huge accommodations would still have been needed, as against premodern tradition, but they could have gone more smoothly. There is at least modest excuse for the pomposity of this hindsight in that there were a few people who actually did see the implications more clearly, but were ignored. Feminist voices were raised before 1800 to argue that changing values argued for more gender equity. They did not, of course, anticipate full modernity, but they were on the right track. Plenty of people saw that sexuality should be evolving toward more open recreational priority; these included early participants in behavioral change but also commune leaders in the mid-19th century who deliberately flaunted Victorian prudishness. Old age advocates were admittedly fewer in number, but the general notion that progress should include not only longevity but happy productivity was part of the Enlightenment framework.

Almost no one, however, predicted or could predict the full implications of modernity in redefining human nutritional issues, though even here there were a few hints early on. While the emergence of obesity as a key modern problem was largely unexpected, it followed from a miscalculation so focused on adequate food supply that obesity too long went unrecognized save as a purely individual dilemma—with results that are very much part of the anxieties of modernity in the world today. This particular trap, however, would have been hard to avoid, because the goals that did receive priority were also legitimate, and indeed remain legitimate in many parts of the world today.

Many of the optimistic forecasts of the 18th century assumed growing agricultural productivity, partly because of the application of scientific discoveries but more from the general glow that surrounded the idea that human production could improve on virtually every front. Agricultural changes occurring already in the period provided some reasons for hope, as age-old procedures in Western Europe, like leaving a third of the land uncultivated each year to restore fertility, could be replaced with greater land utilization and as efficient new crops, many from the Americas, received growing attention. The focus on greater food production was central to any progressive vision, for recurrent famines had bedeviled agricultural societies from their outset. Huge general famines hit periodically, but smaller, regional crop failures occurred, it's been estimated, almost one year in seven, and while some compensatory supplies could be brought in, transportation for bulky food products could not fully remedy a local disaster. Riots over food deficiencies and/or the rising prices that accompanied them were one of the most common forms of traditional protest, from Europe to Asia.

So when hopes began to become reality, with the continued gains in agriculture during much of the 19th century, it was hardly surprising that societies reacted by shifting their tolerance for hunger, rather than looking under the modern rocks for an unexpected new challenge. The late 1840s saw the last famine to hit the Western world save as an immediate consequence of war, and while leaders might have been quite cavalier about hunger before that point—as evidenced by substantial British neglect of Irish suffering during the potato blight—change was on the way. Increasingly—and obviously this was fully in line with Enlightenment optimism—people turned away from the idea that hunger was somehow ordained by God or the result of individual bad behavior. Pessimistic economists briefly argued that hunger would alone teach people to obey their leaders and work hard, but this too was increasingly rejected. No one should have to be hungry in a properly organized, modern society. And, given improved agricultural productivity and transportation systems now capable of shipping bulk foods around the world, almost no one in modern settings had to be.

The huge shift in both goals and realities has shown through in various ways, most of them taking shape a century and a half ago and simply confirmed over time. Governments began to take increasing steps to assure food supplies. Famines in other parts of the world began to draw sympathetic (if often inadequate) attention and various kinds of charitable donations, though of course agonizing problems might persist. Certain kinds of protesters, aware that the dominant norms now reduced tolerance for lack of food, might begin to go on hunger strikes to goad their superiors. Feminists did this in the early 20th century, as did Indian nationalists a bit later on: the result was truly challenging to those in power, and often led to force feeding as preferable to watching someone even voluntarily starve. But the whole scenario depended on significant changes in the acceptability, and shock value, of hunger—the tactics would have made little sense earlier. Less politically, a new kind of domestic protest arose among some middle-class girls, first identified in Western Europe and the United States in the 1860s, through the modern incidence of the disease anorexia nervosa. In a society built now around abundant eating, girls who had trouble articulating their discontents might inchoately lash out against their parents by defying the abundance norms. Earlier, when hunger was actually prevalent, the disease would have made little sense, save as an extreme religious gesture. Clearly, food and hunger were being rapidly redefined.

Scientific discussions of food began to proliferate, with growing attention to proper nutrition and the prevention of hunger even in crisis times. The social focus resolutely targeted hunger, not the more subtle dangers of abundance. From the late 19th century onward, massive efforts to feed poor children emerged in all the industrial societies, reflecting both modern thinking about hunger and some real humanitarianism, along with concerns about debilitated populations and the need to nurture children at a time of falling birth rates, Many societies established school meals and other programs to carry the fight against hunger even further. Recurrent inquiries that showed how hunger, or at least inadequate nutrition, continued to persist among certain groups posed challenges that helped

keep a spotlight on this key issue. The advent of the Depression and atten-
dant hunger marches served as notice that social goals in this vital area
were still not being consistently met. Even more obviously, on a worldwide basis, the attention of agencies like the Food and Agriculture Organization or of NGOs like Oxfam, drawing attention to agonizing deficiencies, not only drew forth a certain amount of charity but helped maintain
the realization that lack of food remained a dominant issue. More than
formal organization was involved: any middle-class American kid growing up right after World War II, particularly if a finicky eater, would
become intimately familiar with the mantra "think of the starving children
in . . . " first Europe, then India, as a goad to clean the plate. And while the
ploy often failed, the focus on hunger rather than restraint could easily
carry on into adulthood. It would take time to reposition guilt.

Well before this juncture, however, the initial modern response was
actually being rivaled, in societies like the United States, by a historically
unprecedented situation: the possibility that not just a few individuals
but substantial segments of a modern society might face not too little
food, but far too much. And for this the initial modern response, though
admirably attuned to historic problems and ongoing needs in much of
the world, has proved ill suited and at times positively distracting once
advanced industrial societies began to move toward high-gear obesity.

For the simple facts are that, first, the challenge of rising obesity rates
is purely and simply a brand-new issue in human society and, second, no
modern society has yet figured out how to cope with it. Individuals may
manage quite well, and here some new patterns emerging a century ago
proved quite helpful; but societies more generally have failed, and the failure deepens, and extends over a wider geography, with every passing year.

The fundamental turning point in this vital area began to emerge in the
later 19th century. By this time food supplies were more than adequate
for the bulk of the population in Western Europe and North America—
though pockets of severe hunger still accompanied poverty or economic
downturns. Classical famines had ended, given the improvements both
in agriculture and in global transportation: what hunger remained was a
function of economic inequality, not supply.

For many people, not only more assured supply but also the emergence
of new commercial food producers had crucial impact on eating potential. Here, the United States unquestionably led the way. It was in the
1890s that packaged snacks began to become available, from companies
like Nabisco. These cookies and crackers were hailed not only because of

their obvious convenience but also presumably because they supported good health and nutrition. In fact, the clear advantage was that they could be eaten not only anywhere but anytime—and also eaten rapidly, in a society that was already widely known for fast meals. Snacks were a great innovation if the problem was defeating hunger—the old issue—but they actually helped tip the scale, quite literally, toward the more characteristic food issues for modern societies. Wrapped cakes were urged for "bicyclists, students and tourists," who might feel the urge to eat at odd moments. Packaged hot chocolate was similarly touted as a food for any time of the day, "The Greatest Invention of the Age, Every Family Should Have It." Chewing gum won growing attention, on the assumption that having something available for the mouth at all times, on top of an initial sugar rush, was an important gain. By the 1920s the appeals about the ready availability of snacks and their role in preventing any but the briefest pang of hunger, gained increasing emphasis. "Keep a supply of Sunshine biscuits handy and give them to your children regularly," went a common type of commercial refrain. And there's no need to belabor the obvious: from this inception, snacks became an increasingly important part of American life, filling (along with sodas, also a late-19th-century product) 10% or more of grocery store shelves. More food, more of the time became an American staple, and while other modern societies followed these trends at a certain remove, they too were pulled into the commercial food orbit to an increasing extent.

Huge changes on the supply side were matched by often diminishing needs on the intake front. The tragedy was that new food availability occurred at precisely the time when a growing minority of modern people—and soon a majority—saw their need for physical exertion reduced by machines, commuting trains, buses, and cars, and the rapid rise of white collar work. Never before had so many spent so much of their working and traveling time simply sitting. Here was the second jaw of the modern food pincer.

And finally, the characteristic modern food challenge, of abundance combined with reduced physical demands, coincided as well with the equally fundamental transitions in health, away from a primary focus on communicable disease and toward attention to degenerative illnesses such as cancer, heart attack, and strokes—illnesses in turn often associated with body type and nutritional quality. Signaling some new awareness, hospitals began weighing patients routinely for the first time, while by the early 20th century bathroom scales became available for individual homes; and at the same point the idea of an annual checkup spread more widely and included such other new experiences as regular tests for blood pressure. This huge health transition, linked to changes in longevity patterns, had implications well beyond weight and food, but it helped form the context in which the changes in food supply and need could take on additional personal and social meaning.

Not surprisingly, in the United States and elsewhere, the modern food dilemma began to generate comment fairly quickly, by the second half of the 19th century—on both sides of the Atlantic—but for a long time the problem was incompletely defined, and presented almost exclusively in individual terms. Several signals marked the first realization that modern people faced food issues that were far different from those of traditional societies. A few doctors in Europe (not, initially, the United States, with its then-lagging medical education) began to work on nutritional issues, generating new knowledge about calories and other components of the relationship between eating and health. The growing life insurance industry began publicizing actuarial tables clearly demonstrating that lower body weights correlated with longevity, though the relationships were not as rigorous as they have since become. A number of food faddists and diet experts began to ply their trade. On the American side, for example, Horace Fletcher began advocating massive amounts of chewing for each bite of food (amounts varying with type of food). His argument was that taking lots of bites would reduce intake—and he was surely right—and he demonstrated his own resulting fitness by annually climbing all the stairs in the Washington Monument. It was true that, as late as 1910, the average American newspaper still had as many ads for products and procedures that would help people gain weight as for those that would aid in loss, but the tide was turning at the gimmick level, complete with formal weight-loss books that began their ascent on bookstore shelves.

The results of these efforts were not as swiftly translated into medical practice as might be imagined, though Europeans were quicker in response than their American colleagues. Many American doctors continued to value plumpness as a sign of health, while quite legitimately questioning both the motives and the efficacy of many of the diet gurus. Some were turned off by women who seemed to want medical help mainly for beauty reasons: doctors might find their quest frivolous or might in fact share in the growing disgust about fat people more generally. Pediatricians were slow to pick up weight concerns, long more interested in making sure that kids were saved from malnutrition. Setbacks like the Depression of the 1930s, with its vivid images of hunger, helped prolong a lag between the basic modern food transition and widespread medical practice.

All this helps explain why the focal point, in this transitional phase, was not really explicitly on health. Rather, the trump cards settled on a compelling redefinition of desirable appearance, with the social decision increasingly taken—again, on both sides of the Atlantic—that fat people looked bad and, by extension, that fatness probably reflected defects of character.*

Thus a great corset debate opened up around 1900, in Europe and the United States, spurred by Parisian fashion designers. Should women be urged to acquire natural slenderness, to fit the increasingly demanding dress styles, or could they continue to use mechanical aids? The specific furor had inclusive results, with many women continuing to use girdles and other devices, but the idea that nature was preferable to artifice in fact gained ground steadily. By 1914 magazines like *Vogue* concluded that "the image of the corsetless figure is an established one." Other developments such as the emergence of specific swimming suits—though far less revealing than their counterparts today—pressed in the same direction. In the United States the 1890s unveiled a new fashion standard with the immensely popular images of the Gibson Girl, relaxed, fit, and willowy thin. And while women, as arbiters of beauty, received greatest attention, male fashion standards were involved as well. A Fat Man's Club in Connecticut, formed in the 1860s, closed soon after 1900 because no one wanted to be publicly associated with this kind of image. And new slang terms, like "slob" or "butterball," or, a bit later, "broad" as a derogatory term for women, began to gain ground, a sure indication of a massive change in popular preferences: it began to be fun to deride the fat guy or gal. An American magazine noted in 1914 how "[f]at is now regarded as an indiscretion and almost as a crime." A *Philadelphia Cook Book*, selling 152,000 copies a year at the outset of World War I, noted that "an excess of flesh is to be looked upon as one of the most objectionable forms of disease."

---

*It's worth noting that a similar aesthetic transformation, though without as much character reference, emerged around skin: traditionally, just as plumpness had signaled success, so had a pale complexion among Caucasians, a sign that the individual was not compelled to outdoor manual labor. By the later 19th century, when growing numbers of people were cooped up in factories and offices and pale of necessity, fashionability—though not best health, as it turned out—turned to the value of a tan. Modernity prompted intriguing and basic redefinitions of what beauty should represent.

What was happening, clearly, was a major change in desirable body image corresponding to the sea change in the nature of the food problems confronting modern societies. Whereas in traditional societies plump people demonstrated that they had overcome the characteristic food challenge—dearth—and by the same token could use their bodies to display good health (and often, material prosperity as well), in modern societies the equation was precisely reversed. Now, slenderness showed the capacity to defy overabundance, and was increasingly equated with beauty and health alike. And the timing was exactly right, though how explicitly aware the new dress designers and fashion gurus were of the overall shift in food supply and characteristic diseases is anybody's guess. The suddenness of the transition was remarkable, as some of the women who lived through it noted, but equally important was the depth of feeling attached. For some people, at least, fat was now truly ugly, or as one ad put it, "a disgusting fright."

Fat was also, particularly in American formulations, a visual symbol of moral or (soon) psychological issues. Far from their traditional image as jolly and good humored, fat people now were seen as harboring real personal weakness. The fat person, one 1930s offering specifically noted, is "a sad heart, black with melancholy." Most obviously, they were lazy. Anyone with adequate gumption would be able to keep the pounds off or show enough "courage" to diet them off should they arrive. The growing popularity of psychologizing added to the general homilies about lack of discipline. "Psychiatrists have exposed the fat person for what she really is—miserable, self indulgent and lacking in self control." Being fat was a "sickness," a "resignation from society."

And of course slenderness became increasingly associated with happiness: by the 1950s Americans were regaled with stories of dramatic weight loss that led immediately to better jobs and marital success. The omnipresence of enviably trim movie stars and models drove the new goals home on a virtually daily basis.

Once the modern aesthetic was established, the continuation of the story becomes familiar enough—though it has two parts. First, invitations to live up to modern body standards persisted with growing vigor. With very few brief regressions, major fashion changes, particularly in leisure wear, urged compliance. Massive numbers of people—45% of the American adult population by the 1990s—claimed to be actively involved with dieting, spending billions of dollars on diet products and surgeries.

But the second part of the story is even more important: collectively, the campaigns simply did not work well. A transition in principle did not turn out to govern actual eating and exercise habits in affluent societies—with the United States in the forefront here. Various individuals and groups actively resisted the new pressures, claiming they were exaggerated or contrary to individual rights (another modern goal)—people should be free to be fat if they so chose. Most obviously, the traditional and quite human association of more eating with more happiness overrode the dramatically new modern standards, and the distinctive modern food context.

By the later 20th century, despite many decades of widespread bombardment by the various advocates of the new standards, levels of overweight and obesity began to rise clearly and steadily. By 2002 the average American gained twenty pounds during adulthood, twice the amount characteristic in 1970. The percentage of overweight and obese combined mounted to 62% of the population, up from 48% in 1980. Rates of childhood obesity expanded at an even more rapid pace. American trends were particularly ominous, but the basic patterns spread to modern societies generally. By the early 21st century obesity rates in France had increased by 17%, to almost 10% of the population, while childhood obesity had nearly doubled, to 13% of the total. Mounting obesity was also reported throughout Western Europe and Australia, and now among middle-class children in modernizing settings in places like China and India as well.

Calling the result a false start admittedly risks oversimplification. People have to eat. Food has become more abundant in modern societies, and food producers have clearly become increasingly skilled in inducing people to eat more than they should—as in the larger serving sizes in American restaurants from the 1980s onward. Quick snacks, including those provided to kids by harried parents, apparently provide more direct happiness than the more abstract delights of slenderness. But the problem was compounded by the lure of traditional standards: the pride in making sure that everyone had (more than) enough to eat and the continued association of childhood plumpness with health. Even specific modern revisions—for example, against the customary argument that a pregnant mother was "eating for two"—prove hard to implement. Against the weight of the food industry and the inertia of older eating styles, a successful transition to modernity, though vivid for many individuals, was still-born for society at large. Aesthetic standards proved insufficient, and moral pressures, though successful in making many feel guilty about their bodies, might be actually counterproductive, generating the phenomenon of eating as consolation for breaking one's resolution.

The outcome, most obviously, was a growing public health problem but also a real toll on personal happiness, as many people became victims of the disparity between standards accepted in principle and the reality of modern bodies. Polls of white female adolescents in the United States, for example, showed massive dissatisfaction with corporal reality. Failed dieting often overshadowed adulthood—the lag in adjusting to this aspect of modernity and the larger happiness gap clearly overlapped. The question, can a more effective modern transition be devised? remained unanswered, however. By the 21st century, appeals for further innovation became more strident, particularly in the area of social regulation. Special taxes to alter consumer behavior, controls over food advertising, requirements that schools weigh children and publicize results (introduced in Australia and six American states) all suggested the growing need to rethink the adequacy of initial responses to this stubborn facet of modernity.

Dealing with Modern False Starts

Gender, sex, eating, aging—modernity has forced changes in very basic aspects of personal and social experience. Not surprisingly, in these cases and others, first responses often confirmed and even elaborated more traditional cultural patterns—even though for the long run they were inappropriate. The resultant false starts, however understandable, have significantly complicated adjustments to modernity and constrained personal happiness in the bargain—both for groups that sought more rapid change and for those who remained comforted by the persistence of older norms and shocked that they could not hold their ground. Disputes over images of dependent women, negative presentations of sexuality, or even the appropriateness of "all you can eat" extravaganzas continue to burn bright, not only dividing groups within modern societies but also placing conflicting expectations on individuals. The result, obviously, is no small amount of personal or familial anguish, when the path toward later age is unclear or when bodies resolutely refuse to meet personal and social goals, or even when echoes of earlier ideas about gender or sexuality intrude. Here, in turn, in the ongoing impact of false starts in responding to modern change, is a key source of the gap between modernity and personal satisfaction.

But false starts can be recovered. Those that intruded early, as with gender or sexuality or aspects of leisure, began to be redone within a century, and while the process is far from complete even today—hence continued disputes and confusions—the disparity between cultural response and modern demand has been lessened. We do not know whether comparable adjustments will prove possible for the modern dilemmas that emerged more gradually, where adjustments remain measurably out of whack. Overall, the lesson of false starts is twofold: they help explain why modernity has not generated more abundant happiness, but they may also—encouragingly—demonstrate the possibility, in a huge process of change that is still relatively young, of gaining a second chance.

Further Reading

On the modern history of sex, several excellent inquiries for the United States: E. Freedman and John D'Emilio, *Intimate Matters: A History of Sexuality in America* (Chicago: University of Chicago Press, 1998); Beth Bailey, *Sex in the Heartland* (Cambridge, MA: Harvard University Press, 2002); and Rochelle Gurstein, *The Repeal of Reticence: America's Cultural and Legal Struggles over Free Speech, Obscenity, Sexual Liberation, and Modern Art* (New York: Hill and Wang, 1999). A relevant older study, mainly on culture, is Paul Robinson, *The Modernization of Sex* (Ithaca, NY: Cornell University Press, 1989). See also Dennis Altman, *Global Sex* (Chicago: University of Chicago Press, 2001); and Peter N. Stearns, *Sexuality in World History* (New York: Routledge, 2009). On other important cases, Igor S. Kon, *The Sexual Revolution in Russia* (New York: Free Press, 1995) and Sabine Frühstück, *Colonizing Sex: Sexology and Social Control in Modern Japan* (Berkeley: University of California Press, 2003) .

On old age, some of the best work was done a few decades ago, though with renewed attention to aging I expect additional scholarship. A fine recent example is Pat Thane, ed., *The Long History of Old Age* (London: Thames and Hudson, 2010). See also Andrew Achenbaum, *Old Age in the New Land: The American Experience since 1790* (Baltimore, MD: Johns Hopkins University Press, 1980); David Troyansky, *Old Age in the Old Regime: Image and Experience in 18th-Century France* (Ithaca, NY: Cornell University Press, 1989); William Graebner, *History of Retirement*, rev. ed. (New Haven, CT: Yale University Press, 1980).

For recent work on what might be seen as the first anticipations of the new modern problem on weight, see Katharina Vester, "Regime Change: Gender, Class, and the Invention of Dieting in Post-Bellum America," *Journal of Social History* (Fall 2010). Other relevant works include Naomi Wolf, *The Beauty Myth* (New York: HarperCollins, 2002); Peter N. Stearns, *Fat History: Bodies and Beauty in the Modern West* (New York: New York University Press, 2002); Sander Gilman, *Fat: A Cultural History of Obesity* (Cambridge, UK: Polity Press, 2008); and Amy Erdman Farrell, *Fat Shame: Stigma and the Fat Body in American Culture* (New York: New York University Press, 2011).

Women's and gender history has become a massive field. For larger introductions to the complexities of modern change, with further references attached, see Merry Wiesner-Hanks, *Gender in History: Global Perspectives*, 2nd ed. (Malden, MA: Blackwell, 2011). See also S. J. Kleinberg et al., eds., *The Practice of U.S. Women's History: Narratives, Intersections, and Dialogues* (New Brunswick, NJ: Rutgers University Press, 2007); Bonnie G. Smith, *Women's History in Global Perspective*, vols. 1-3 (Urbana: University of Illinois Press, 2004); Anne Cova, *Comparative Women's History: New Approaches* (New York: Columbia University Press, 2006); Kathleen Canning, *Gender History in Practice: Historical Perspectives on Bodies, Class, and Citizenship* (Ithaca, NY: Cornell University Press, 2006). On the United States specifically, see Mary Beth Norton, Ruth M. Alexander, and Thomas Paterson, *Major Problems in American Women's History: Documents and Essays*, 3rd ed. (New York: Houghton Mifflin, 2009) and Linda K. Kerber and Jane Sherron DeHart, *Women's America: Refocusing the Past*, 6th ed. (New York: Oxford University Press, 2003).

6

The Dilemmas of Work
in Modernity

Polls taken of British factory workers by the 1950s and 1960s neatly
defined the problem of figuring out how work stands in modern society: a majority professed some real job satisfaction, but nearly as large
a majority said they hoped their kids would find different opportunities.
The sense that options should exist, rather than parental footstep-fol-
lowing, was distinctly modern, but the clear ambivalence may have been
modern as well.[1]

Modern work patterns emerged with industrialization, though they
ultimately spread well beyond the factory setting. In contrast to most pre-
industrial norms, they involved speed, subordination, and specialization,
and they could prove quite unpleasant. The key trends have gone through
numerous iterations, with changing technologies and changing job categories, but the links between contemporary patterns and the early-19th-
century origins are clear cut. Efforts to accommodate to characteristic
modern work problems stretch back as well, including a few false starts;
at no point thus far, however, has an entirely acceptable arrangement
developed for most workers. In many ways, modern work replicates, and
in part produces, the larger relationship between modernity and happiness, but in somewhat darker hues. Workers themselves note, usually,
that modern jobs serve satisfaction less well than modern families do—
despite all the issues in many modern families. Distress for some, qualified adjustment for the larger number: here is a fairly consistent response
to modern work over what is now many decades.

For workers on the front lines of change, modernity in work got off to a
screechingly bad start, bringing far more obvious deterioration than that
attached to the false starts discussed in the previous chapter. For the rising, articulate middle classes, however, problems were masked by a particularly vigorous appeal to happiness and good cheer, which continues

to hover around modern work even today—at an extreme, producing a kind of false consciousness where work is concerned, an inability to face problems squarely. The most important question is what has happened to the work experience after the bad start—which is where the challenge of interpreting ambivalence comes in. It is tempting to argue that a worsening of work life is a durable product of modernity, but there would be many workers themselves who would contradict this. At the least, it is clear that work has not improved as much as some early optimists hoped, and that the results play into the gap between modernity and satisfaction overall.

Modern work, then, involves a deliberately harsh launch, masked only by optimistic rhetoric. Measures taken since the later 19th century have addressed the core issues tangentially, by cutting job hours or adding human resources coatings. The result is less a false start than a recurrently inadequate response.

The Nature of Modern Work

Anyone with a dim memory of history lessons about the industrial revolution will recall the many miseries that attended this central pillar of modernity: low wages and slum living in crowded cities, problems of sanitation and safety, and abuse of child labor, just for starters. Many workers accepted factory jobs only because they had no options, and readily fled back to the countryside for agricultural jobs whenever possible. Similar patterns emerge with industrialization still today, as in China, where millions of rural migrants crowd into urban factories.

In fact, however, though these birth pains are significant, they are not the main point of the work experience in modernity. Successful industrializations, within a few decades, see improved wages (though with troubling pockets of poverty still); urban conditions ameliorate at least a bit, as measured among other things by better health levels; and abuses like child labor begin, if slowly, to recede. In significant ways, there is progress over time.

It's also important, on this vital topic as with others, not to overdo the beauties of premodern work, even aside from outright slavery. Jobs in agriculture and the crafts could be physically grueling; manual weavers, for example, frequently became permanently deformed because they had to activate looms with their chests. Not surprisingly, one of the boasts of modern work optimists involved the reductions of physical effort that machines could produce. Premodern jobs also frequently involved abuse of apprentices and common laborers, including harsh physical discipline as well as low pay. While in theory craft work allowed people to rise from training to paid labor to shop ownership, the ladder frequently broke down, leaving many in lifetime subordination.

Still, with all the qualifications and even aside from temporary setbacks that were later corrected, modern work, for many people, involved at least three systematic areas of deterioration that became all the more apparent when initial disarray passed.

✦ First, compared to premodern opportunities for the majority (slavery again aside), modern work placed people under the orders of supervisors lifelong, and not merely during years of apprenticeship. Most modern workers never gain full control of the organization of their working day and must always account directly to a boss.

✦ Second—and this was an accurate perception by Karl Marx, even if he overdid it a bit—much modern work becomes far more subdivided and specialized than premodern work was. This in turn makes it difficult for a worker to identify the product or end result he or she might claim as his or her own. It is arguably much easier, as a result, to wonder whether—aside from the need to earn some money—the whole effort is worthwhile. The contrast with generating craft products or bringing in a harvest remains telling.

✦ Third—and over time this may be the worst aspect of the three, or at least the one that continues to deteriorate most clearly—the pace of work accelerates, with machines or machine-like rhythms, rather than human needs, setting the standards. The directors of modern work deliberately pressed workers to abandon premodern work habits like gathering for a chat, wandering around every so often, or even taking a nap. Workplace clocks helped enforce a modern sense of time and punctuality. Early in the industrial revolution a French factory owner awarded a bouquet of flowers each week . . . to the most productive machine (one assumes they wilted quickly); no human beings need apply. A hundred years later, in the early part of the 20th century, the efficiency engineers who began to run the show in the United States deliberately set as their aim to make human motions as machine-like, as removed from individual will, as possible. The priorities were clear.

It's not hard to paint a stark modern picture: pressed to work by bosses rather than one's own determination, and urged on to an increasingly rapid pace, the modern worker specializes in a corner of activity with results that are hard to determine or identify with. And all of this occurs as work is also increasingly separated from family, with the tensions of trying to assure adequate attention to the domestic side added in.

Not surprisingly, at many points in the past two centuries, workers directly or indirectly have responded to these reductions of the human dimension of the job. Many continued to flee modern work settings at the first opportunity. Massive turnover rates, of 1,000% a year or more, were common for decades in factory industry, and other workers eagerly settled for lower pay in preference to engaging with modern work in the first place. From Luddite raids on technology onward, workers also periodically attacked the conditions of modern work—as in the 1960s sit-down strikes in the United States and Europe that briefly insisted on greater variety and worker control on the job. Individual agony could be real, as with a late-19th-century German worker who claimed that after a day on the job his "eyes burned so" that he could hardly sleep and lamented, "the work is becoming increasingly mechanical, no more incentive, we are worn out and mindless." What Karl Marx described as alienation was a very real human experience for many modern workers.

And in contrast to initial low wages, exploitative child labor, and slums, the three basic deteriorations in modern work have never been really repaired. Working under others' supervision, at a specialized job slice whose purpose is not always clear, and amid pressures for a rapid pace—these three modern patterns continue to define modern labor for most people, even in a vaunted "postindustrial" economy. It is tempting—and I truly believe, partially accurate—to claim that one key reason for the shaky relationship between modernity and happiness involves the modern constraints on work satisfaction.

Palliatives: How to Survive Modern Work

Yet without further exploration, the claim ignores a number of complexities, not the least of which is the fact that most modern people, workers themselves, would not fully recognize it in their own lives.

First of all, even during the harsh birth of industrial work, situations and personalities varied, and this continues to be the case. Locomotive engineers, though tied to many modern work characteristics, were distinctively proud of their role in powering mechanical giants through the countryside, which at least at first overrode concerns about speedup or specialization. Except in the direst circumstances, happy personalities (remember the genetic component) could and can often find value in various modern work situations.

Over time, as well, people began to get used to modern work conditions, no longer finding them newly distasteful, while also forgetting premodern comparative standards. Employers in most industrial societies reported that the first generation or two of factory workers were the hardest to accommodate, since their expectations had been shaped by preindustrial conditions. Experiences like clock-based work time, for example, no longer seemed strange to third-generation personnel.

It's also vital to note that a minority of modern workers—even more than the locomotive drivers—found modern work more rather than less fulfilling than its premodern counterpart had been. Modernity creates an important cluster of jobs involving managerial power or wide-ranging professional competence that can be deeply satisfying, indeed life-consuming. (These are the same categories, today, that are most reluctant to retire.) Premodern societies had not offered the number or range of these opportunities, which means that for a significant group of people modern work measurably improved, providing sources of interest or power that overrode the often hard effort involved. And since the work beneficiaries tended to populate the upper reaches of society, shaping broader opinions, they tended, intentionally or not, to inhibit or ignore any wider realization of the work deteriorations experienced by the majority.

Further, the arrival of modern work was accompanied by a widely trumpeted new work ethic, whose proponents deeply believed that everyone—not just the managerial and professional minority—should be able to find life satisfaction in job commitments. From the middle of the 19th century onward, articulate business leaders and many popularizing publicists, like Horatio Alger or the aptly named Samuel Smiles in England, argued and often deeply believed that modern work brought joy, and that there was something wrong with those who did not appreciate its pleasures. A chorus of cheerleading voices, some sincere, others manipulative, tried to persuade all comers that work had deep purpose. We're all familiar with this ethic—essentially, the translation of new happiness hopes into the world of labor—for elements reverberate still. In its initial forms the ethic showed through in Ben Franklin's injunction about early to bed, early to rise making a man healthy and wealthy; or in Horatio Alger urging that devotion to work would lead directly to improvements in life and station. Publicists, even children's story writers, pushed this value system tirelessly, insisting that work should be the centerpiece of a meaningful existence.

The modern work ethic had real consequences. It helped convince new businessmen and professionals that their own toil was justified: many people, particularly but not exclusively in the rising middle class, tried to center their day and life around work, and still do so today. The ethic also made it more difficult for others, who could not buy into the values entirely, to complain successfully. Work, after all, was a good thing, so why grumble? Even more: the ethic's proponents easily argued that people who did not succeed in life were personally faulty, because by definition they had not worked hard enough and/or had frittered away their earnings on distractions like drink or gambling. Discontent, in this view, was not a valid comment on modern work but a sign of individual failure. Of course, not everyone believed this: protests about work continued. But the idea that complaint reflected on the complainer, not the system, was hard to shake off entirely. It would resurface for example in the 20th century, when a new breed of industrial psychologists, brought in to reduce workplace grievances, argued that work issues reflected a person's problems off the job, perhaps in family life, not any intrinsic employment problem.

It's also worth remembering that even noncapitalist modern work systems—notably, the Soviet—generated their own varieties of work boosterism, designed to undercut and delegitimize complaints about the nature of modern work.

Thus far: modern work generated significant new constraints, but not equally for everyone, and the system's proponents also tried to mask the trends by making new appeals for satisfaction on the job. Here is part of the explanation for the incomplete impact of modern deteriorations at work: not everyone experienced them, and even those who did might be partially distracted by pressures to look toward the positive. Modernity has also provided enough oscillations in employment, or fears of unemployment, that many workers are periodically grateful just to have a job, and duly distracted from the chore of evaluating its quality.

The big majority adjustment to modern work, however, was a growing, sometimes grudging, willingness to trade full job satisfaction for money— a process called instrumentalism, by which workers turned away from premodern expectations of much intrinsic meaning on the job toward a view that work should be an instrument for a better life in other respects. Obviously, premodern workers must sometimes have taken pleasure in the earnings a good job provided, but a systematic and approved commitment to instrumentalism was a modern development, a crucial adjustment to what was otherwise an intimidating set of trends. Historians have found the first explicit signs of instrumentalism toward the middle of the 19th century, in Western Europe and the United States, and obviously as a tactic it has thrived ever since.

Instrumentalism could take several overlapping forms. Workers might simply—as early printers' unions were doing around 1850—say that they would accept new technologies that made their work duller if they got higher pay in return. Or, as a second variant, workers might gain comfort in their role as breadwinners: the job isn't much, but at least I can take pride in supporting my family. The breadwinner idea was pushed hard in the 19th century from various sources, helping to sustain male workers amid the various changes modernity brought, including the new physical separation of work from family. In the middle classes, these first two approaches might combine, with earners expecting to provide measurable improvements in living standards for their families—bringing home the bacon, and not merely bread.

A third variant of instrumentalism involved expectations of upward mobility. Horatio Alger, after all, praised the value of work but also insisted that diligence would pay off through improvements in station, either for the worker or his children or both. Stories of rich people with humble beginnings circulated widely, in the same vein. Newspapers—a key part of the cheerleading chorus—began carrying accounts like the following 1830s Massachusetts entry, as successful people mused on their origins:

> My father taught me never to play till all my work for the day was finished. . . . If I had but half an hour's work to do in the day, I must do it first thing, and in half an hour [the modern time touch here]. . . . It is to this habit that I now owe my prosperity.

The mobility theme struck a particular chord in the United States, where it became part of national self-image. By the 20th century Americans became revealingly likely to exaggerate the amount of upward mobility in their society, in contrast to Europeans who just as systematically minimized. But every modern work situation has generated some people who are willing to overlook shortcomings on the actual job because they think they can get ahead.

Instrumentalism, in its various forms, clearly explains why work deteriorations do not show up more explicitly as people evaluate modernity. Yet, as a solution to the modern work dilemma, the approach has its limits. First, of course, it clearly depends on an ability to see external rewards accruing: in periods where living standards do not rise, instrumentalism can produce less satisfaction, not more. The same holds true for mobility aspirations. By the 20th century, scholars were identifying what came to be called white collar alienation, whereby service workers who expected to climb into managerial ranks thanks to their labors realized, around age forty, that they were going nowhere, and soured measurably as a result. Americans, with the national symbolism of mobility, were particularly vulnerable here.

At least as important was the fact that, even when it functioned well, instrumentalism had its sad face. To the extent that workers, of whatever collar, were implicitly or explicitly giving up expected satisfactions from the job itself, based on real or imagined premodern standards, they were clearly surrendering some aspect of happiness. The trade-off could work, but it was not an entirely pleasant compromise—not in keeping, for example, with the more stirring injunctions of the middle-class work ethic itself. Happy was the worker who both enjoyed his job *and* gained greater rewards, but instrumentalism suggested, probably correctly, that this was not the standard experience.

Other changes in modern work, accumulating from the later 19th century onward, provide the final set of cushions for the work experience—here, essentially modifying, though not entirely eliminating, initial false starts. Reduction in work hours was central. Initial beliefs that only standard premodern work days, or a bit more, would allow machine production to pay off gradually yielded to the realization that the down sides of modern work—particularly, its pace—could be managed only if there was less of it. A modern pattern was established whereby in principle a day was divided among work, sleep, and leisure (though commuting time and household tasks could cut into this latter), rather than a longer but more relaxed work stint, premodern fashion, punctuated by sleep though also embellished by periodic festival days. Vacations, also gradually introduced, amplified work reductions. The whole notion of regular retirement was also a response to the need to reduce the work experience.

Other managerial tweaks might also ease some pressures. Newly established personnel offices, by the 20th century, worked to promote greater worker satisfaction and also began to limit abrasive practices by supervisors. Foremen, once heavy-handed bosses, were taught to become more adept in human relations. Modern work still operated under supervision, but it became more velvet-gloved, while new methods, like prizes and picnics, were promoted to make workers feel that their contributions had real meaning. The rise of white collar work, gradually surpassing factory labor in the most modern economies, might also modify some of the worst modern work pressures. Employers exerted great effort to make white collar workers feel different from factory workers, more part of a middle class with dress to match. Inherently, office work provided more opportunities for informal socializing than factories did. For both real and manipulative reasons, many white collar workers did gain a sense of superiority over their blue collar cousins, and even when, as Marxists argued, this was a false consciousness it might produce more perceived satisfaction. More recently still, introductions of more flexible work schedules, including telecommuting, have sought to modify the most rigid pace of work and blend family and work concerns more constructively.

There were, however, clear limits to these important changes, for the fundamental character of modern work was not transformed. The pace of work continued to mount. Industrial psychologists might reduce the pain a bit—piping music in was a way to get workers to move more quickly without full awareness—but they strove mightily to speed things up. Henry Ford reified instrumentalism by improving pay while insisting on adherence to the new assembly line. Night work became increasingly common into the 21st century, another source of conflict between work and the normal functioning of the human body. Office and sales work—the white collar staples—was increasingly pressed into the modern mold. New equipment, like typewriters (and, later, computers) allowed new work speed and productivity requirements—how many words a minute?—while reducing skill levels and variety on the job. It was no accident that coffee drinking became intractably linked to many office jobs, in preparing employees to meet the mounting pace. Foremen rigorously supervised sales personnel. Many white collar categories, like sales personnel, were also subjected to new emotional standards, pressed for example to keep smiling regardless of customer provocation—a new installation of the notion that work should seem to be fun whether it was or not. Here was an explicit application of the general promotion of modern cheerfulness in the workplace, and it could be emotionally costly. An American telephone operator put it this way: "You can't be angry. . . . You have to be pleasant, no matter how bad you feel." With computers, finally, for some employees, boundaries between life on and off the job were even challenged, potentially cutting into one of the modern compromises.

Furthermore, attempts to insist on apparent work satisfaction continued essentially unabated, complicating efforts to complain or even objectively assess. Industrial psychologists were joined by many human resources popularizers in urging a happy adjustment to the job. Protests continued recurrently, particularly with the rise of trade unions, but it proved particularly difficult to make major strides on grievances most directly related to work quality; instrumentalist gains came more easily. And work-based protest itself trailed off, in Western societies, after the 1950s and 1960s, partly because the growing white collar segment proved hard to galvanize. A *Saturday Evening Post* writer, fulminating against the union movement, restated the work ethic in terms many Americans would readily accept: "Most of the trouble in the United States will end when the people realize that the cure is useful work. . . . Work will buy life and happiness. There is no honest alternative. Sweat or die!"

Stress

Adjustments in the worst features of modern work, combined with instrumentalism and limits on work time, all help explain why the most painful forms of alienation have not afflicted the majority of the labor force. Emphasis on work as a positive source of satisfaction, including specific injunctions on white collar personnel to keep smiling, might reinforce an accommodation process—though it might also complicate.

The clearest sign, however, that something continued to misfire in modern work involved the surprisingly persistent need to identify real or perceived psychological damage, in ways that had no counterpart in the premodern world. The problem first surfaced clearly in the later 19th century, after the dust had settled on the most disruptive, initial features of industrialization but as the pace of work inexorably moved forward. It was at this point that distress signals shifted from individual workers alone—like the German miner cited earlier—to medical professionals and publicists.

First impressions emerged literally around 1850, though with no formal apparatus or terminology available. A *New York Times* article in 1852 describes a young businessman who has to be always busy, constantly checks his watch, and becomes impatient at the slightest delay. Never at rest, he becomes always a bit weary, and finally his health fails. The "vigor of his youth" becomes (revealing phrase, as this evaluation later developed) "burnt out" well before his time.

The first named candidate to capture this modern condition was rather cumbersomely called "neurasthenia," a disease first identified in the United States in 1869. The target was a generalized fatigue, plus loss of concentration and efficiency, caused by the various stresses of modern society. Work was not the only culprit, but it played a primary role, particularly where middle-class men were concerned, and of course the reference to declining efficiency linked to modern work requirements as well. Writing in 1920, one American doctor took neurasthenia as an established fact:

> That not only America, but every part of the whole civilized [read: *modern*] world has its neurasthenia is an established fact. . . . Modern life, with its hurry, its tensions, its widespread and ever present excitement, has increased the proportion of people involved. . . . The busy man with his telephone close at hand may be saving time on each transaction, but by enormously increasing the number of his transactions he is not saving HIMSELF.

Neurasthenia was widely publicized for decades, which both reflected its status as a result of modern work and encouraged people to think they were suffering from it. It served to reinforce the need for vacations and other compromises with modern jobs.

But the term itself did not last, and for a time was replaced with the popularity of the idea of nervous breakdown—a concept first described in 1901, and then promoted by what was learned about battlefield trauma in World War I. Like neurasthenia, breakdown (with a more modern, mechanical ring to it) described all sorts of causes and symptoms. Emphasis again went to fatigue and increased difficulty in functioning, with work therefore a particular locus. As before, primary reference highlighted the "pace, pressure and uncertainty of existence" in modern life, though productive work was sometimes taken as a cure as well as a sign that breakdown did not impend. Indeed, more than with neurasthenia, nervous breakdown drew comments that, while the psychological collapse might be quite real, the individual him- or herself was responsible

122 | MALADJUSTMENTS IN MODERNITY

for rallying and getting a grip. As with neurasthenia, however, extensive popularization made it clear that the disease served a real explanatory or exculpatory need, in a variety of modern settings.

Nervous breakdown, however, never caught on fully with medical professionals, unlike its predecessor. It generated more popular than expert appeal, and this helps explain why—along with new tranquilizer drugs that could reduce or mask some of the problems involved—this term too began to decline by the 1960s, though it survives to an extent even today.

In its place rushed the closely related concepts of stress and burnout, both products of the 1950s that retain currency even today to explain the need to let up on work, change jobs, or at least explain why individual performance was deteriorating. Stress, as a category, began to receive popular notice from the late 1940s onward, with a major book issued by its leading proponent, the Canadian endocrinologist Hans Selye, in 1956. More than with nervous breakdown and even neurasthenia, stress featured some clear physical symptoms, most notably high blood pressure but also risks of heart attack. It also derived from a distinct line of research on animals. But like its predecessors it was clearly linked to the perils of modern work life—"primarily a disease of stepped-up living and urbanization," as one *Time* magazine article put it. And it had the usual symptoms of fatigue and decreased effectiveness, though through the specific mechanism of stress hormones. Popular articles on stress began to crop up in the 1950s, accelerating steadily into the 21st century.

Burnout was a close companion, in meaning and chronology alike. The term was first used early in the 1970s, to denote long-term exhaustion and diminished interest, with job function high among the causes. A study in 2000 referred specifically to burnout as "largely an organizational issue caused by long hours, little down time, and continual peer, customer and superior surveillance"—that is, by common features of modern work.

Stress and burnout have required a bit of flexibility in their continued evolution. Stress, particularly, initially highlighted the most pressure-filled, executive jobs—President Dwight Eisenhower's heart attack was attributed to stress. Lower-level workers were held to be exempt. Over time it turned out that people at the managerial summit, who work very hard but encounter few job frustrations, suffer lower levels of stress and disease than many other kinds of workers, who are the clearer victims of this facet of modernity. Still, the concept has proved sufficiently protean, and needed, to survive empirical challenges and adjustments.

Clearly, on the fringe between formal medicine and popularization, a series of concepts has proved essential, for over a century now, to describe the toll that modern work, and more vaguely other aspects of modern life, can take. People have needed some partially approved term to account for why they may feel so bad at work, despite the cheerful work ethic and the various personnel remedies now being applied to prevent stress as well as grievance. They use the term not only to explain how they, or their friends, feel, but also as a satisfactory motivation for changing jobs or retiring outright. They use the term, in sum, to explain the aspects of modern work that, for some at least, have never been repaired.

Polls (Again)

The ambiguities of overall contemporary reactions to modern work flow directly from the history of the experience, with a few more specifically recent twists. Both quantitative and qualitative data can be read to suggest quite a bit of satisfaction, with minority dissent; or minority satisfaction with impressive amounts of majority hesitation or positive distaste. The data, in other words, mirror the conflicted reactions of the British workers cited earlier in the chapter: jobs are endurable, maybe a bit more, but there should be better options. And while American workers may be—or may have been until a few years ago—a bit more positive than their modern counterparts elsewhere, they exhibit similar shadings overall. The polling data do not, unfortunately, interpret themselves, which is where the larger perspectives on modernity in work become vital.

A summary of Gallup, University of Chicago, and Conference Board polls,[2] taken in 2009, restates the dilemma. One survey shows job satisfaction at its lowest level in two decades, but two others cite remarkable stability for a half-century. No one claims that happiness in work has been going up in recent decades, particularly at the full satisfaction level. In the Conference Board venture, less than half of all Americans were now marking "quite happy" or "fairly happy" with work, down from 61% in 1987: tellingly, the respondents said that the most enjoyable part of the job, other than the company of coworkers, was the commute, which as the pollsters noted was a rather shocking comment on the work itself. But the other polls claim that 85% or even (Gallup) 95% of American workers are either completely or somewhat satisfied with their jobs, with the least happy in some of the more unskilled occupations (only a quarter of all roofers claim satisfaction). But even here, it is necessary to probe a bit more deeply: though teachers claim high levels of work pleasure, like the other helping and creative professions, in fact large numbers leave the calling within five years of starting, so what do the poll claims measure?

British materials, though slightly different, are also confusing. A quarter of all workers claim to be very happy at work—the American figure usually ranges between 30 and 40-45%—but only 20% describe themselves as unhappy (American figures are somewhat lower here). Most folks, in other words, find a mixture of pleasure and annoyance in their jobs. What satisfaction there is derives overwhelmingly more from friendships on the job than from the job itself. Smaller companies work better than large for job happiness in the United Kingdom, and happiness declines the longer a person stays with an organization. By the same token, despite widespread if partial satisfaction, job changing is common—men take four to six different posts in their lifetimes, women even more, and many stick to a given job three years or less. (Similarly, in the apparently happier United States, a third of all workers actively believe that another job might well be better for them.) Britons spend much more time worrying about work than love life. Over half believe that a perfect job for them exists—the happiness rhetoric in action?—but over half also believe that they have yet to find it.

The intriguing American interviews conducted by Studs Terkel in the 1970s produced arguably similar—and similarly ambivalent—results.[3] Most interviewees took pride in doing a good job, whether bus driving or bank management was their calling. But lots of workers found their supervisors unduly critical or simply ignorant, which cut their pleasure considerably and might lead to active discontent; and a sense of boredom increased after a few years on a job. Formulating a grievance, however, was difficult, lest one be labeled a "troublemaker." Most people tended to get through the day thinking about other things: "So you just go about your work. You have to have pride. So you throw it off to something else. And that's my stamp collection." The hectic pace of work came in for considerable, and clearly adverse, comment. On the other hand, many workers professed a real measure of contentment, and not just the rich and famous: an ironworker talked of his pleasure in looking down at the world from a skyscraper scaffold: "It's a challenge up there, and that work's hardly ever routine. . . . I'm a good man and everyone on the job knows it." In between the disgruntled and the complacent—and perhaps most typically—a garbage man says he can't complain: "You have to work to make a living, so what's the use."

In sum: many contemporary workers clearly don't like their jobs, particularly when, because of close supervision or lack of meaning, modern conditions apply most bleakly and where instrumentalist rewards are meager as well. A probably larger number, particularly in the United States, really cherish their work, because they are happy people to begin with, or because they are encouraged to favorable response because of cultural pressures to be positive, or because the job is intrinsically interesting (and sometimes well rewarded). A subset of this important minority like their work in part because of its modern qualities—the challenging pace, particularly—but for a larger number other aspects of work, some of which, like companionship, had been present in premodern settings as well, form the primary appeal. The largest numbers still are in between. They are somewhat satisfied, but usually in spite of modern work characteristics—except for instrumentalist opportunities—rather than because of them. Stress and burnout are concepts close to the surface for this group. And the members of this majority are tentative: they often wish different work fates for their children, they often change jobs, they depend heavily on instrumentalist cushions and the ability to daydream about them. And, as already noted, they are eager to retire.

Age-graded results may add a bit to understanding. In the American data workers in their forties are least satisfied—despite the fact that instrumentalist rewards are usually greater than for younger categories. This is the age when disappointment at not finding the conceived-of perfect job, not matching one's own mobility aspirations, bites particularly hard. Workers in their fifties, in contrast, are most satisfied: they've either achieved a desired result or figured out how to adjust expectations—and of course the cushion of retirement around the corner undoubtedly helps as well.

Trends

If there had been polls of workers in factory or other modern categories a hundred years ago, they surely would be less positive than they have become over the past fifty years. Modern conditions were more raw, older standards could be more actively remembered, and instrumentalist responses were less well developed. Even then, however, a minority would have expressed active satisfaction—because their slice of modern work was genuinely engaging, because their personalities were sanguine in the first place, and/or because the positive work ethic (and its promise of mobility) made real sense to them. Whether this minority has grown or not is impossible to determine.

While reactions to work have improved, however, key aspects of the modern work condition still provoke hesitation or dismay, with pace and the vagaries of supervision at the top of the list. Some data suggest stagnation over the past half-century, others suggest some deterioration. One American study shows widening gaps between relatively satisfied and less satisfied, reflecting growing income inequality and, through this, the dependence of contemporary job responses far less on the work itself than on the instrumentalist system. For many, changes in real income or in lifestyle expectations become the driver to poll results, supplemented in the United States by particularly sensitive beliefs that work negativity might reflect badly on the respondent—not on the qualities of work per se. For work in itself, some sense of personal pride in performance and, often, enjoyment of the social contacts available balance unfavorable features to create a neutral to slightly positive tilt.

This evaluation is consistent with one final bit of evidence. The last great outburst of work-based protest, in the West, occurred in the 1960s. Among the many currents in that intriguing decade was a serious movement, by many workers themselves though backed as well by some (not all) labor leaders and many students, to seek a positive change in work arrangements geared toward greater satisfaction. Key targets involved giving workers themselves greater autonomy and more opportunities to suggest improvements, while also facilitating regular movement to different sets of jobs, in order to expand variety and interest and reduce narrow specialization. The result was an interesting series of work experiments in a number of factories, particularly in Europe, soon supplemented by the introduction of some new management techniques on the Japanese model, where encouragements to worker suggestions about production processes were further enhanced and where managers introduced new emphasis on open communication. Some of the changes seemed to reduce boredom and job turnover. But there was no revolution here: basic modern features persisted, and many employers found it easier to talk about raises—more instrumentalism—than to tinker too deeply with modern work arrangements. In the United States, furthermore, where a particularly bitter conflict arose in an automobile plant in Lordstown, Ohio, changes were further stifled by worker concern that rearrangements, though generating greater job variety, might threaten earnings levels. After a bit of turmoil, the majority of workers decided that jobs as income sources took precedence over jobs as sources of interest. It was hard to zero in consistently on modern work itself.

Overall, the relationship between modern work and happiness remains tentative. The three characteristic modern deteriorations have been modified, considerably masked through off-job rewards and other adjustments, but not reversed. For a minority, often armed with semimedical terms to shield against the modern pace, real distaste is close to the surface. And, for a variety of reasons, including cheerfulness pressures as well as instrumentalism, basic tensions are not easy to discuss in any systematic way. Here, most broadly, is a clear source of the partial disconnect between modernity and happiness.

Further Reading

For a general evaluation of the emergence of modern work, Peter N. Stearns, *From Alienation to Addiction: Modern American Work in Global Historical Perspective* (Boulder, CO: Paradigm, 2008). A famous historical comment on reaction to modern work is Edward Thompson, *The Making of the English Working Class* (New York: Penguin, 1991); at least as famous as journalistic commentary is Studs Terkel, *Working: People Talk about What They Do All Day and How They Feel about What They Do* (New York: New Press, 1997). Jonathan Goldthorpe, et al., *The Affluent Worker in the Class Structure* (New York: Cambridge University Press, 1969) is a classic study on degrees of alienation. See also Daniel Nelson, *Managers and Workers*, 2nd ed.: *Origins of the 20th-Century Factory System in the U.S.* (Madison: University of Wisconsin Press, 1995); Jürgen Kocka, *White Collar Workers in America, 1890-1940: A Social-Political History in International Perspective* (Thousand Oaks, CA: Sage, 1980); and Daniel Rodgers, *The Work Ethic in Industrial America, 1850–1920*, 2nd ed. (Chicago: University of Chicago Press, 1978). A recent study of expert efforts to speed work up is Matthew Stewart, *The Management Myth: Why the Experts Keep Getting It Wrong* (New York: Norton, 2009); Jonathan Gershuny, *Changing Times: Work and Leisure in Postindustrial Society* (Oxford: Oxford University Press, 2000); Amy S. Wharton, *Working in America: Continuity, Conflict, and Change*, 3rd ed. (New York: McGraw-Hill, 2005); and Kerry J. Daley, *Minding the Time in Family Experience*. Vol. 3, *Emerging Perspectives and Issues* (Stamford, CT: JAI Press, 2001).

PART III

Great Expectations

In at least two crucial aspects of life, the huge gains brought by modernity quickly generated additional expectations that equally quickly began to cloud the gains. We turn in this section to the "what have you done for me today?" side of the modern mentality, where real gains are soon eclipsed by ambitious new hopes. Some brief celebrations accompanied the achievement of modern childhood, but they were soon matched by new standards (as well as some objective new problems) that made childhood seem even more challenging than before. The same occurred with death, where the very arrival of modern death patterns generated cultures and behaviors that made what was still ultimately inevitable—there are limits to modernity—more troubling than had been the case in traditional society. We begin with death, which according to many observers has generated the most widespread tension between modern conditions and actual experience and expectation—noted in many different regions by observers like Philippe Ariès. We then turn to childhood, a less predictable source of modern anxiety, where many Americans face some particular concerns in shaping modern approaches to parenting. Finally, we assess the great modern basket for rising and impatient expectations, accelerating consumerism. Alone, but also as a displacement for other modern vulnerabilities such as work or childhood, consumerism readily illustrates the difficulties of combining modernity and satisfaction.

7

Death as a Modern Quandary

Modernity and death are not friends. The relationship is not as dreadful as some observers have claimed, citing death as the "new modern taboo," for some constructive adjustments have occurred. But death does not have a clear modern welcome and, ironically, earlier ideas of a good death have gone by the boards. Many adults die less well than their counterparts did in the past, and the dominant personal wish for best death—quick and unexpected—results from the new disjuncture, leaving many loved ones in the lurch in the process. In fact, huge disparities between people considering their own death and those (often the same) people considering the deaths of family members denote the modern dilemma. Death and happiness, never boon companions to be sure, are farther apart than they were traditionally, in part because happiness itself has been not only emphasized but redefined. Death fits awkwardly when happiness is phrased in terms of earthly pleasures and pursuits. It interrupts work; it contradicts the normal joys and lures of consumerism. Without question, from the 18th century onward, definitions of modernity worked best when death was simply ignored.

The problem centers on expectations, not real, material change where, save in wartime, modern societies have a lot to brag about. By any reasonable objective standard, death is an area where modernity has brought huge improvements by massively reducing its onslaught before later age, and while as we will see there was a somewhat exaggerated initial response to the key changes, earlier in the 20th century, there's no serious question either of dramatically false starts. Most people welcomed the obvious reduction of death, without reservations; there was no clear or immediate down side to modernity here. But sorting out the details— clearly a work in progress still—raised a host of issues, some of which seriously complicated happiness at least in key phases of life. The question boils down to reaping the benefits of modernity without befouling them by too many layers of unrealistic hopes.

The modern death revolution took shape between 1880 and 1920 in the Western world, and similar patterns have emerged or have begun to emerge in most other parts of the world since that time. In the West, however, some intriguing reconsiderations of death occurred before clear material change. They were not fully modern, at least in the 20th-21st-century sense, but they reflected modernity more broadly, and they need to be briefly evoked as more than a historical footnote.

For even before there was any huge change in the actuality of death, a modern discomfort with death and with traditional responses to death began to take shape. Some caution is necessary. Historians used to assume that, since death was so common in traditional societies, people took it in stride, cushioned by pervasive fatalism. And it is true that traditional Western society did fail to take some preventive measures that modern people would find automatic: children, most obviously, were not protected against certain kinds of accidents, like falling into unguarded wells, and doctors were not usually called when a child (as opposed to an adult, assuming the means to pay) fell ill. But death had huge impact even in an obviously different culture. Parents bitterly mourned the death of a child, despite the fact that some children inevitably died in almost every family. Organizing a "good death" for an older adult, where family members would visit the death bed (ideal here was a lingering, wasting demise, often from a respiratory disease) to express sorrow and resolve any lingering family tensions, was a crucial ritual. Death was indeed common—remember that the majority of people, as farmers, also routinely experienced animal death—but this does not mean it was easily absorbed. After all, the reason modernity brought such welcome change in this area was that it reduced traditional levels of encounter with death.

Projections of modernity, and associated progress and happiness, included important assumptions about change where death was concerned. Enlightenment optimism had a great stake in the belief that longevity could and should be substantially extended. The more hopeful pundits thought that death would be largely eliminated before later age, thanks to scientific advance and more abundant food, and there was great fascination with redefining later age itself, where greatly improved longevity would mean that death could be kept at bay. Haltingly, Western societies did begin to put some new policies in place: in the 18th century better border controls temporarily reduced the path of epidemics from the Middle East into Europe, and then from the 1830s onward new experiments with urban sanitation showed a constructive interest in reducing more ordinary forms of contagion. No massive results accrued as yet, but the interest was there.

The first big changes, however, were cultural, not directly medical. More and more people, headed by the growing middle classes, came to believe or were told to believe that many traditional aspects of death, starting with high infant and maternal mortality, were simply unacceptable in a modern, progressive society.

The starkest sign of change emerged in an unexpected format: the new genre of magazines for women that began to blossom on both sides of the Atlantic from the 1830s onward. Along with recipes and dress designs, the magazines, as we have seen, began to issue commentary about how good mothers should prevent the deaths of babies. Many, perhaps most infant deaths, a new group of semimedical advice givers claimed, resulted from bad practices like careless feeding or smothering with excessive clothing. There was no practical breakthrough here: the magazines really had nothing much to offer anyone, save for a truly heedless parent, that would actually reduce infant death levels. What was new, however, was the sense that somehow good arrangements should cut into traditional death levels in one of the key categories—babies—and that when death did occur, someone might be open to blame. Clearly also, an audience began to develop for this kind of criticism. Women may have bought the magazines for other reasons, but they were clearly not so incensed by the notion that they bore new responsibilities as mothers that they turned away.

The most interesting symbolic shift in the response to death—and here the United States led the way—involved significant redefinitions of burial sites, with a complex set of meanings involved. In the first place, cemeteries now began to be located away from concentrations of population, at least in the growing cities: a suburbanization of death preceded suburbanization in other forms. Partly this reflected urban growth and crowding, partly it reflected some new concerns about contagion. But, whether as cause or effect, a desire not to be so routinely reminded of death was involved in the shift as well. Whatever the mix of reasons, death should now be distanced, and ordinary people were spared daily encounters of the sort that traditional churchyards had once routinely supplied.

More than location was involved. The new suburban cemeteries were now to be dressed up, rather than focused on the starkness of death. Beginning with the Mount Auburn cemetery outside Boston, in the late 1820s, a garden cemetery movement arose (later followed by park cemeteries, different in design though very similar in purpose). In the modern cemetery, 19th-century style, the dead were to be rested in a landscaped environment, where the sights of nature obviously distracted from too much emphasis on the reality of death and where emblems of decay, so prominent in Western death art and memorials traditionally, were nowhere to be seen. If death could not exactly be portrayed as a happy event, at least it could be camouflaged with serenity. As one early commentator noted,

> When nature is permitted to take her course—when the dead are committed to the earth under the open sky, to become early and peacefully blended with their original dust, no unpleasant association remains. It would seem as if the forbidding and repulsive conditions which attend on decay were merged and lost in the surrounding ceremonies of the creation.

The notion of diverting unpleasant association with death simply accelerated as the 19th century wore on. The new breed of professional cemetery directors saw their calling as a form of art, "and gradually all things that suggest death, sorrow, or pain, are being eliminated." Carrying the happiness theme to extremes, one landscape architect even hoped to "put such smiles" into cemeteries that visitors would see them as positively "cheerful places." Even weeping willows, staples of the earlier garden cemetery, became suspect.

Other important trends pushed in the same direction, of masking death with more positive, if not always smiling, connotations. Mechanical devices could now lower coffins, reducing the ugly sense of finality that came with gravediggers and manual shoveling. More obviously still, the growing art of embalming provided opportunities to portray dead bodies in lifelike fashion, rather than seeing the first signs of decay. Here, too, new kinds of professional pride came into play. Thanks to embalming and cosmetics, one funeral director noted, "when I come for the last time to look upon my dead, they will look to me as natural as thought they were alive." And finest Sunday clothing was now used rather than the traditional shroud, again to minimize the sense of death as a shock. Funeral homes, taking dead bodies out of the domestic environment, sought a subdued air but again, "as cheerful and pleasant as possible." Caskets, finally, became more elaborate, with particularly interesting attention to comfortable upholstery—the corpse should not have to suffer from unadorned wood that might suggest aches and pains even after sensation had ceased. Huge changes in symbolism and practice reflected the obvious desire to reduce the contradiction between death and normal happiness.

One other innovation, this time in belief rather than ritual, showed the desire to reduce any sense of pain in death, to make death as compatible as possible with happiness. Increasingly, Americans were encouraged to think of the afterlife as a place where families could reunite. The pain of loss could be modified by this unprecedented, and highly unorthodox, belief that loved ones could all reassemble in the great beyond. Earlier beliefs, that death could provide a transformation of existence and a hard-to-imagine union with the saved, now gave way to a conception of heaven that really translated idealized earthly and familial joy.

There was however one huge problem with all this readjustment before 1900: death rates remained quite high. Few families, to take the most vivid example, would be spared the death of at least one child. To handle this new disparity, between cultural hopes and harsh reality, 19th-century standards also expanded the displays, and possibly the experience, of grief. Elaborate mourning outfits and rituals became common in the middle classes, and girls might even be given training kits, complete with black clothes and coffins, for their dolls. Emotion for a time helped bridge between the modern desire to distance death and the fact of its ineluctability.

Then, however, came a fuller opportunity for reconciliation, when a death-averse culture finally encountered a real reduction in death. Here is also where the crucial dilemmas of modernity took clearer shape.

The Modern Death Revolution

The facts are a progressive dream come true. New public health measures—spurred by urban problems but also the basic Enlightenment commitment to social improvement—pushed strongly against traditional sources of death. So did gains in living standards, including the food supply, and public education. So did certain advances in medicine, including (after a bit of a lag) germ-theory-inspired hygiene for physicians in delivery rooms and advances in surgery. Visits to doctors and hospitals became more productive, in contrast to premodern patterns.

In 1880, 25% of all children born in the United States would die in infancy; by 1920 the figure was down to 8% for whites regardless of social class.[1] New Zealand had already achieved 5% by that point. Steady improvements thereafter, throughout the industrial world, would push levels toward 2% or even below, and while nonindustrial regions could not match these gains, there were changes there as well. Where modernity had full hold, families by the 1920s could reasonably expect to encounter no child death, a huge change for parents and siblings alike.

Based primarily on the virtual elimination of child mortality, average life expectancy began to soar, into the seventies and even eighties by the later 20th century. By this point, other changes added in: inoculations (besides smallpox) and antibiotics provided new treatments and preventatives for common diseases for older children and adults. New medicines to control blood pressure had vital impact on death rates from heart attacks and strokes, without of course eliminating them. Maternal deaths in childbirth became extremely uncommon, thanks not only to hygiene but to medicines that could control puerperal fever and other infections. Due to international controls and public health measures, plus some inoculations, killer epidemics virtually disappeared. To be sure, new threats emerged by the later 20th century, like AIDS and SARS, but particularly in the industrial world, control measures and medicines prevented massive mortality, so the achievement, though battered a bit, still prevailed. Even new problems, like obesity, did not, at least yet, check the progressive tide, though they began to limit it a bit. It was the decline of death in middle age as well as the drop in birth rates that propelled later-age population segments, notably people in their eighties, to become the most rapidly growing demographic group by the final decades of the 20th century.

These changes were accompanied by two others. Most notably, death began to occur primarily outside the home. With urban crowding but also improvements in hospital hygiene and gains in anesthetics and surgery, hospitals began to become far more positive places, moving away from their older role as custodians for the very poor. It now made sense for everyone to seek hospital treatment for serious illness, and this in turn meant that death was now likely to occur in that setting as well. Along with the decline in death rates before later age and the growing use of professionals to organize burials, this contributed immensely to the reduction of death's impact on ordinary life routines. Many people could now reach mature adulthood with no immediate contact with a death situation of any kind—another first in human history.

Finally, the causes of death shifted, away from the common contagious diseases plus digestive ailments (historically, the leading single killer of infants) and toward degenerative diseases spiced by automobile or industrial accidents. Killers now came from within, from cancer or arteriosclerosis, from agents feared but often not perceived—which made dependence on medical tests all the more pervasive. Death through degeneration represented progress in one sense, in that it heralded the new success against more conventional sources of mortality. But the unseen qualities could be troubling, at least from middle age onward, particularly to the extent that symptoms might be unrecognized, that a doctor's visit might always uncover some unexpected news of terminal illness. Here was potential for new kinds of fear that were not readily compatible with modern happiness and that could modify—though not, rationally, eliminate—an appreciation of the huge gains in the modern context for death overall.

Modern death patterns constitute a truly powerful package, by historical standards, one of the really fundamental changes in the human experience for several millennia. It's hard to argue that the changes were not positive. Death in hospital obviously has some big drawbacks over death in more familiar surroundings, so this point can be debated. And fears of internal deterioration certainly affect the quality of life, though whether this is worse than the prospect of periodic bouts of mass contagions is doubtful. But the core changes, in the death rates themselves, form one of the clearest reasons why almost no person living amid modernity would seek to go back to the premodern past. The problem centers in the unexpected complications and unrealizable hopes that the core changes generated. Here, in turn, lies the clash between the modernity of death and the levels of satisfaction that might have been expected—aside from the obvious fact that people quickly forget the burdens of even a proximate past that they have been spared.

Redefining the Modern Death Culture

Responses to the retreat of death were swift and dramatic, settling in widely by the 1920s. Clearly, for example, doctors began to replace priests as the authorities people turned to when death threatened. In turn, doctors, by training and inclination, emphasized their commitment to keeping death at bay, rather than reconciling the dying and their families to the inevitable. Death fighting, beyond the reductions already achieved, became a keynote of modern societies.

Hopes could run high. Early in the 20th century an American popularizer tried to turn undeniable gains into a formula for future near-perfection: "[The] burden of woe has now been lifted. . . . Man has cast off fear and finds himself master of nature and perhaps of all her forces." The decline of death and the parallel rise of science projected a vision of earthly satisfaction far greater than what the Enlightenment progressives had ever ventured: a vision in which serious risks and uncertainties could be eliminated and mortality kept at bay until a comfortable old age. The idea that happiness could now embrace an absence of fear pushed the boundaries of optimism to new levels.

More was involved, however, than simply enjoying the continuation of modern trends. Specific attacks focused on cultural traditions that now seemed unnecessary and even repellent. It wasn't enough to herald a new era for death. The compromises that had been essential in the 19th century, to reconcile a growing aversion to death with its omnipresence, could now be overturned. A new death culture seemed imperative. And this meant, front and center, a major offensive against Victorian-style grief and mourning. American periodicals began to highlight the emerging new wisdom as early as the first decade of the 20th century. An article in *Lippincott's Magazine* in 1907 urged that death be stripped of any particular fuss. After all, it was now occurring almost entirely in old age (which the conventions of the time were depicting as an age of decrepitude in any event), and family members would be reunited in heaven anyway, so everyone should take the whole thing in stride. Neither fear for one's own death nor grief at the passing of an older relative made any sense. Now, emphasis rested on the idea that the "hard facts of science" urged that the end of life was not only inevitable but no big deal, and people should stop surrounding the whole event with so much emotion.

The great target was grief. It was ridiculous, the new modernists argued, to waste money or feelings on a death. As a 1908 article noted, "Probably nothing is sadder in life than the thought of all the hours that are spent in grieving over what is past and irretrievable." Modern "psychotherapeutics" were available for emotions that, just a few decades ago, Victorians would have found normal, even desirable, along with medical attention to make sure there were no physical causes of "melancholic feelings." Any prolonged bout with tears suggested "something morbid, either mental or physical." Another popularizer summed the approach up quite simply, in calling for a cultural "abolition of death."

Sentiments of this sort, which commanded a great deal of ink for about three decades in the United States (and there were some similar trends in Western Europe, though Americans for a while took to bragging that they were more modern on this crucial topic than their hidebound cousins), were revealing in several ways, even though, in their intensity and smugness they constituted a minor version of a false start. The attack on grief was, in essence, a celebration of the genuine changes in death—in rates and in family involvements now that the experience moved increasingly out of the home. The attack also celebrated the older theme of modern happiness, now that this could be unencumbered with any sense of death as part of normal daily experience. Progressive optimism, always interested in stressing the pleasures of this life, could now be simplified given what was actually happening to the patterns of death.

There were several durable results from this now-forgotten campaign to revolutionize attitudes toward death. First, the idea that intense or at least prolonged grief was a sign of imbalance unquestionably gained ground. Therapeutic "grief work," to this day, means helping people get over the emotion and defining the emotion as a problem. We have noted already that, in contemporary American culture, a significant minority of those diagnosed with depression are simply, by less stringent standards, normally sad, and the persistent modern prompting to get over grief enters into this situation vividly. "Chronic grief syndrome" was a revealing new term in the medical lexicon, and the basic idea of encouraging people to get on with things took strong hold.

Second, though here personal reactions could obviously be even more varied, the new approach also urged that people who were experiencing grief not intrude too blatantly into the lives of others. With a bit of a lag, etiquette books, once havens for recommendations of the elaborate manners desirable in dealing with a grieving individual or family, began to turn tail. Emily Post was admitting, by the 1930s, that too much mourning simply stirred up undesirable emotions. Amy Vanderbilt, in 1952, was even more up to date. Friends of the bereaved should certainly show sympathy, but they must also be as matter-of-fact as possible so as not to encourage grief: everyone would benefit from less emotion, not more. "It is better to avoid the words 'died,' 'death,' or 'killed' [even] in condolence letters. It is quite possible to write the kind of letter that will give a moment of courage and a strong feeling of sympathy without mentioning death or sadness at all." Most revealing was the modernist advice to the bereaved themselves, who now had an obligation to keep strong feelings to themselves, to exercise real self-control. Grief risked being impolite, in the new formulas. As Vanderbilt put it, "We are developing a more positive social attitude toward others, who might find it difficult to function well in the constant company of an outwardly mourning person."

The ramifications of this second impact were extensive and durable. By the early 21st century, American funeral customs had evolved to include, frequently, comments on the recently deceased from one or more family members. Some broke down, others did not even try: but the standard was the ability to speak reasonably coherently and while expressing grief make it clear that emotions were sufficiently under control that the audience need not feel burdened. It was a demanding but revealing exercise. Even earlier, the need to avoid impinging on friends drove many people to seek solace not simply from therapists, but from groups of strangers. By the 1940s and 1950s Thanatos societies, Compassionate Friends, and other groups formed in many American cities, populated by those who had lost a loved one (sometimes the categories were more specific, as in loss of a child) and who needed sympathy but, in a modernist context, could not expect adequate response from friends and relatives. The best recourse—and a very odd one by any traditional benchmark, though quite possibly highly desirable in modern conditions—was to seek out those who could form bonds based not on any prior acquaintance but on shared experience and a common realization that actual friends could not be expected to tolerate what needed to be expressed. Modern death could create strange bedfellows.

The most obvious link between the new conventional wisdom and actual death practices, finally, involved significant and fairly steady changes in rituals that took shape from the 1920s onward. If the new goals were maximum possible matter-of-factness and minimal burdens on others, Victorian mourning had to be toned down if not eviscerated. Special clothing or markers were progressively abandoned—out with veils or armbands, and certainly emblems on a home. By the early 21st century even somber attire at funerals themselves was increasingly optional. Employers became increasingly reluctant to allow time off for mourning, beyond a day or half-day for the funeral itself, not just for blue-collar workers but even for respectable middle-class folk, though sick leaves might be manipulated. As women began to reenter the labor force, work restrictions often limited anyone's availability—besides that of the funeral professionals—to organize extensive displays of grief or remembrance.

Not surprisingly, though the linkage would not have directly occurred to most of those involved, other and often even older rituals that had evoked death were now tamed: Halloween, most notably, was increasingly turned into a banal opportunity for kids to eat too much candy, rather than be reminded of the mysteries and fears of death and its minions.

The whole subject of children and death now had to be reconsidered. With very few young people now dying, and with no need, normally, to expect a child to witness the death of a sibling, innovation was essential. Experts and popularizers alike, and in their wake many parents themselves, began to argue that children and death should not mix at all. More than the decline of death was involved here: with lower birth rates, individual children began to be more highly valued, increasing the stakes in keeping death and childhood entirely apart. An urgent new expertise contended that grief itself was too much for kids to handle—and this just a few decades after the availability of mourning paraphernalia for dolls. By the 1920s *Parents' Magazine* was advising that even sugar-coated messages about death could be overwhelming for kids: emphasizing angels and family reunions in heaven might unintentionally spark actual thinking, and therefore fear, about death. Death itself became a bad word because of its starkness. Avoidance was the key. A nursery school might even ban reference to the "dyeing" of Easter eggs, lest children misinterpret the term. Certainly, in the wisdom of the mid-20th century, children should be kept away from funerals, just as they were banned from most hospital rooms for emotional as well as practical reasons. The goal was a combination of circumlocution, concealment, and blandness so that, as one expert put it, "the child . . . will meet many minor death references as just one more interesting phenomenon."

Correspondingly, children's stories began to be revised or rewritten, so that 19th-century staples, like a tragic illness or a life plucked away too soon, were eliminated. This was the context in which, from 1932 onward, new breeds of children's heroes, beginning with Superman himself, were defined in part by their immunity to death. Even the deaths of animals began to be minimized in fiction and in the real life of family pets, with dead carcasses disposed of secretly and replacements purchased as soon as possible to paste over any grief.

Finally, even for adults, there was substantial silence. After the impressive surge of popular commentary during the first third of the century, the topic disappeared from view. It's always a challenge to interpret the absence of a phenomenon, but in this case the challenge can plausibly be met. Once traditions had been substantially dismantled, there was no reason to keep death in view, a few flurries—such as recurrent discussion of funeral costs—aside. Indeed, it was consistent with the overall message that the subject be dropped. Fascination with medical advances proceeded apace, for this was fully compatible with modernism; indeed, by the later 20th century medical discussions, mainly in the progressive mode, were displacing not only consideration of death but even more conventional national and international news. But with the modernist agenda established, there was scant need to return to an unpleasant phenomenon. Much of the tone of the few comments that did appear became increasingly triumphal: as a *Scholastic* magazine article put it in 1940, "Modern knowledge . . . offers to the intelligent person today a conception of living which is a positive answer to the old death fears." Mainly, death might be ignored. Medical professionals eagerly cooperated, for many decades often concealing imminent death from both patients and family members in order to avoid encounters with unpleasant emotions.

It's important to remember that the basic changes were modern, with at most some modest national variants. Unfamiliarity with death spread widely. An older Japanese person noted, later in the 20th century, "Look at young people today in the presence of death. . . . The first thing they do is call a funeral company. They act like helpless children. Such an embarrassing situation never arose in the past." The attractions and problems of avoiding death became increasingly widespread.

All of this could create the impression, as some critics began to note by the 1960s, that death had become a modern taboo. Children were to be bypassed as much as possible. Alterations in death rates and locations allowed the topic to be viewed as a rare and unwelcome intrusion. A modern society that discussed almost every conceivable subject largely omitted death, once the modernist assault on tradition had been completed. There were few regular opportunities or available authorities for people to talk with about their own death, though religious professionals or psychological therapists modified this void; this might be all the more troubling when anxieties were redirected to the silent degenerative killers that now replaced more public threats, like epidemics, as the key source of death. Probing death with one's friends or relatives was not normally in good taste, particularly if emotions surfaced; special groups of strangers might be the only recourse here. It was hard to think of modern contexts where discussion of death was appropriate. Even the word risked vanishing from the preferred vocabulary, beyond the niceties urged on adults who had to deal with children. Talking about people "passing," most obviously, seemed oddly preferable to direct references to death.

American modernism, after the brash mood of the 1920s passed, may have been less extreme, even so, than that of parts of Western Europe, where the taboo label might have been even more applicable. The continued vitality of religion in America, and associated rituals once death had occurred—such as Catholic wakes or the Jewish practice of sitting *shiva*—often modified the modernist thrust. This was the conclusion of some critical students of modern death. The more rapid gains of cremation in places like the United Kingdom—a hugely nontraditional response to death in the Western context, prompted by a desire to reduce ceremony and expense and also respond to levels of crowding that made cemetery expansion difficult—suggested a greater openness to innovation than was true across the Atlantic. The fact remains that the modernist response to the objective changes in death had made serious inroads throughout the Western world, creating additional adjustments in turn. There was no better indication of this development than the emergence of a serious effort at counterattack in the 1960s, as the down sides of successful modernism became increasingly inescapable.

Adapting Modernism

Modernism in death was too stark for many people from the outset, and initial modernist statements also created problems that in turn prompted some modifications. Even by the early 21st century, however, adjustments of modernism had not really deflected some of the main trajectories. If death was not literally taboo, for example, it certainly was not an easy or common topic of conversation, despite the best efforts of the culture critics.

In the first place—and here an unexpected American ability to develop and maintain some viable traditions may have facilitated a more constructive adaptation than some other modern societies managed—funeral home arrangements, well established by the early 20th century, offered a definite if transient exception to any general movement to distance death. Obviously the venue confirmed the separation of death from home, with careful embalming and cosmetic work intended, whether successfully or not, to dispel any images of decay. But the somber, somewhat old-fashioned trappings of the home, often located in a converted mansion, conveyed a distinctive and nonmodern flavor. More important, while funeral home professionals worked to cushion any excessive emotion, the sedate tone of the site provided opportunities to convey and share in grief, typically for several evenings of viewing leading up to the funeral itself. Here was a definite ritual occasion, not a brush-off, with a sense of community and emotional support—time-limited, to be sure, but very real. Modernist critics paid the new death rituals a backhanded compliment by noting their high cost and outdated overtones, but most American brushed these quibbles aside. Spending some money, indeed, was part of doing death right in a modern context.

Particular American communities added to the funeral home ritual. African American funerals offered particularly abundant opportunities for emotional expression, and by 2000 were adding other elements like theme funerals that assembled some of the deceased's favorite foods or sports equipment, with the specific goal of making it "like home." As one participant noted, "It makes it just a happy place to be." The accumulation of pictures and slide shows from a person's life, gaining popularity by the early 21st century within the funeral home context, showed that modern death rituals, far from disappearing, had a power and evolutionary quality that added to their substance.

Indeed, with the funeral home, it became clear that Americans were reestablishing their own definition of a good death, a death that would allow most family members to believe they had done the right thing and might console a person contemplating his or her own death that the right thing would be done. The contemporary good death would occur in later age—that had always been part of a good-death concept. It would be fought, medically, for a considerable time, with considerable expense involved (even if a good chunk came from insurance or the government), urged on by loving relatives who wanted to delay the death as much as possible and who sought reassurance that they would bear no guilty responsibility when the reaper finally won out. Then turn to the funeral home, with its rituals and communal grief, followed by a fairly expensive funeral and a definite marker that would permit later visits and memories, in a coffin impervious to dirt and deterrent to too many morbid thoughts about decay. The mixture was intriguing: a bit of genuine tradition (including religious elements in most cases), a lot of modified Victorianism, and some modernist constraints as well, including the fact that the whole process was time-bound, with grief and mourning meant to clear up pretty quickly after the rituals had ended.

Adding to the modern reality came a set of modifications introduced from the 1960s onward, deliberately designed to smooth over modernist excess. The movement of cultural criticism that swept across the United States in the 1960s, though directed most vividly toward issues of war, consumerism, and social hierarchy, opened the door as well to some new comments on death. Spearheaded by widely read authorities like Elisabeth Kübler-Ross, a variety of arguments attacked modernism as both superficial, for society as a whole, and damaging, for many individuals constrained in thinking about their own death or in the emotions they could express about the deaths of others. Doctors were attacked for overdoing the death-fighting approach and neglecting emotional needs, and society at large was called to task for relying too much on doctors. Grief, it was now argued, should be welcomed, not repressed, and Kübler-Ross specifically urged a receptivity to the complex stages an individual must go through to prepare for the inevitable, once a terminal condition is identified. More attention, more emotion, more integration—death must be put back into the fabric of ordinary life.

The critique had a number of results, both at the time and (in some ways more modestly) since. Courses on death and dying proliferated. New books on death appeared, and any bookstore still today (in contrast to its counterparts eighty years ago) has a few interesting titles in a small section on death—nothing to rival the medical self-help materials, but at least available. Children began to be shielded from death less systematically, particularly when it came to attendance at funerals. Conscientious parents still worried a lot about this aspect of child rearing, but the worries now included a realization that appropriate exposure was a good thing, not a source of damaging fear. Medical personnel began to receive a bit more training in handling grief, and condoning it, and a new candor about death, with patients and families, became standard practice—reflecting a belief that death was better faced than evaded, but also a concern about lawsuits. A growing number of American states began to authorize living wills, in which people could not only specify funeral arrangements but also stipulate a desire to avoid heroic medical measures that might prolong life but without either dignity or quality. And while no large movement urged a wholesale embrace of grief, the notion that it was rude or unhinged was modified a bit. Here was a set of important adjustments that suggested a capacity to modify modernism's excesses, as a bit of a false start when modern death conditions first erupted, without complete reversal.

The most important institutional modification was the hospice movement, born in the 1970s in Western Europe but transplanted vigorously in
the United States. Here was an institution deliberately designed to provide
an alternative to death-fighting hospitals when an illness was recognized as
terminal. Emphasis centered on relieving both pain and fear, and providing
a setting in which relatives could easily associate with the dying individual—
including returns to one's home wherever possible (which is precisely what
most hospice patients said they wanted). The goal was to recreate some elements of the older kind of good death, including familial and domestic surroundings, in the process both establishing a more dignified and comforting
environment for the individual involved and facilitating expressions of love
and grief from others in advance of the shock of actual death.

The modifications of modernity, some of which are just now taking
hold, are interesting and arguably constructive. To date, however, they
also have some clear limitations, suggesting that for many people and
institutions the modern culture has been softened less than might have
been expected.

- Item: the impulse to avoid death references still runs very strong.
  A recent innovation, minor but revealing, involves changing the
  words of a classic children's song about the old lady who swal-
  lowed a fly. Traditionally, the final verse has the woman swallowing a horse, after which she "dies, of course." Now, however, the
  politically correct stanza still has her swallowing the horse but she's
  merely "full, of course." More interesting is the attempt of leading
  health organizations to distract from their involvement with frequently terminal illness. Thus the American Cancer Society publicly seeks to distance itself from efforts to discuss mortality: "In no
  way do we wish to be associated with a book on death. We want to
  emphasize the positive aspects of cancer only."
- Item: the hospice movement, though truly significant, faces far
  more limitations than one might have expected, given its multide-
  cade experience. Fewer than 25% of all dying Americans have any
  contact with hospice care, and often so late that there is little real
  cushion to their death experience. The vast majority of Americans
  who are aware of the hospice institution do not realize that home
  care can be provided. Constraints include simple ignorance; hesitations about insurance coverage (which is revealing in itself); lack
  of guidance from dominant medical professionals who dislike giv-

ing up on patients; and insistence on continued heroic measures by well-meaning relatives who can't let go of the dominant modern model. Certain minority groups are particularly hesitant, and obviously a hospice contact is not relevant in all situations in any event. But there is a clear problem in utilizing this modification of the most unadorned modernity in death.

✦ Item: 80% of all American adults say that they know that predeath stipulations, such as living wills, are desirable (this figure may have risen slightly since the American president indicated his commitment in 2009). But only a small minority actually has living wills, mainly because the distaste for thinking that elaborately and specifically about one's own ultimate death overcomes common sense. Because of this hesitancy, and also the even more significant unwillingness of hospitals and relatives to follow through, the vast majority of Americans die in conditions that they did not stipulate and do not like—which is ultimately the most obvious problem with the whole modern approach.

Overall, while the extremes of modernism did represent something of a false start, the basic contours remain, including wide hesitancy about discussing death in the first place. Here in turn is the reason why changes in death do not contribute to the happiness margin over premodern societies as much as might have been expected.

Modernity and Death: Areas for Debate

Precaution and Blame: Redefining Risk

The first issue to emerge from the advent of the modern context for death was really coterminous with the new culture itself. Vivid interest in finding new ways to prevent possibly fatal accidents was a logical and, in principle, desirable concomitant of the growing realization that traditional levels and sources of death could be reconsidered, that risk could be regulated in new ways. Add to this a related belief that, when fatalities did occur, a responsible agent could and should be identified, and a set of interesting changes resulted—with the United States in most respects clearly, for better or worse, in the lead.

We've already noted that, even before the death revolution, changes in outlook in the 19th century led to some new and positive precautions as against more traditional fatalism, particularly where children were concerned. The notion that there was nothing to do about children falling in wells, for example, began to be rethought. To be sure, early factories, with hosts of accidents involving child laborers required to work amid fast-moving machine parts, actually increased accident rates, with lots of absurd comments about how the workers involved had only themselves to blame for carelessness. Overall, however, opinions gradually shifted toward a growing belief that risks could and should be consciously considered and precautions taken wherever possible (a few exploitative workplaces aside). Concurrently, as with the maternal criticism strain in women's magazines, increasing commentary built up around the idea that certain kinds of deaths—again, particularly for children—not only could be but should be prevented, and that if they nevertheless occurred some guilt must be assigned. So a context was established that was clearly ready for extension when the full mortality revolution occurred and with it an opportunity to widen the notion that the boundaries of death could be pushed back still further.

The early 20th century also witnessed the advent of a new round of mechanization, now applying to home and neighborhood as well as workplace. The growing use of automobiles was accompanied, as an unfortunate corollary, by a massive increase in the accident rate, initially including lots of urban kids in the streets. The rise of electrical appliances in the home had the same effect, though on smaller scale. New attention to safety was essential simply to respond to new problems, quite apart from the larger surge in aversion to death. With the United States in the lead in this kind of technical change, and probably also with a particular national sensitivity to child-centered rhetoric, it was no surprise that the nation developed both unusually early and unusually extensive safety consciousness. Somewhat unexpectedly, for a society that also prided itself on dislike of regulation from above, and not always entirely happily, Americans began an evolution toward a network of safety restrictions and admonitions, with the goal, at the core, of reducing vulnerability to death (or serious injury).

In briefly tracing what became almost a mania for protection from risk, it's important to be clear: the basic impulses involved were and are entirely understandable; they responded to real problems—obvious down sides of modern technology, in many instances, as well as the new death culture; and even today they can be viewed—surely will be viewed, since many Americans continue to participate voluntarily—as not only logical but completely desirable. Questions of balance emerged clearly, however, as a new awareness became a near-obsession.

The process began in the 1920s, when places like New York City began calling attention to the numbers of children being killed by cars—"the helpless little ones who have met death through the agencies of modern life." Speed limits and licensing requirements followed, mainly from the 1930s, onward, with the automobile-crazed United States well ahead of Europe in this regard. Later, additional requirements, escalating steadily, involved mandatory seatbelts and child-restraining devices of ever-increasing complexity. Similar trends expanded safety regulations on playgrounds and in the household—the latter with this demanding mantra: "the responsibility rests on mothers for the elimination of home accidents."

Germs focused another precautionary spiral. Concerns about hygiene mounted in the early 20th century, with school programs for example directed particularly at lower-class and immigrant children whose parents presumably were unclean. Often sponsored by manufacturers of soaps and cleansers, these programs regaled Americans with the importance of bathing, tooth brushing, regular hand washing, and home cleanliness. Again, it seemed impossible to do too much, and by the later 20th century the United States was again leading the world, this time in the ubiquity of the use of plastic gloves for food service. Even foods later to be cooked, like fish or meats in grocery stores, should not be touched by human hand (at least in public view; one never knew what happened behind the scenes).

Along with the myriad practical warnings and details, two related new concepts emerged from this fascination with precaution. In the first place, the idea of accident or (in the case of disease) bad luck was increasingly challenged. The idea that good arrangements, in a properly organized modern society, should overcome risk was tantalizing. Both government officials and the insurance industry—each with obvious self-interest—promoted the idea of responsibility: if death or serious accident occurred, someone was at fault. An insurance manual of the 1940s thus emphasized "driver failure or poor judgment" as the cause of most problems on the roads. Or, as with appliances, if users should not be blamed, then problems could be pinned on the manufacturer. Continuing this line of thought, a Department of Transportation statement in 1997 urged, under the general heading "Crashes Aren't Accidents," that the term "accident" be abandoned altogether: "It's not accidental that one person survives a crash wearing a seatbelt and one person goes through a window and dies."

The same thinking entered into the disease arena. After all, if people took proper care of themselves, in terms of nutrition and avoidance of damaging substances, the bulk of heart attacks and cancers might not occur—at least, so claimed some public health/prevention enthusiasts. A Harvard public health survey in 1997 thus asserted that 75% of all cancer resulted from lifestyle mistakes, not simply "getting sick."

The second corollary of this effort to explain fatalities through invocation of human agency obviously led to a growing preoccupation with blame. Cause readily became fault, when it could be assumed that normally fatal risks were under control. And here, change entered not only into public attitudes but into the law itself. During most of the 19th century, accidents might lead to court cases but verdicts were almost always returned (for disasters such as steamboat explosions or train derailments) as "nobody to blame." The notion was that the people were taking their trips (or working in factories) voluntarily, and so assumed all the risks themselves. New legal thinking, however, particularly in the area of tort law, began to widen the idea of responsibility, and by the early 20th century juries were often ready to go along. By the later 20th century, tort actions, and related extensions, ranged widely in the United States. A man jumps in front of a train in an abortive though injurious suicide attempt, and then successfully sues the subway system because the driver did not stop quickly enough. Tort actions soared, during the 20th century, from a scant 1.2% of all filings to a quarter or more.

Lawsuits obviously helped vent grief and anger, particularly when death was involved. They provided a conservative society with an interesting way to attack rich corporations and wealthy doctors, for juries of ordinary people became notoriously willing not just to punish, but to punish big. But underlying the whole movement was an assumption, usually unstated but vigorous, that fatal risks should not be part of the modern world and that when they occurred, someone or some institution had deliberately violated proper order.

The safety mania and the passion for blame were not absolutely inevitable consequences of modernity, at least not at American levels. Particular legal systems and a largely laissez-faire economic system that induced a love-hate relationship with big business were involved as well. But modernity played a role, because of the new commitment to minimize death and (logically enough, in one sense, given the newly low morality rates) to fix blame when things went wrong.

The resultant trends were good in many ways. It's hard to argue against any single safety precaution, for a few lives might indeed be saved. Lawsuits legitimately warned manufacturers, or even individual doctors, who might otherwise have been tempted to cut corners. Even with the tort apparatus, obviously, many products emerged that not only caused sickness and death but did so with the full knowledge of the corporation involved.

But the balance may have shifted undesirably, toward too much protective regulation and too many legal crusades. Many bicycle-riding people—such as the Dutch, who briefly tried helmets but then uniformly rejected them as ugly and cumbersome—manage to do without some of the protective gear that American impose on themselves, without bad results. Malpractice suits visibly drive up medical costs and the nastiness of excessive testing, reducing the actual quality of care; yet, as a society, we seem unable to come to grips with a reasonable compromise, partly because of the pressures of special interests (trial lawyers, in this case) but partly because the public is unwilling to recognize that there are points beyond which the effort to eliminate risk becomes both silly and counterproductive. The worry and expense that go into American safety and blame crusades may not be worth any ensuing gains at the margin. And there may be very real down sides to a society that surrounds kids with so many protections and warnings, so much sense of the external environment as dangerous, in terms of their capacity rationally to assess risks as they mature. This is not one of the most attractive features of modern life, and the excesses do not conduce to happiness.

Young Death

If concerns about safety saddled many Americans with new anxieties, a fortunately smaller minority faced a more direct challenge as an unexpected consequence of modernity in death: when, against the modern odds, death occurred before later age. Modern conditions made the death of a child or young adult infinitely harder to handle than had been true in premodern times, though 19th-century anguish about responsibility for untimely deaths—the aspersions against mothers who did not care properly for their children—prepared the transition. People have usually mourned the loss of a child, so the contrast should not be exaggerated. But when a young person died in the modern context, in which such deaths had become dramatically uncommon, the sense of unfairness or guilt or both could be almost literally overwhelming. And when all this occurred in a culture that urged considerable repression of grief and a minimization of ritual—even if the strictures might be relaxed a bit for unusual circumstances—the result could be virtually impossible to handle.

Here is where many people needed recourse to groups of strangers linked by their shared, statistically rare experience and the need to discuss emotions that could not be paraded before one's own friends, at least for any length of time. But even this might not suffice. Though precise figures are impossible to come by, estimates that the majority of marriages broke up when a child or teenager died, because of mutual recriminations and a sense of grief impossible to share, were at least plausible. This was a marked contrast to the realities of marriages in the past, where divorce admittedly was far less common but where grief and ritual may truly have helped bind a couple together in ways that were lacking in the modern context.

Additionally, many parents who were spared the tragedy of an untimely death nevertheless anxiously recognized how awful it would be, and hovered over young children in consequence. The discovery of new (if still uncommon) problems like Sudden Infant Death Syndrome (SIDS) provoked many a fearful nighttime check on a sleeping child. This problem, first uncovered in 1948 and then widely discussed from the 1960s onward, was almost tailor-made for adult concern. The fact that helpless infants were the victims—people who should not die—and that parents might, through better arrangements, have prevented the death, by checking more often and placing infants correctly, created shudders of anticipatory guilt. Common exaggerations—such as claims in magazines by the 1970s that over thirty-five thousand American infants were dying from this cause annually, at least five times the actual rate—both reflected and encouraged the understandable, if statistically unnecessary, alarms. Untimely death, in other words, given its scarcity quality in the modern context, reached beyond death itself.

And it was not only adults who were involved. The death of a sibling could have a traumatic impact on a surviving child, unprepared for death and easily convinced that somehow his or her survival was a monstrous fault, given the fact that no one of the sibling's age should really be called upon to die. Hesitations still about how to expose children to death and funerals, despite some relaxation of the constraints of the 1920s and 1930s, compounded the difficulty in assimilating that which should not have happened. Psychiatric help became standard in such circumstances, in the broad American middle classes, but even it might not suffice.

This particular modern conundrum is probably impossible to resolve, though more open communication about death, in more normal circumstances, might provide better resources when modern probabilities do not hold true. The fact is that one of the vital gains of modernity—the elimination of children as a common death category—had a tragic flip side, deeply affecting only a few people but capable of touching a wider range of family members.

An intriguing corollary to the dilemma of death of the young involved the rapid evolution of attitudes toward military casualties. While patriotism officially blanketed reactions to military deaths in the two world wars, this umbrella began to fray during the Korean conflict, when media reports began to dwell on individual profiles of slain soldiers and on the tragedy of wasted life. The Vietnam War revealed even more fully how the unacceptability of any significant losses could turn the tide of public opinion, and also generate unprecedented pressure to retrieve the bodies of those missing in action. Military efforts to reduce wartime deaths, and to avoid excessive publicity (as in the decision to bring coffins to the domestic airbase only during the night, to bypass television cameras), redoubled by the time of the Iraq War. Here was a new way that even limited combat could touch a modern public and challenge the levels of modern satisfaction. A 2006 opinion poll captured the new mood: when asked how many casualties were acceptable in a war, the majority of the American public said none at all. Yet, of course, modern war did not cease.

Death of Others: Letting Go in the Hospital

Critical care decisions have come to constitute one of the most pervasive tests of modernity in death. Hospitals, though remaining the most common sites of death, continue, understandably enough, to associate themselves with life preservation and the capacity to hold death at bay. Medical personnel, in the main, still receive little training in dealing with the dying process or with family members. They have learned to be more candid about death, and individuals with particularly sympathetic personalities may work hard to console all parties as death nears. But this is not the hospitals' or the physicians' main job.

The profusion of tests and technologies further complicates the act of saying goodbye to a dying loved one. Critical care units are not friendly to visitors, nor is the sight of a family member plugged with tubes and wires a comforting one. Visiting hours may be constrained, though hospitals have made some concessions to family needs in the case of possibly terminal illness. Increasingly, even the determination of death becomes a function of technology; though humans (doctors) interpret, only machines, in the past several decades, can reveal the contemporary definition of death in the cessation of brain activity. The result is perfectly rational, but leaves the layperson loved one even further on the margins.

Hospitals and physicians themselves feel increasingly compelled to complicate the days or weeks of approaching death with batteries of additional tests and heroic medical measures. There is always a chance that something will work, but often the more compelling goad is the fear of lawsuits if every conceivably relevant diagnosis is not deployed, every possible measure taken to provide a few extra days through the grace of breathing devices or resuscitation methods or medicines themselves.

In this context, unnatural and confusing, loving relatives themselves often become the crux of the problem: they cannot decide that enough is enough, and they constantly press for this or that additional remedy. The result may well delay the inevitable, but with genuine and various costs.

There is, first of all, the expense itself. In a society that prides itself on pushing death back, mentioning money may seem churlish, but facts are facts. It has been estimated that as much as 25-40% of all medical expenses in the United States (25% of all Medicare payments alone), unusually high as a percentage of national income in any event, revolve around the treatment of terminal illnesses, and while some of this involves initial diagnosis and care and then palliative measures, a great deal derives from lengthy hospital stays and the tests and heroic measures that relatives cannot bring themselves to do without. Arguably, at risk of oversimplifying a complex equation, we are willing to spend a great deal of money (admittedly, often funded in part by the insurers, which helps mask financial reality) to indulge our desire to keep relatives alive just a little bit longer.

The result adds to the anguish and confusion of the final days for the key relatives themselves. Often battles ensue, with different relatives displaying differential willingness to bow to the inevitable. The focus readily turns to the frenzy of tests and procedures and the intrusion of additional technology, rather than concentration on comforting and saying goodbye—and sharing the process with others. An inherently unhappy time easily becomes an exhausting and bewildering crisis. Hopefully, at the least, the result demonstrates a willingness to do whatever it takes to prolong life as much as possible—reducing if not eliminating opportunities for subsequent guilt. But grief itself may mount from the tensions involved, and from the inability to focus on the process of separation. Emotional costs can be considerable.

Of course there is variety in this aspect of modern American death. Some individuals yield earlier. The hospice movement, though still a minority phenomenon, provides alternative advice and alternative settings. Sometimes there is opportunity to move from the frenzy of heroic measures to some weeks of calmer departure, before death finally ensues.

But there is little question that, particularly in the United States, a death-fighting, death-avoiding culture risks running amok as loved ones confront but refuse to accept a final illness. Many relatives, even when not directly faced with decisions about plug-pulling, are unable to concentrate on bidding farewell and preparing acceptance—the kind of acceptance that, many death studies show, dying individuals themselves attain—because of the haunting sense that they should be organizing even more death-fighting measures.

One's Own Death

Here is the crux of the modern quandary: too many people do not die as they wish to, not because of vastly unreasonable expectations but because so many well-meaning participants prefer fighting death over an emphasis on calm and dignity.

The goals of Americans (and most moderns) that are dying are clear enough. Comments emphasize "relationships and belonging," "having control," and "being human." Emphasis does not center, in most instances, on maximization of the life span once serious illness or decrepitude sets in. But what the dying want, and what they get, too often differ strongly. This is a key reason why, in contrast to premodern societies, most modern people would prefer to die suddenly and unexpectedly (even though the resulting burdens on relatives are in many ways far greater, save in the general ability to avoid prolonged hospital stays and apparatus). The preference is to evade the dilemma of a dying process, rather than to master it.

A second, related means of reconciling wishes with modern realities involves the efforts to legalize euthanasia. Approval of medically assisted death, in cases of terminal illness, has advanced farther in Western

Europe, particularly the Netherlands, than in the United States, with Oregon the lone exception amid widespread national disapproval. The Dutch carefully screen requests to make sure that a terminal condition definitely exists and that the decision is voluntary, but partially in 1985 and fully in 2001 they have allowed assisted deaths as a means of countering the loss of dignity and excessive dependence that modern death can otherwise involve. Requests for this resolution have mounted steadily in the Netherlands, particularly when cancer is involved, though most applications continue to be disapproved. By 1995, nevertheless, already over 2% of all deaths in the Netherlands were medically assisted. Whether the pattern will extend in Western Europe is open to question, but at least the option is on the table for discussion. Not only the Netherlands but also Belgium and Switzerland (and, far away, the Northern Territory of Australia) also moved to legalize certain kinds of physician-aided deaths. The United States, again with the one anomaly, is far from any similar agenda, thanks in part to more powerful conservative political movements and greater conventional religious commitment. Doctors who briefly publicized their participation in assisted deaths, as modern death fighting accelerated in most respects in the 1990s, were successfully brought to trial. Legislative proposals in both California and Rhode Island failed outright, and even more states saw no formal political attempts at all. Privately, a larger number of doctors debated: one poll suggested that an interesting handful, 4% of the total in the state of Washington, did quietly collaborate with patients' requests to be allowed a speedier death than nature provided. But while future developments cannot be predicted—some global polls suggested over 50% support for new opportunities to attain death with dignity—short-term prospects for widespread change are not good.

This meant that lots of modern people are left with a daunting combination of circumstances when the end approaches, some of them inherent in modern death causes and incidence, some of them more clearly man-made. In the inherent category: large numbers of people now die in later age, of diseases like advanced cancer or Alzheimer's, which either directly or through pain-killing medication reduce or eliminate any real capacity to voice opinions about how the final weeks of life should be handled. Age and debility in many instances make it inevitable that doctors and well-meaning relatives would take decisions over with results that often clash with the probable continued interest in dignity and humane surroundings.

And this is where the physical nature of much death (when not simply sudden or induced) joins hands with human and cultural factors. Many dying people have become vulnerable to control by others because they have simply not taken the time to prepare any statement about how they wished to die: the possibility of avoiding the contemplation of death, during so much of a long life, trumped any kind of reasoned preparation. As we have seen, vague awareness of a problem and the will to act, in a culture that did not encourage much thought of death, remained widely separate.

Even more troubling are the many cases where people *have* legally stipulated, through a living will, a desire to avoid heroic medical measures, where "DNR" (do not resuscitate) is clearly marked on the patient's chart, yet where doctors and relatives combine to override the intent. The attending physician goes right ahead and attaches the tubes and apparatus, uses defibrillators repeatedly to restore temporary life, with the result that the last days are spent, helpless, in intensive care units, amid the fearful machinery, with relatives coming in quickly to say last goodbyes that cannot be heard. Antideath triumphs, not over death itself, but over the desired death. Small wonder that, as an Institute of Medicine report put it rather drily, "a significant number of people experience needless suffering and distress at the end of life."

We do not know how much an awareness of this possible scenario affects the normal course of adult life before serious illness sets in. The fact that a minority is aware of the importance of a legal effort to control conditions in advance and that a large majority hopes that luck will let them opt out through sudden and unexpected demise, suggests at least some realization that the inevitability of death, already an unwelcome prospect particularly in modern culture, may be worsened further through machine-aided frenzy. Certainly, witnessing the "needless . . . distress" of others compounds the final burdens on loved ones, when it turns out that insistence on heroic measures did not fight death so much as deteriorate it.

This aspect of modern death seems simply out of whack, reducing contentment (happiness, admittedly, would be too strong a hope) in the final weeks and days for all concerned and possibly, periodically, disrupting modern distractions with brief but recurrent panic over what one's own ending will entail. The invitation to further adjustments in modern trends is compelling.

Not for Discussion

A final problem, surfacing strongly in the United States in 2009, both reflected the constraining elements of modernity and complicated any effort at revision. It turned out that references to modest reassessment of modern death American-style, in the interests of cost containment and personal dignity combined, generated a political combustion that almost certainly precluded calm discussion in the near future. Part of the furor was politically manipulated. But part of it resulted from death fears and evasions that continued to be part of the modern process.

The occasion was the latest round of discussion of national health care reform. Included in Democratic proposals was a provision for insurance (including Medicare) payments to doctors for advising patients on end-of-life planning. The proposal followed patterns common in some parts of Europe, but also in American locations like La Crosse, Wisconsin, where the town's biggest hospital had pioneered in trying to assure that the care provided to people in their final months of life complied with their wishes. The La Crosse initiative had developed over two decades, in response to what local officials recognized as a "troubling pattern" when family members struggled over decisions about what to do for a loved one after a crippling stroke or advanced cancer—whether to continue life-support measures such as dialysis when there was really no chance for recovery. The alternative, urging individuals and families to provide guidance when they were still healthy, was designed to limit economic and emotional costs alike, and those involved attested to the success of the shift. Consultations might be fairly lengthy, which is where the idea of some insurance reimbursement for doctors' time came in, but they were widely welcomed. Many people spontaneously agreed that they would not want further treatment "when I've reached a point where I don't know who I am or who I'm with, and don't have any hope of recovery." Ensuing directives gained force of law and protected hospitals and family members alike against liability suits. Over 90% of the adult population in La Crosse had established provisions by the early 21st century, over twice the national level. The result was an average terminal illness hospital stay of thirteen days, as opposed to forty-sixty days in major urban hospitals elsewhere. Those involved professed relief at being protected against ending life hooked up to machines, while families welcomed directives in advance that would shield them from guilt when heroic measures ceased.

The idea of expanding on precedents of this sort as part of a national reform aimed at spreading medical coverage but also cutting costs sparked a firestorm. Former Alaska governor Sarah Palin seized on the measure as a compulsory introduction of what she called "death panels" that would make decisions denying health care to the elderly and the disabled. Normally sensible Republicans joined the chorus, talking about opposing the proposals that risked "pulling the plug on grandma."

People actually involved in end-of-life planning, as in La Crosse, were dismayed at the political gamesmanship. Hospital officials insisted that "these things need to be discussed"; far from heavy-handed impositions of death, they argued, "it's just the opposite—it's giving you a choice of how you want to be treated."

Whatever the reality, the death panel image struck a national chord in a hideously partisan atmosphere. Democrats pulled in their horns, and an opportunity for a calm national discussion of improvements in modern death disappeared—unlikely, given the lifespan of successful political ploys, to revive anytime soon.

Obviously, judgments about this episode are complex. This is hardly the first case in which an issue has been distorted and exaggerated for reasons that went well beyond the actual subject, in this case a more sensible approach to death. Many people might legitimately worry, particularly in a society historically nervous over government initiatives, indeed about any kind of federal guidelines, even if the intent was not to recommend any particular response to heroic medicine beyond providing new opportunities for discussion.

What's relevant is the extent to which the quick popularity of Republican distortions of the concept reflected a continued national aversion not just to the federal government but to the possibility of exploring, publicly, what's been happening to death. A journalist got it right, in commenting on the contrast between community openness and common sense in places like La Crosse and what happened when the same ideas went more public upon reaching the national stage: "The debate has underscored how fraught the discussion is on end-of-life care in a country where an optimistic ethos places great faith in technology and often precludes frank contemplation of mortality." The quest for happiness ironically makes reducing unhappiness around actual death immune to wide or candid discussion. There's something wrong with death and American modernity.

Public Grief

One final development, emerging from the late 20th century onward in many parts of the world, suggests the fluidity of reactions to death in modernity. Here, it's important to note, there's nothing necessarily amiss. Intriguing changes in public grief behaviors, following consistently from the larger modern culture but in new ways, suggest that modern societies are still experimenting, still trying to figure out how to handle the dramatically altered contours of death.

Beginning in the 1980s, new signs emerged of an intense desire to gain opportunities for social mourning for certain kinds of victims of death and also, particularly in the United States, a growing need to memorialize some of these victims as well. Targets were clear, if not always predictable: the deaths must attract vivid video attention, providing real media guidance in the kinds of emotions that should be displayed, and the victim or victims of death must be seen as dying in undeserved ways at a too-early stage of life. The reactions were novel, but there was consistency with modernity more generally in the beliefs that death simply should not happen to people before later age—so the reactions provided additional ways of demonstrating social shock that such inappropriate deaths still occurred.

Important precedents existed for public mourning, but always in the past the figures involved had gained attention through public office. Elderly kings sometimes commanded sincere signs of affection and grief when they died, even from people for whom they had (according to cynical historians) done little or nothing in their lifetimes; hence the sorrow among Bohemian peasants at the death of Francis Joseph of Austria. Dead presidents have sometimes had a similar aura, particularly when they amassed a real record of achievement and/or were assassinated. Mourners along the route of Lincoln's funeral train back to Illinois come to mind most obviously, but also the nationwide shocked weekend following John Kennedy's death.

But the recent phenomenon, though it may build on these precedents, often involves more ordinary people whose deaths seem so obviously unacceptable that a public response is required. Reactions to the shooting of John Lennon, in 1980, provided a foretaste: in contrast to the death three year earlier of Elvis Presley, which had brought mourners from various places to Memphis for the funeral, Lennon's death sparked scenes not only in New York, where the shooting occurred, but also in Liverpool and elsewhere. Large crowds, with tens of thousands of people, gathered at various sites on the day after the news was broadcast. And permanent memorials were quickly established, including the Strawberry Fields section of Central Park, which became a site for other public manifestations of grief later on.

The literally global and intensely emotional response to the death of Princess Diana, by car accident, represented perhaps a less clear-cut case, in that she did have a semiroyal mantle. Still, the range and extent of public grief were literally unprecedented, with monuments established in various places, tributes of flowers maintained in some cases for months, and an endless stream of anguished comment on the news. Within days after the accident, flowers piled five feet deep surrounded the princess's London palace, along with many teddy bears. Flowers were also piled at the Paris accident site, with the bouquets renewed for months. Six memorial structures were established in London. A charitable foundation in the princess's name quickly gained $150 million in donations worldwide. Global telecasts of the funeral claimed half the world's population as viewers, while millions directly lined the funeral route. Here was public grief (and, admittedly, curiosity) at a previously unheard of level.

The 1990s also brought new manifestations of public grief for ordinary people who were victims of acts of terror. The 1995 bombing of the federal building in Oklahoma City generated an outpouring of grief and sympathy. Teddy bears, key chains, and poems were stuck in a fence that surrounded the site, with contributions renewed by visitors for many years. Even more revealing was the unusually swift and extensive commitment to construct a memorial to the innocent victims. The whole downtown site—a valuable piece of urban property—was turned into a national memorial, which opened in 2000 as the largest of its kind in the world to that date. The memorial included 168 empty chairs, each inscribed with the name of a victim, along with a National Memorial Museum and a remnant of the memento-stuffed fence. Remembrance services are conducted annually on the anniversary of the bombing. As with many such contemporary grief recollections, the names of victims are read out one by one; this is an innovation now applied retroactively to other tragedies, such as the Holocaust.

The terrorist attacks of September 11, 2001, occasioned even more massive and enduring grief. Immediate efforts were launched to build extensive memorials, though in New York the project was snarled with controversy. Annual ceremonies became something of a national occasion, complete with presidential speeches and visits and, again, the reading of names. (How long will the pattern continue? Ceremonies in 2010 suggested some lessening of intensity, but no willingness to let go of a now-traditional opportunity to protest death.) The shock and magnitude of this particular event may make the public outpourings seem more obvious than, say, the Oklahoma City case, less demanding of explanation, but it remains true that the intensity and duration of the public impulse do not have clear historical precedent.

Further, it is possible to measure the change of public mood and the growing intensity of the need for emotional outpouring with more humble examples. The 2009 death of Michael Jackson generated noticeably greater reaction than had followed the killing of John Lennon. Startled communications literally overloaded Internet sites (ironically, dampening global reactions to a major Iranian protest movement). Public gatherings took shape literally all over the world—not only in the United States and Western Europe but also in Australia, Ukraine, and Japan. Some of the emotional furor simply reflected the earlier popularity of the King of Pop's music, some mere curiosity about the mysterious circumstances of his death; but there were widespread expressions of grief as well.

The 2008 killings of thirty-two students at Virginia Tech, by a crazed undergraduate, offer a final test case. Just forty-one years before, a similar mass murder had occurred at the University of Texas in Austin, with twelve dead and thirty-one injured. In the Texas case, local sympathy and shock were strong, with canceled classes and closure of the tower from which most of the shootings occurred. But while media reports spread globally, there was no indication of any public gatherings or ceremonies elsewhere. Efforts to raise funds for the victims were not particularly successful (eleven thousand dollars was the total sum accumulated), and there was no effort to establish a memorial despite pressure from families of the deceased, though a garden was finally created in the 1990s. Great concern quickly emerged about avoiding panic or reputational damage to the university, and voices were quickly raised to urge the reopening of the tower: why should normal operations be disrupted by the acts of a lunatic?

The Virginia Tech contrast, in a new age of public responsiveness, was almost complete. Within hours of the shooting, donations began to pour in, from all parts of the nation and beyond—a million dollars came in within six months. A ribbon campaign was organized to help strangers express their sympathy, and offerings of stuffed animals (another interesting contemporary motif, showing a desire to comfort, without question, but also perhaps a somewhat childish emotional regression) were widespread. Memorial vigils occurred on many campuses, even distant from the tragedy site. The university did resist pleas to tear down the building in which most of the killing had occurred, but it vowed to avoid general classroom use in future. Plans for temporary memorials were almost immediate, and quickly as well efforts were made to organize a more permanent monument. The extensive payments granted to victims' families were another move away from the Texas pattern, where no such notion emerged at all. Death of this sort, somehow, had become more horrible in terms of public emotion and a sense of public responsibility.

The basic change—the unprecedented surge of public mourning—may be a welcome innovation in the modern approach to mortality. Rapid and extensive sympathy with the victims of untimely death can be taken as a desirable contrast to the selfishness and individualism characteristic of so many aspects of modern society. The capacity to feel real grief at the death of strangers may be an important extension of more general sentiments of humanitarian empathy whose origins can be traced to earlier periods in the emergence of modernity. To be sure, there is some expense involved, and the sense of emotional attachment also generates new and questionable efforts to develop heightened levels of security. The emotions can be readily manipulated, by politicians among others. Equally interesting, the public grief does not necessarily provide much comfort to the families of victims, and it may even exacerbate raw feeling. Relatives of the Texas victims, to be sure, have remained (or become) concerned about the lack of memorial response. But relatives of the Virginia dead have complained mightily about inadequate compensation and insufficient punishment for real or imagined negligence on the part of university officials, so if they're comforted, they seem to be concealing it well. The "best" public response is not easy to determine.

More to the point for our purposes, however, is the question of what is going on with these interesting and novel manifestations of public emotion amid modernity (particularly, though not exclusively, in the American version of modernity). Interpretation is challenging, precisely because of the innovation involved, and surely some combination of factors must be cited. But these factors include both a new instantiation of the modern aversion to death and the obvious need to continue to experiment over grief in the modern context. Participation in the new manifestations of public grief may provide catharsis beyond the specific occasion for mourning, possibly releasing some wider modern fears about death and to that extent reducing this source of dissatisfaction. The clearest conclusion is that modernity and death, those uncomfortable but inescapable companions, compel continuing change and adjustment. The process is ongoing.

The Modern Problems

Difficulties with handling death in modern societies reflect the novelty of basic problems: we continue to try to come to terms with a death revolution scarcely a century old. In this sense it is small wonder that the needs of the modern context, quite different from those that prevailed even amid the experiments of the 19th century, are still being defined, that initial recourses need to be softened and reshaped. Adaptations continue, for example with the new approaches of the hospice movement or efforts to provide more rounded training to the medical personnel that now play such a role in managing death.

Some aspects of the modern conundrum probably cannot be resolved. In a situation where so few children die—a benefit of modernity—it is hard to imagine that parents who do suffer this unusual loss can be readily consoled. Guilt, adding to grief, is virtually inevitable.

Other modern tensions would seem to permit further improvement. More effort to encourage people to spell out their goals for treatment at the end of life and to encourage others involved to respect these goals is surely within the realm of possibility. Difficult decisions will not be eliminated, but they can be eased. Opportunities for farewells and for more nuanced expression of grief can be encouraged. The modern barrier—the obvious difficulty in encouraging both personal and public contemplation of death—is quite real, but it need not be insuperable. There is no reason to wish to return to premodern death conditions, but this does not mean that modern complications cannot be confronted.

Modern conundrums about death do not yield a clear comparative story line. Particular cultures face distinctive problems. Japanese hesitancy about turning to definitions of brain death was an interesting case in point. Many critics once argued that, because of greater religious ballast, Americans managed to retain more salutary death responses than West Europeans did. There was more willingness to tolerate death ceremonies, less or at least more gradual involvement with disruptions of tradition such as cremation. Yet there is evidence that innovations like cremation can generate their own rituals and meanings, so their popularity need not be taken as a shallow dismissal of death. Fascination with medical progress and technology and the more general distaste for death may make it harder for Americans than some other modern societies to confront some of the drawbacks of modern death, beginning with excessive medicalization itself. The inclusion of death, in 2009, as yet another component of the intractable liberal-conservative disputes over what is euphemistically called the "social agenda" was not an encouraging sign for this particular national culture. It also seems probable that American fears of death, in responses for example to terrorism, harbor some distinctive and not necessarily constructive elements.

But the big issue is modernity itself, and not some particular national susceptibility. Huge gains are widespread in modern societies, but so are the needs for fine tuning and for a willingness to confront topics defined as unpleasant in the modern context. Opportunities for further adjustment will clearly exceed particular national contexts as well, providing occasions for experimentation with best practices and for a certain amount of global learning.

Death and Happiness

It's easy enough to see, finally, that death and modern happiness don't go well together. This is another disjuncture that's not likely to be fully fixable, though the tension might be narrowed. But how much do changes in death qualify modern happiness? How much do they contribute to the happiness gap already outlined?

A couple of points are clear. The reduction of death, thanks to the death revolution, is surely one key reason people in modern societies are happier, on average, than those in more traditional settings. Not having to mourn the deaths of children, not having to be reminded constantly of death's threat, even (probably) not having to deal with death directly, at home, are all pretty clear benefits of modernity, despite some down sides. It would be totally misleading to claim that death's modern problems compare to the issues death raised in premodern societies.

Further, to the extent that modern societies manage to distance death from becoming a daily preoccupation, they may continue to contribute to happiness (though also, arguably, shallowness—modern happiness hardly defines every desirable goal in a meaningful life). When modern people respond to happiness polls, it's unlikely that death intrudes significantly, if at all, unless some personal tragedy has recently struck.

The newer kinds of tensions about death, however, do affect happiness levels in three and possibly four respects, even if polling data probably pick up these shadows incompletely at best.

First, and most tragically, the people exposed to the statistical improbabilities of modern life, those who do lose a child or young spouse, inevitably confront the gap between normal standards of happiness and their misfortune in ways that are difficult to manage. Their sense of unfairness is fully understandable. The contrast with earlier settings, in which death brought sorrow but not a sense of unfairness or disruption of normal expectations, is obvious but hard to remedy.

Second, the traumas so often associated with the final weeks of even older relatives, with difficult decisions about treatment levels and the disorientation imposed by many hospital settings, create their own, if temporary, gulf between conditions of death and what may be reasonably regarded as normal life satisfactions. Death must always qualify happiness, but smoother mediations can be imagined that would lessen the starkness of the contrast. Subsequent ritual, including funeral home gatherings and periodic remembrances, reduce the tension—again, there's no reason to exaggerate the modern dilemma. But many death scenes do suspend normal expectations in modern life, and the suspension is clearly painful precisely because the contrast has been defined so starkly.

Third, the anxieties associated with efforts to secure against death clearly qualify happiness at some points for some modern people. Worries about the safety of children generate minor annoyances—the current need to put kids in some kind of restraining device in cars well past the toddler years—and deeper fears as well—the fears that bring parents to the crib at night, to make sure the newborn is still breathing. Belief in the possibility and responsibility for preventing death also encourages fearfully gloomy responses to tragedies encountered in the news, where the quick transferability to "what if it happens to me and mine next?" clearly darkens happiness, sometimes for extended periods of time. Add to this the fact that modern life does generate some undeniable new threats— like car accidents—even though overall mortality continues to be pushed back, and there are some definite clouds on any reasonable horizon. Some individuals, perhaps some whole regional cultures, seem to play up the anxious hovering theme more than others, but there is no doubt that both reasonable and unreasonable fears can flourish, even with death receding, given the new awareness of risks and the new desire for prevention.

How much—and here is the fourth category, potentially the most important but surely the most difficult to plumb—do death fears for oneself qualify happiness amid modernity? It's easy to make a case that modern unfamiliarity with death, plus the reasonable need to worry about unseen health damage associated with degenerative processes (again, is it more crippling to contemplate an undetected cancer or, as in past periods, the next epidemic?), plus the equally reasonable concern about facing an end of life in which one's wishes are ignored or not known and in which one may be powerless to abandon life gracefully all add up to a recurrent, largely silent confrontation that intrudes unbidden on the daily, hopefully happy routine. Certainly, modern people find death difficult to discuss, but it is no less inevitable for that fact. Do we shadow our happiness through private encounters with death's new strangeness and uncontrollable qualities? Probably sometimes, depending much on personality and age. Do we blithely dismiss the topic, until confrontation becomes inevitable, enjoying the fact that death is not a daily intruder in modern life and hoping that one's own end will come without warning or any need to prepare? Probably often, depending much on personality and, to some degree, on age.

Death, in modernity, blots happiness massively in some deeply unfortunate but atypical situations. It qualifies happiness, arguably to an unnecessary extent, in some life passages and amid some projected fears. It may periodically intrude in contemplation of one's own end. Whatever the encounter, there is no question that modern conditions make it difficult to share or air uncertainties, and in the process may worsen their impact. The various facets of modern death history center on the gulf between rising hopes and expectations and the real, but finite, change in material reality.

Further Reading

There is some classic work on the history of death. Philippe Ariès, *The Hour of Our Death*, 2nd ed. (New York: Vintage Books, 1982) developed the most elaborate historical perspective on modern discomfort with death. Elisabeth Kübler-Ross has also written extensively on the subject; see *On Death and Dying,* rev. ed. (New York: Scribners, 1997); *On Grief and Grieving: Finding the Meaning of Grief through the Five Stages of Loss* (New York: Simon & Schuster, 2005); and *On Life after Death,* rev. ed. (Berkeley, CA: Celestial Arts, 2008). But see also Arthur Imhof, *Lost Worlds: How Our European Ancestors Coped with Everyday Life and Why Life Is So Hard Today* (Charlottesville: University Press of Virginia, 1996); David Stannard, *The Puritan Way of Death: A Study in Religion, Culture, and Social Change* (New York: Oxford University Press, 1977); James Farrell, *Inventing the American Way of Death: A Study in Religion, Culture, and Social Change* (New York: Oxford University Press, 1977); and Ralph Houlbrooke, ed., *Death, Ritual, and Bereavement* (London: Routledge, 1989). Other reliable work includes Robert Wells, *Facing the "King of Terrors": Death and Society in an American Community, 1750–1990* (Cambridge: Cambridge University Press, 2000), and Ernest Becker, *Denial of Death* (New York: Free Press, 1973). For more recent surveys, see Suzanne Smith, *To Serve the Living: Funeral Directors and the African American Way of Death* (Cambridge, MA: Belknap Press of Harvard University Press, 2010); Gary Laderman, *Rest in Peace: A Cultural History of Death and the Funeral Home in Twentieth-Century America* (New York: Oxford University Press, 2005); and Peter N. Stearns, *Revolutions in Sorrow: The American Experience of Death in Global Perspective* (Boulder, CO: Paradigm, 2007).

%% 8 %%

Century of the Child?

Childhood, Parenting, and Modernity

Many American polls from the later 20th century onward suggest that the happiest kind of married couple is childless, a truly striking finding and an obvious change from the good old days, when having children was a fundamental goal of marriage. A study by Daniel Gilbert suggests that the average American mother's happiness drops steadily from the birth of her first child until the last child reaches eighteen and leaves home (at which point it may pick up again, in the parental equivalent of retirement). And if parenting *is* a marital goal, recent canvasses suggest that a single child is best for adult happiness.[1] Many grains of salt may apply here: people may be confusing a shallow kind of pleasure, based for example on more free time and resources for leisure and consumer pursuits, with deep life satisfaction that polling cannot really capture. But there is also some striking confirming evidence: polling data also show a decline in parental expressions of enjoyment from the 1960s onward: the only parental category claiming that their commitments were improving were divorced dads, possibly because fathers' rights were gaining a bit or possibly because so many divorced dads did little with their offspring save an occasional amusement park fling. Lots of parents asserted that, were they to do life over again, they might not get involved.

The point here is not to abuse polling data or letters to advice columnists, which might on occasion simply reflect a really bad day. It is accurate to note, however, that parental satisfaction has definitely not matched the many positive gains in modern childhood—gains that were being painstakingly achieved and heralded by progressive folk just a century ago. It's worth pointing out, as well, that parental anxieties have in many ways mounted, which affects not only opinion polls but basic adult happiness. Seventy-seven percent of contemporary Dutch parents, for example, claim literally daily worry about their adequacy with their own children.[2] Here, more clearly than with death, it's possible to show not only how modernity raises new and unexpected complications but also how new standards really cut into daily life experience as well.

But the comparison with death is useful in a few respects. As with death, childhood in the modern context involves some genuine new difficulties, and though these do not explain the core reactions, they certainly contribute a bit. More problematic, however, has been the emergence of dramatic new expectations. Rather than enjoying clear gains over premodern conditions—including the effective conquest of infant death—moderns turned distressingly quickly to more demanding definitions of the successful childhood, definitions that have proved hard to achieve with any degree of satisfaction. Along with new problems and escalating expectations has come a set of misperceptions—areas where parents readily conclude that considerable threats exist without foundation in fact. Problems, misplaced fears, and disappointed expectations add up to a powerful package.

As with death as well, however, modern people continue to experiment. Key modern aspects of childhood and parenting are still relatively new, a century at most in full bloom, and there's reason to watch a process of continued adjustment, and hopefully to introduce a dash of recent-history guidance.

Childhood, obviously, involves a variety of participants. The most blatant down sides of children's modernity, particularly on the expectations side, really apply to adults. The process of modern parenting—granting various specific circumstances and personalities—is simply not as pleasurable as it arguably should be. Claiming less-than-happy childhoods, however, is another matter. There are certainly some troubling symptoms at the edge, for example in the rise of suicides among older children in a number of modern societies. But the relationship between many children and modern happiness is complex, and it's best to let some evidence roll in before returning to this category.

A particular American twist, finally, seems to apply to the modern conundrums of childhood and parenting. Many aspects of contemporary childhood, and their contrast with traditional patterns, apply to all modern societies, and these general features are important. Schooling and limited family size are modern constants, and they do force some issues quite generally. It's worth noting, for example, that the shrinkage of the birth rate, and the expansion of longevity, automatically reduce

the importance of children in modern societies from a purely percentage point of view. Obviously, compensation is possible through higher
standards of adult attention and responsibility, and that is indeed part
of the modern story, but it's worth asking if one of the modern tensions
doesn't involve the extent to which adults have to develop non–child-centered interests simply because there aren't as many children around to
involve them, and because a smaller portion of their life will involve child
care. Claims of heightened valuation of children—which are common as
modernity advances—thus war against the fact of lessened quantitative
significance.

Against the modern-in-general, however, emerges the American variant. These teasers:

⚬ The United States is the only society in the world that requires traf-
fic to stop when school buses load and unload their charges. The
symbolism is intriguing: only in the United States are children
regarded as so precious that normal activities should be suspended
around them (or, alternatively, only in the United States are children regarded as so incompetent that they must have artificial protection).

⚬ And second: as mothers began to enter the labor force outside
the home in large numbers throughout the Western world, from
the 1950s and 1960s onward, an obvious response was the establishment of day care centers. American parents, however, were
far more reluctant to use these services than were their European
counterparts, and felt far guiltier when they did so.

⚬ Third and finally: only in the United States did a significant movement develop against homework, based on concerns that teachers
were overloading innocent children both physically and mentally.
Granted, this particular pattern has largely yielded to modern educational necessities, though there are still flare-ups every so often,
but the fact that significant resistance developed, over several
decades in the early 20th century, represents an intriguing national
hesitation.

Again, there seems to be something distinctively protective about many
American responses to children, at least in principle. We will see that the
same distinctiveness applies to American variants of many other issues
associated with childhood in modernity.

Modernist Hopes and Boasts

A desire to transform childhood was central to the modernist impulse from the Enlightenment onward, and it had as inevitable accompaniment a belief that traditional childhood had been badly handled. We've already noted how naming practices changed, including abandonment of the idea of reusing names of dead siblings, signaling a new appreciation of children's individuality. But there was far more involved. While the larger modern-traditional contrast has faded today—one reason we take less pleasure in basic modern gains than might otherwise be the case—most modern adults probably believe that traditional uses of children were ill founded even though they may also believe that there was an earlier stage of modernity, say the halcyon 1950s, when childhood conditions were superior to what they are today. In other words, to the extent that there is any historical sense at all, many Americans would probably feel some pride in improvements over the bad old days in colonial times, while also worrying about some contemporary declension as against a simpler though definitely already modern recent past.

What was wrong, to the increasingly modern eyes that visioned childhood from the Enlightenment onward, with childhood in the traditional past? The first point was cultural. Western culture had long, and rather distinctively, looked at childhood through the lens of original sin. How ordinary parents acted on this impulse is not entirely clear, but the connection certainly justified uses of anger and fear in calling children to account, given their naturally sinful natures. And there are important surviving subcultures in the United States today, particularly associated with evangelical Christianity, which maintain many of these beliefs. On balance, however, Enlightenment thinking, which by the later 18th century was influencing the emergence of a more moderate Protestantism, argued that children were at the least morally neutral at birth—a blank slate—or (increasingly, when rationalism was supplemented by the glow of Romantic sentimentality) positively and charmingly innocent. The first quarrel between modernists and a sense of earlier tradition, then, involved the conception of the basic nature of the child, and it was easy to slam the past in light of the more positive valuation now attributed to children and childhood. In the United States, a quiet battle took shape in the 1830s and 1840s over the abandonment of original sin, but most mainstream groups picked up the more optimistic approach, which encouraged a sense of cherishing rather than chastising the child.

The idea that traditional parents harbored a mistaken judgment about children's character often made it easy as well to point accusing fingers at past discipline, and to call for a more humane approach. Reformers, writing for example in a new secular literature on how to raise children, cited several points. First, they emphasized that it was wrong to try to scare children as a means of correction. This attack on fear tactics, including familiar invocations of bogeymen, continued, in the United States, into the 1920s, when it began to trail off, presumably because most middle-class parents had internalized the message. But concerns about scaring kids continued in other venues, for example the 1930s Disney efforts to make classic fairy stories less frightening, with more benign little elves and forest animals and more happy endings. In the West, modern opinion also moved against traditional uses of shame and, at least in part, physical discipline.

A second consequence of the recasting of children's nature fed a fundamental redefinition of function. During the Enlightenment, education and the appeal to children's rational capacity became basic building blocks of progress more generally: here was a launching pad for improvements in technology, here was a way to eliminate superstition and put political life on a solid footing. By the early 19th century, emphasis on the importance of educating children was increasingly paired with attacks on children's traditional work commitments. Learning, not labor, should be the goal of respectable childhood. Increasingly, middle-class families realized that a period of formal education was essential for their offsprings' future. More hesitantly, child labor laws and, soon, actual primary school requirements moved this redefinition into the experience of other social classes as well. Resistance was inevitable: many workers and peasants resented this intrusion into their parental control and economic expectations, but gradually legal pressure and an understanding of what modern jobs demanded increased the number of parental converts. Less progress occurred in the *nature* of education: rote learning and strict discipline continued (and in some ways continue still), but even here there were experiments toward more student-participatory systems.

The growing appeal of childish innocence plus the new emphasis on schooling created a growing commitment to childhood as a space very different from adulthood. Here, too, traditional emphases came in for attack. After all, when work was the prime obligation of children in most families, rapid maturation was a desirable goal. Most agricultural societies, and not just in the West, rather liked children who were serious before their time, and found little durable merit in childish qualities per se. They also tended to place a high premium on obedience, and while 19th-century guidance literature continued to drive home the importance of obedience, the theme might already be diluted by goals such as creativity.

By the later 19th century, at least at the rhetorical level, modernist spokespeople were defining a childhood considerably different from the previous, largely agricultural model. Modern enlightenment, so the argument ran, opened the way for acknowledgement of childhood as a separate and blissful stage in life, defined by innocence, free from harsh discipline, and devoted to learning rather than work obligations inappropriate for children's health and development alike. For the first time in human history, children could be treated as they deserved, to their benefit but also, through expanding education, to the benefit of social progress.

The modernist picture, however sincere, concealed key complications. First, probably inevitably, it oversimplified the traditional past. Doctrines of original sin colored approaches to childhood, but they did not fully define them: lots of parents developed deep and positive attachments to their children—as witness their sorrow at the high rate of infant mortality—untouched by religious niceties. Historians have particularly disputed the disciplinary assumptions associated with modernity. Use of fear and physical punishments were quite real, and of course modern parental advances have not fully eliminated them. But many experts argue that spankings, for example, if administered moderately and fairly, do not necessarily distort a childhood (this is not a recommendation, simply a recognition of the validity of different approaches). And, as we have seen, some historians believe that outright abuse of children was far less common in the premodern context than it has become since, mainly because tight communities monitored the behavior of individual parents in ways that prevented excess. Finally, while it is true that a certain amount of work defined most premodern childhoods, and while (by modern standards) real exploitation undoubtedly occurred, the contrast with the results of modern schooling are not as clear-cut as moderns might like to believe—a point to which we will return.

Furthermore, the modernist version of the past omitted some features of the premodern environment that were arguably more constructive than what has occurred under modernity's sway. A number of scholars have argued, for example, that opportunities for expressive play were greater in traditional societies than they are now, and that modernity is a villain of the piece in this regard—beginning as early as the first decades of the 19th century. Most children did work, from five years of age onward, but they also had a considerable amount of free time, and they were able (under the general gaze of the village or neighborhood, but without direct adult monitoring) to play with each other quite creatively. Once the idea took root that a prime characteristic of children was educability, this traditional openness began to be restricted in favor of adult-sponsored activities. Already by 1800 middle-class parents were beginning to buy books designed to build children's character, and the notion of monitoring some recreational activities in favor of constructive learning emerged soon thereafter, though gradually. By 1900 experts were suggesting that even objects around infants should have educational value and that open-air activities should be channeled into properly supervised playgrounds and rule-bound, organized sports and games. None of this was ill-intended, though some of the reform efforts reflected fear about children's impulses and particular concern about the parenting qualities of the lower classes and immigrants. But it is true that explicit adult oversight did increase and that adult goals began being imposed on what was still, sometimes, called play time. And there may have been losses involved, for the kids themselves and for their creative development.

Modernist hymns to the glories of modern childhood around 1900 also frequently overlooked the slow progress, in fact, of the overall vision. Schooling advanced in the 19th century, but despite legal requirements it remained far from universal. Child labor persisted widely, particularly for young teenagers; the year 1910 saw the largest amount of child labor ever in the United States. In schools themselves, harsh discipline and shaming techniques, like dunce caps, arguably limited learning even for those who did attend.

This was the context, in turn, early in the 20th century, for a fuller modernist transition amid a new reformist push. The lead dog in this accelerated modern mood was the final big thrust against child labor, at least in the United States and Western Europe. Reformers had already succeeded in passing a variety of child labor laws and school requirements in industrial societies, and gradually also factory inspection had put some teeth in the prohibitions in the most modern economic sectors. But children continued to work extensively in agriculture, in crafts and shops, and in street trades such as newspaper vending. The affront to the self-styled definers of proper modern childhood had become too much to endure. Major new associations formed to root out the evil once and for all, with arguments ranging from children's health and morals—"the ranks of our criminal classes are being constantly recruited from the army of child laborers," as a new American advocacy group put it—to the transcendent need to free time and attention for schooling. Under this onslaught, plus the ongoing changes in business and industry that reduced needs for children, child labor finally receded. By 1920 in the United States, only 8% of all children between the ages of ten and fifteen were at work, and by 1940 the figure was down to 1%. Premodern traditions finally gave way.

The Flowering of Modern Childhood

What was happening, in the first decades of the new century, was the culmination of a real modern revolution in childhood, launched earlier but now gaining full momentum and adding important additional facets. Reformist rhetoric and patterns already spreading among the middle class now bore fuller fruit.

First, obviously, the age-old association between children and work effectively ended save for occasional part-time or summer jobs for some older children (where, increasingly, those who did work thought in terms of personal gain, not the family's economy). Additional laws, growing recognition of the importance of schooling, and the complexity of many modern work situations that precluded useful childish involvement combined to redefine the core functions of childhood. This huge change was soon amplified, in most industrial societies, by a steady decline even in domestic chores for urban children. Fewer young children to care for, new household appliances (dishwashers were central here), even a growing parental sense that, given the primacy of education, children should not be overburdened with additional assignments—here was another combination that increasingly removed children from effective work. This shift, admittedly, was gradual, but by the end of the 20th century boys were contributing almost no household labor (particularly by the time they were teenagers), and girls very little. There was considerable evidence that many modern parents became too impatient to wait for children to take care of even trivial chores; it was quicker, in the short run, to do it oneself. The rate of family arguments over chores also went up, doubling between the 1920s and the 1970s; here, too, many parents largely gave up, particularly since many reported increasing difficulty simply thinking up things for kids to do.[3] As one mother put it, "there's just so much to do [with schoolwork and lessons] that I don't want to fight about it." Childhood was meant for other things.

And primary among the other things was school. Education had been expanding for many decades, in all the industrial societies, so further innovation built on extensive foundations. But here too there were decisive additions in the early decades of the 20th century. First was the much more serious effort to enforce school attendance requirements. Even middle-class families had sometimes eased up on individual children who displayed behavioral difficulties in school, and certainly many other families had long been lax even where on-paper regulations were clear. By the 1920s, increasing uniformity prevailed. Second, changes in habits and laws alike pushed a growing number of children into significant engagement with secondary as well as primary schooling, and over time the rates not just of high school attendance but of actual completion pushed up as well. Whole childhoods, and not just portions, were now devoted, in principle as least, to education. New efforts were poured not only into attendance but into punctuality as well. College attendance also accelerated its steady climb, gradually becoming an expectation for a majority of American children. Finally, and most interestingly even for the middle classes, school requirements themselves often became more serious, as educational bureaucracies ramped up across industrial nations. Most 19th-century schools had operated on a loose pass-fail basis, sometimes also mingling diverse age groups in ways that encouraged at most cursory evaluations of rote learning. In contrast, report cards emerged as standard practice in the 1920s, aimed of course as much at parents as at children. College Board tests were introduced in response to the growing diversity of interest in colleges, and while they did not initially carry the weight they would gain by later in the century, as sentries into the most desirable schools, they certainly added to the impression that schooling was now a serious business. Finally, school subject matter expanded and in many ways increased in difficulty, with emphasis shifting from merely the 3 R's and a bit of moral instruction to more serious work on foreign languages, science, and social studies at least by the time of high school.

Education's development was sometimes masked by a recurrent sense of inadequacy. Thus at various points, from the early 20th to the early 21st century, student knowledge of American history and government (or lack thereof) was lamented, as if it had once been far better. In fact, insofar as evidence exists, contemporary students on average know at least as much as their predecessors did, and in some areas, like math, are expected to know more. It is still possible to claim that their learning fell short, or that too many segments of the student population drop below now-acceptable standards, or even (as was often unfortunately the case) that national performance standards were lagging behind those of other societies. But there should be no confusion about basic trend: more students were expected not only to be in school longer but to measure up to higher criteria, virtually with each passing decade. The fact that this was so often beclouded by disappointment reveals one of the unexpected complexities of the new equation between childhood and education. Progressive hopes were not easily achieved.

The intensification of schooling and the effective disappearance of a major commitment to work were accompanied by the other basic components of childhood modernity. First, the same period that witnessed the massive attack on child labor saw the rapid decline of infant mortality and the resultant new norms concerning childhood and death. Soon, additional inoculations developed to push back not only death but many forms of serious illness, and even before this, in the 1920s, middle-class parents began to blaze a trail toward regular consultation with the new medical specialty of pediatrics. (The American Association of Pediatrics formed in 1930.) Every decade from this point onward saw new ways not just to reduce now-modest mortality rates but to improve children's resistance to disease in general. Only the onset of rapid increases in children's obesity, at the very end of the 20th century and beyond, represented a serious setback in an otherwise progressive path. Measles, polio, ear infections—all the common diseases of childhood could now be prevented altogether or quickly cured. Here again, a massive transformation became almost a matter of routine.

Along with improving health came the rapid reduction of the average birth rate. Here, too, gradual changes had developed during the preceding century, as new middle-class prudence was emulated by farmers, workers, and peasants—sometimes, as we have seen, at real cost to sexual expressiveness at least until modern birth control devices became more widely accepted and available. By the early 20th century the familiar modern pattern of 2.5 or 1.8 kids per family was beginning to be standard fare, as most people adjusted to the new facts that children now consumed rather than produced revenue and that there were other drawbacks in trying to raise too many offspring in modern conditions. Even the famous baby boom turned out to be a blip, not a permanent new trend, and by the 1960s modern societies were heading back down to essentially population-stable reproduction rates or even a bit below.

Small average family size had many implications, but the most obvious consequence, or potential consequence, for modern childhood was to free up more parental attention and investment in each individual child. The investment, in turn, was relatively safe given the new unlikelihood of death before maturity. The implications were, admittedly, double-edged, and tensions over the development of each individual youngster could actually rise. But the common modern interpretation of this important change emphasized that parents with only one or two kids to care for could really do a proper job for the first time in history, surrounding their small brood with the material, educational, and emotional support that provided the best chances for effective upbringing and parental satisfaction alike.

The final component of modernity, particularly pronounced in the United States, involved the emergence of a new breed of scientific experts and popularizers in the child-rearing field. New research could be brought to bear on the process of dealing with children, within the family, within the school, within society at large. The many flaws of traditional treatment could be dissected—experts had every self-interest in making it clear how much they could improve upon the past (including the previous generation of experts, as things turned out; this aspect might become a bit confusing). Providing advice about children was not new: preachers used to do it from the pulpit, and then in the 19th century a new breed of popularizer—often, a member of a pastor's family—provided mixtures of practical and moral advice. Now, however, the genre was taken over by psychologists, social workers, and pediatricians (some of them sponsored by new government agencies like the Children's Bureau), or by publicists relying on this kind of expertise. The nature of advice changed, its range expanded immensely, and the sheer volume of available materials began to multiply. Whole bookstore sections began to be devoted to child-care books, some of them fairly hefty. *Parents Magazine*, established in the 1920s with its motto "on rearing children from crib to college," was dedicated to translating research into advice even for middle-class parents, and it quickly won hundreds of thousands of subscribers (it now has two million). While Dr. Spock's book-length venture, coming out first right after World War II, was the most famous and influential contribution to the overall modern advice genre, it was part of a much larger movement to frame modern childhood with external expertise.

The new level of scientific or pseudoscientific guidance added considerably to the setting in which modern childhood was defined and emphasized. Experts in all industrial societies, for example—including newcomer Japan—began to insist on separate judicial and disciplinary treatment for young offenders, helping to define a category of juvenile delinquency regarded as quite separate from adult criminality. At least for a time, hopes for rehabilitation of this special category burned bright, so long as the distinctiveness of childhood, even errant childhood, was maintained. But the ordinary process of parenting was affected as well. Sales of key manuals—successive editions of the Children's Bureau publication, *Infant Care*, proved to be the most popular federal publication ever, even as its topical coverage progressively expanded—suggested that consulting expert advice was becoming an increasingly standard recourse for up-to-date parents eager to do the right thing, somewhat suspicious of conventional sources of advice (like grandparents), and open to guidance with the science seal of approval. Parenting could be made better.

The combination of the modern strands of childhood easily promoted a further sense of progressive celebration: the bad old days were behind us, and for the first time in history a new and proper approach to children was becoming possible. By the 1920s, a full hymn of modern self-praise could be advanced, citing not only the basic gains but the hope that thanks to better scientific advice and training, and the reduction in birth rate, more parents would be up to the task of progressive parenting and more schools could be entrusted to step up, not only in education but also in hygiene and character training, whether parents were adequate or not. Even before this, in 1907, a Swedish school teacher, Ellen Key, coined the classic modern phrase "century of the child," in which a "new consciousness" would at last realize the full potential of childhood.

Key's book was widely taken as a key marker in the triumph of modernism. It was, in a way: it certainly blasted the past and held up a series of new standards as guarantees of potential progress. But it was not a cheerily optimistic book, and not only because it reflected some Scandinavian gloom. The path of progress to modern childhood was clearly marked, but it had not yet been traversed. The glass of modern childhood, in other words, could be seen as half empty or half full. Great strides were possible, great achievements could be claimed, but there would always be a way to go, a gap between what the experts knew and what ordinary mortals actually did. It was, and is, hard to be satisfied, which is one reason why the huge changes in childhood have not generated as much consistent satisfaction, or parental pleasure, or even positive response from children, as might have been expected. The gaps, visible even at the height of progressive contact with a backward past, has only widened with time, and they apply directly to the space between happiness and modernity.

The Tensions

Three basic aspects of modern childhood, in adult conception and in children's experience, help explain why modernity has not generated as much cheer as reformist rhetoric seemed to promise. First, modernity birthed some genuinely new problems; these did not erase the gains, but they certainly caused their own anxieties. Second, even the apparently positive modern achievements had some unexpected down sides (which also meant that the past had not been quite as retrograde as some enthusiasts were wont to imply). But third and most interesting: almost immediately the huge modern gains were dwarfed by new sets of expectations that proved not only hard to fulfill but productive of recurrent parental distress. And all three of these complexities emerged amid the sheer magnitude and novelty of change. Even positive aspects might take a while to assimilate, contributing to the divide between what was hoped and what has happened.

New Challenges

Modernity generated several brand-new causes for parental and societal anxiety about children. We've already touched on the legitimate new concern about accidents. Automobiles are not child-friendly devices, and modern societies, headed by the United States, must continue to make adjustments to reduce the safety hazards involved. There's an odd ambivalence about the American pattern, as realistic fears for children's safety, from infancy through teenage driving, compete with the deep suburban need to let kids drive. New worries unquestionably result: though the problems do not significantly affect the huge statistical gains in children's overall health and survival, statistics and worry are not the same.

Various social changes, even including global trade patterns, feed greater levels of concern over children's access to alcohol and drugs. Problems here are not brand-new—children could encounter alcohol even in earlier times—and modern societies sometimes exaggerate levels of increase in youth access to drugs. But some genuine issues can be checked off in the modernity-deterioration column. Even more recently, the childhood obesity problems add another category of difficulties never before encountered at more than an individual level.

More pervasive still are the lures of consumer culture targeted directly to children, again with the United States, with particularly unfettered media heading the list. The problem first began to surface late in the 19th century, when easy-to-read, often rather violent "penny dreadfuls" were published with an adolescent audience in mind. By this point some child workers had a bit of spending money of their own, and it was at this juncture that, in middle-class families, parents began granting allowances; this, coupled with literacy, provided the source for products now intended to bypass adult supervision. From the early 20th century onward, a familiar list of ever-ascending efforts sought a childish audience: comics and comic books; special radio shows; comics again; movies, in escalating bad taste particularly once producers discovered a summer audience for junk; accessible television shows ostensibly intended for adults; and of course video games and Internet fare. Each wave sought to draw children's attention through violence or sex or both. Each demonstrated to concerned parents that controlling their children's leisure time and purchases was difficult if not impossible. Each drew waves of criticism about its capacity to lure children into inappropriate behavior, but with little resultant control. A 1910 comment, directed at comics, might aside from word choice have been applied to the video games of a near-century later: "a carpet of hideous caricatures, crude art, and poverty of invention, perverted humor, obvious vulgarity and the crudest coloring . . . which makes for lawlessness, debauched fancy, irreverence." Never before had parents and other adults faced this kind of problem in dealing with children, for never had a commercial apparatus developed so widely with the capacity to target youngsters directly. Demonstrably, most parents did not know how to respond, even after over a century of basically repetitious experience. Mild efforts at censorship periodically surfaced but almost always failed.

New sources of accidents; new risks of ingesting damaging products; and the dilemma of taste control legitimately and widely provoked new levels of anxiety and a concern that good parenting was in some ways more difficult than ever before. None of the problems seemed fully resolvable, particularly after infancy when children had to be released to a wider world if only to go to school (though the small but interesting home schooling movement, late in the 20th century, sought to address even this problem head on). Here, then, was a key source of the disjuncture between modernity in childhood and adult satisfaction.

Down Sides of Progress

A second source of parental discomfort, and in some cases childish concern as well, involved the unintended consequences of the major gains in modern childhood—consequences that rarely erased a positive margin but that nevertheless generated problems that more traditional societies had not faced.

The unanticipated worries that the decline of child mortality caused ˙ are an obvious case in point. There's no question that an actual child death heightened guilt and grief in modernity. Worries about children's survival in general probably declined—since there were far fewer risks here to anticipate—but the gains, in terms of parental relief, were less unalloyed than might have been predicted. And while keeping children healthy was easier than ever before historically, new standards imposed more specific duties than before as well, beginning with the regular pediatrician visits and careful lessons in personal hygiene. It was harder than might have been imagined, amid the earlier hymns to progress against disease, to feel secure.

The reduction in the family birth rate also caused problems, for smaller family size could put pressures on children and parents alike. From the adult standpoint, there were fewer sibling intermediaries between an individual child and parents, and this meant fewer household caretakers for the child and potentially either more burdens on one or both parents or more inattention or both. This issue was compounded, in the middle classes from the 1920s forward, by a fairly rapid decline in live-in servants and a steady trend toward separate residences for grandparents, who reversed 19th-century patterns by becoming less routinely available. This might improve grandparent-child relations, in that it was easier to be indulgent when contact was more limited, but it could place added burdens on parents. A key reason parents began to depend more on outside expertise was that other sources of advice and collaboration became less readily available. Households with only two siblings also increased rivalry for parental attention. The 1920s saw a massive level of concern about what was now dubbed "sibling rivalry," with dire warnings about the damage jealousy could do through aggression or personality distortion. Another score for unanticipated problems.

Expert advice itself could be a problem. A generation ago historian Christopher Lasch worried that parents were overrelying on outside guidance, which reduced their own confidence in their capacity to deal with offspring. His concern may be warranted, though which came first—declining confidence or successful external interference—is a bit of a poser. Expert advice also fluctuated, both on specific aspects of child rearing and on general tone—as in shifting approaches to strictness and permissiveness. This could be confusing in and of itself, and also raised issues of intergenerational dispute (successive parent sets disputing with their own parents on what modern child rearing should consist of). Even within the same social class, neighbors might disagree over what advice was best, compounding parental guilts and uncertainties. None of these issues was unmanageable, with a good dose of parental commonsense and decisiveness, but there were tensions involved.

The big gorilla, however, in terms of unanticipated problems, was education. For over a century, Enlightenment-inspired enthusiasm for the benefits of schooling and learning as the core feature of childhood, and the indignation that had crested over the evils of child labor, largely precluded careful discussion of some of the problems this huge conversion might entail, beginning with the clear reduction of parental authority. Even now, a century into the full impact of the modern educational experience, a number of issues have surfaced that were simply not considered even by earlier detractors.

The complexities must be faced, even in a book authored by someone who has devoted a lifetime to promoting education. Something like modern schooling seems essential to the functioning of contemporary economic and political systems. There are no grand alternatives to propose, in the context of modernity. But it is also clear that modern schooling works very badly for some kids—that child labor, appropriately monitored, might be motivationally preferable were it still a valid option. And it is clear that for many children who do make it through the system, or even thrive—and for their parents—there are important stresses and costs.

Some children simply don't like school and do consistently badly in school performance. Judgments here are complicated by social class: many well-intentioned middle-class observers believe that inadequate and unsupportive home environments cause these problems, and in some cases they are doubtless correct. Some societies, however, particularly those more comfortable with formal tracking than is true of the United States, have simply decided that some students—about a quarter of the total, in France—are better off being placed predominantly in a work apprenticeship by the time they reach their early teens, with only a small amount of continuing formal schooling up to the official school-leaving age. Mismatches between student abilities and motivations, and the pressure to continue schooling at least through the secondary level, cause obvious problems for schools, students, and parents, and they are not easy to resolve. There's no question that it's harder for many kids, when school replaces work, to identify what they currently do with what they hope to accomplish as adults, and this can further a sense of confusion about life more generally. The issues are disproportionately male and disproportionately lower-class, but they can spill over more widely in individual cases.

Other discomforts cropped up relatively early in the full conversion to modern childhood, to the dismay of parents and teachers alike. Problems began to be noted, informally, as early as the mid-19th century: it was in the 1850s that a German children's book featured a character called Fidgety Phil, a hyperactive boy who could not sit still in school and whose behavior problems clearly threatened a successful future. Special classes for children of this sort began in several European countries early in the 20th century, when new research established that students of this sort might in fact be quite intelligent but were not going to function adequately without some help. Research on the issue intensified by the 1930s, which was also the time during which the first efforts at medication began. To be sure, some experts continued to argue that the problem here was not kids, but school itself: "If anything should change in this equation, it is the school, not the child." But school demands seemed inexorable, and the focus tended to shift to parents, who should be able to keep their offspring in line: "If parents recognize . . . a child's feelings as natural, helping him at the same time to control his actions, he will make progress." This was the context in which, during the 1950s, a new drug, Ritalin, seemed to offer salvation for troubled parents and difficult kids alike, a way to reconcile personality difficulties with the schooling requirement without too much extra exertion on the adult side, after an often agonizing transition in which the problems were acknowledged in the first place and a decision made to seek expert medical evaluation. By the 1990s Americans were using 90% of the world's Ritalin total,[4] a sign of the acuteness with which this particular school tension was recognized— though also, arguably, a dangerously indulgent acceptance of the easy way out. It was hard to be entirely comfortable with the way this particular modern incompatibility was being addressed.

Even aside from special problems—the students who can't wait to drop out or those burdened with hyperactivity—it's clear that American society, perhaps more than most as modernity has advanced, remains uncomfortable with the burdens of schooling even as it embraces education in principle and devotes massive resources to it. Specifics have varied over the years, but an undercurrent of worry has persisted. School desks might distort children's posture—a lament of the late 19th century. Homework—a new phenomenon in the 20th century—might ruin children and childhood alike by its imposition on physical stamina and mental energy, a source, as one parent put it around 1900, "of nervous exhaustion and agitation, highly prejudicial to body and to mind." For several decades, many school districts restricted homework by law: it was only the Sputnik crisis of the 1950s, by calling attention to global educational competition, that put most of these concerns officially to rest. By the later 20th century, however, the attention of many parents was shifting from protesting homework itself to spending considerable amounts of time guiding their children in its completion—or simply doing it themselves. By 2000, 58% of American parents claimed to be helping their children considerably, some noting that their kids would not work otherwise: "He won't have it any other way. It's like 'If you don't sit down with me, I'm not going to do it.'"[5]

Effort levels were not the only issue. Many American parents also resented the imposition of school judgments on their children, whom they tended to regard, as *The Prairie Home Companion* radio show mocked, as "all above average." Experts and parents alike increasingly agreed, by the 1960s, that schools should systematically strive to preserve children's self-esteem. As a 1960s self-esteem guru, Stanley Coopersmith, put it, "ability and academic performance are significantly associated with feelings of personal worth."[6] This meant that parents had to be careful to build up their children's confidence, but also that they could expect responsible teachers to do the same. Small wonder that many parents increasingly badgered teachers to award good grades and that they expected other measures that would bolster a sense of self-worth. At an extreme, a group of Connecticut parents in 2008 even objected to the use of red markers to correct their children's papers, because this kind of colorful criticism might adversely affected tender egos. And if all else failed, there was always the supportive bumper sticker, another distinctively American product of the desire to reassure children about the benignity of the school experience: "I have an honors student at Clearview Elementary School." Without adult watchfulness and support, school could be a crushing experience, and a variety of compensatory efforts became part of the process of being (or seeming to be) a good parent.

Schooling, in sum, as the central obligation of modern childhood, did not fit all children comfortably. Some of the problems may prove to be transitional—reactions to the fact that the obligation is still fairly new, still requiring unexpected adjustments. Over time, smaller minorities of children may feel adrift at school; high school completion rates have already improved greatly over the past half-century (though this is not necessarily the same thing as a fully positive adjustment), and still-greater comfort may develop, in more families, in the future. Just as they have come to accept homework, at least to a degree, more American parents may reduce their suspicions about the burdens of school on their precious offspring, possibly even allowing national educational demands to come closer to the standards already developed in other modern societies in terms of academic intensity. For the moment, however, some real problems, and a wider tentativeness, remain.

Finally, even where school acceptance runs high, indeed partly because it runs high, new problems have surfaced, further embellishing the unanticipated consequences category. Preparing young children for school was arguably a less natural activity than comparable effort to ready them for formal child labor: the latter could involve assistance jobs for parents; the former meant a more deliberate investment in enhancement. Already in the 1920s and 1930s parents began to show interest in furthering the cognitive abilities of young children, by sending them to "better" nursery schools, buying educational toys, or (in the case for example of adoptees) using the new art of intelligence testing to make sure one was getting top-college material. By the 1960s, the baby boom surge into colleges, plus increasing awareness of the pecking order among universities, created still greater interest in loading the dice as early as possible. New books about *How to Raise a Brighter Child* or *How to Multiply Your Baby's Intelligence*, products of the 1970s, both reflected and encouraged a new intensity applied to young children. Sports activities and music lessons were increasingly sold not just as intrinsically interesting but as contributors to intellectual development. School performance, in this more demanding view, did not just happen, but must be carefully prepared.

Then, at the other educational end, there was college itself, and the examinations leading thereto, providing clear evidence to parents and children alike of how well the schooling process had gone up to that point. Most modern societies offered a series of future-determining examinations, one set to channel entry into secondary school tracks, and the next (particularly for those who made it to the academic path) to determine university options. Both exam portfolios involved intense, competitive effort, usually with considerable parental support; Japanese mothers, for example, came to tolerate all sorts of high jinks from their offspring as release from their concentrated study. In the United States, pressure to get into an appropriate "best" college mounted gradually during the 20th century. In the 1950s, universities like Harvard deliberately cultivated a national recruitment base, and new demographic groups began to aspire more widely as well, both of which expanded levels of competition, and then in the following decade the sheer numerical pressure of the baby boom, and the growing percentage of adolescents seeking college access, began to complicate entry. Many families came to believe that it was far harder to get into college of some sort than was in fact the case, because it was indeed becoming harder to get into the presumably "best" institutions. Multiple applications to colleges soared, as families tried to assure some entry. Training courses for College Board exams expanded widely, and more and more kids began to take the tests many times in hopes of score improvement. *U.S. News and World Report* began to publish its annual rankings of colleges and universities in 1983, and the wide sales and attention both reflected competitive concerns and furthered these concerns in turn. Colleges, for their part, busily resented the rankings, playing up how difficult it might be to get into their own precious enclaves. Parents began to be described as "frantic" during the college application year, because of their own aspirations combined with some understandable reluctance by their kids to get too caught up in the whole process.

The same recent period also generated new symptoms of educational and associated stress at its worst—minority phenomena, to be sure, but significant in their own right and potentially troubling to wider populations—including school-worried parents. School-based shootings, particularly but not exclusively in the United States, seemed to reflect combinations of mental illness and tense peer group dynamics, rather than education per se, but they certainly added a new layer of concern to the whole educational process. Some new diseases arose in direct association with schooling, even beyond attention deficit disorder: early in the 21st century, several thousand Japanese children each year were reported as suffering from *hikikomari*, an inability readily to leave home and function normally. Essentially, they were on a physical and mental strike from the pressures of education. Even more starkly: in all modern societies, youth suicides went up: by 22%, in 2003 alone, in Japan, but also ominously in the United States. American suicide rates for adolescents, at .8% in 1970, reached a peak of over 1.3% in 1990; they did then drop, presumably particularly because of more attention to counseling and to antidepressant medicines, but annual oscillations in the early 21st century, apparently because of fluctuations in medication use, remained troubling. Here many factors might combine: mental illness, family disruption, including parental divorce, as well as medication patterns. But school and related peer pressures loomed large, another sign that the glories of education were not as unqualified and as widely distributed as modern progressives had originally hoped.

Adding Expectations and Resetting the Parental Agenda

Unintended consequences and unforeseen problems are a standard part of the process of historical change, and particularly—given the soaring optimism so often involved—with the changes that form modernity. From the vantage point of the early 21st century, modern childhood turns out to be a good bit more complicated than hopeful observers would have predicted just a century before—and this is one reason why many parents express at most qualified satisfaction with this aspect of their lives.

Particularly noteworthy about the down sides of childhood in modernity, however, were the ways they combined with, and burdened, the new expectations that quickly arose on the heels of modern gains. Progressive experts, and many ordinary parents, were not content with urging more care for the individual child and trying to assure basic school success: they wanted new responsibility for children's emotions and—even more brashly—positive happiness for children as well. Both of these new domains further complicated the definition of being a good parent while further altering the experience of childhood as well.

NEW RESPONSIBILITIES FOR EMOTION

We have already glimpsed the camel's nose. New anxieties about sibling rivalry and larger issues of controlling jealousy, or the discussions of keeping children away from grief, were two early outcroppings of what became a systematic effort to promote greater parental responsibility for explicit emotional socialization. Experts and parents alike ultimately joined in the campaign, which among other things began to swell the pages of child-rearing manuals.

Several assumptions underlay the new agenda: that quite ordinary children—not just problem cases—faced emotional issues that they could not easily handle alone; that earlier advice on how to deal with children emotionally was largely wrong and sometimes dangerous; and that (implicitly) being an emotionally mature adult was more complicated than was once assumed—that active and purposeful socialization was required.

Obviously, parental involvement with the emotional development of their children was not new with modernity. The wide traditional insistence on obedience had all sorts of emotional implications and consequences. Victorian child-rearing advice, with its strong dose of moralism, had even more emotional contours (though instillation of obedience remained central): emotional goals were an important part, for example, of gendered expectations in the 19th-century middle class. But the Victorian approach did not assume massive adult intervention: sound advice and role-model examples would normally suffice. Victorians might easily worry about children's physical health, about their sexuality, or about their moral development, but the list of specific emotional targets was both far briefer and far less anguished than it would become with the full onset of 20th-century modernity.

For, by the 1920s, it was as if child-rearing experts and parents alike decided that, since some of the older problems associated with childhood were receding (notably, the high death rates), it was about time to introduce a new batch of worries. Obviously the connections were not so simple, but the anxieties did indeed ramp up at exactly the point where they might logically have begun to recede considerably. Lots of people had a stake in making sure that childhood was still seen as demanding, indeed newly demanding, in the modern context, and American culture, with its rhetorical fascination with privileging children, was a great incubator.

Targets of concern were numerous and varied, stretching from jealousy through anger and grief and reaching fear and even guilt as well. The invention of jealousy as a major childhood problem was a key case in point, as experts urged the need for a "lot of effort" on parents' part to deal with a challenge that could lead to dangerous behavior by kids themselves (in attacks on siblings)—"there is no limit to the depths" to which jealous children might sink—and a damaging personality defect later on (for jealousy "indelibly stamps personality and distorts character"). Children simply could not navigate these emotional waters on their own. And while psychological studies pushed the issue, parents quickly agreed—as a 1940s poll listed this aspect of emotional management the second most pressing problem families faced with their children.[7]

But this was only one corner of the new emotions agenda. Parents needed new exertions to help children control anger—by the 1930s, child-rearing manuals indeed replaced "anger" with "aggression" in their contents lists, to designate the emotion's risks. Children's fears required attention, as older advice (at least for boys) simply to urge greater courage yielded in favor of more nuanced behaviors. This was another emotional category kids could not face on their own. "Unless some grownup helps" fearful children, "each frightening experience leaves them weakened for the next assault." Even guilt must be reconsidered, lest children be overwhelmed. Here again was an emotion that might generate "a harmful effect on their mental health as long as they live."

The new emotional agenda for parents and adults had several consistent features, beyond the strictures about individual emotions and their management. First, obviously, was a pervasive assumption that children were, by nature, emotionally frail and needy, requiring lots of support and guidance. This partly reflected the strong focus on emotional socialization in early childhood, given a growing belief that waiting until more rational controls set in might be waiting too late. Errant emotional responses, if left uncorrected, might not only lead to childish misbehavior but would surely distort adulthood. Discussions of emotional management were dotted with terms like "festering." It was not enough, traditional-style, to coerce children into concealing damaging emotions in the home; a more active manipulation was essential, so that silent emotional boils would not develop that would inevitably burst forth later on. And finally, by logical extension: lack of capacity firmly to control a batch of damaging emotions marked an adult as childish and immature. Childhood might be a delightful stage of charm and innocence, but emotionally it was a thicket to be navigated. Revealingly, by the 1930s teenagers, when polled, proved eager to demonstrate their own awareness that they had moved past the stage of jealousy or anger or fearfulness, using terms like "immaturity" to mark their own progress from earlier phases of childhood.[8] The wisdom now ran: emotionally vulnerable children must be actively managed lest emotional fires persist, in order to make it to an adulthood marked by ample capacity for self-control. A tall order, adding considerably to the list of basic parental responsibilities.

Two principal factors generated this new list of parental obligations, besides the growing power of psychologically based expertise: the efforts to respond to novel demands on children, particularly in school settings; and the realization that adults themselves were being called upon to develop new emotional modulations, which it was logical—and which it might seem to be imperative—to launch in childhood.

School settings placed a new premium on emotional control but also provided a new, external source of emotional assessment, with teachers more than ready to call problem children to the attention of parents. Here was a direct link between modernity and emotions management. "Works and plays well with others," that standard kindergarten grading category, was now singled out for particular attention. Revealingly, worries about controlling bullying behavior—and making sure other kids weren't emotionally damaged by it—began to emerge in the 1920s, and this would become a recurrent theme in the children-school equation from that point onward. The modern definition of juvenile delinquency, as separate from normal adult crime, was probably a step forward for judicial systems, but it also called for new recognition of the importance of controlling hostile and angry emotions lest one's own children fall into this troubled camp. And well-meaning experts, particularly by the 1950s, were not reluctant to use delinquency warnings as part of their guidance to parents. Widespread concern about the commercial culture being directed to children could also motivate and shape the new attention to managing children's emotions. Parents might find themselves unable to keep comic books or dubious television fare away from their kids, but at least they could try to make sure that their charges were not becoming overstimulated emotionally—whether in the direction of undesirable levels of aggression or equally undesirable fearfulness. In various ways, modern childhood itself seemed to call for new levels of emotional oversight.

But it was the redefinition of adulthood, in combination with beliefs about the centrality of childhood socialization, that most obviously motivated the belief that emotions must be handled in new ways. In a real sense, adulthood was now being perceived as more different from childhood, emotionally and in other respects, than had previously been the case, and this put new pressures on parents to get their children ready even while recognizing the special qualities of childhood. Take jealousy, for example: by the 20th century, all modern societies were calling for new levels of intermingling between men and women. This was increasingly true in the schools themselves, and also in workplaces such as offices and department stores. By the 1920s, the same principle also began to apply to adult socializing, as couples mixed for parties and other entertainments. The importance of being able to control jealousy—ideally, not to experience it at all—obviously increased when domestic seclusion began to break down.

From this, it was entirely logical to urge that the process of identifying and mastering the emotion must begin early in life: the parents who were exercised over the new malady of sibling rivalry were in part playing out new emotional demands of their own on their offspring. More generally still, key changes in the middle-class economy, and particularly the rise of large corporate bureaucracies and the service sector, called for new emotional skills. The importance of getting along with others, in a management team, was increasingly obvious, and this could call for new abilities to damp down both anger and jealousy and indeed to overcome emotional intensities of virtually any sort. Experts in salesmanship, like the tireless advocate Dale Carnegie, with his injunctions about "winning friends and influencing people," were even more explicit about the importance of keeping a surface smile on the face whatever the provocation. The successful middle-class adult was, increasingly, the adult skilled in personal emotion management. Small wonder that the child-rearing advice literature constantly urged on parents the relationship between their ability to hone children's emotional skills and later-life success. Small wonder that, by the 1950s, American studies showed that the families most open to advice about the importance of emotional guidance and monitoring were those in the managerial and service sector—as opposed to working-class or even more traditional professional families who were less quickly persuaded that a more laissez-faire parental approach must be rethought. Key features of ongoing modernity, in other words, created an eager audience for new warnings about the burdens of children's emotions.

The result, of course, was a growing list of things to do, particularly with the very young. Parental availability for reassurance was vital in all the areas of concern. Lots of explanation was called for: explain carefully that a baby was coming, to anticipate jealousy; use appropriate circumlocutions to avoid exposure to grief. Lots of listening was essential as well, in an atmosphere of studied parental calm and restraint: experts urged that a key means of preventing festering was to let children verbalize their emotions without acting out, particularly important in the case of anger, "to prevent emotional sores from bursting." The idea was to listen to expressions without any action or hostility involved: as Dorothy Baruch put it, in a popular 1949 manual, "You don't want to worry or irritate anyone else when you use your Rage Release." "The more the child releases the anger, the less of it will remain, provided it has been handled in an acceptant way that doesn't make new anger take the place of what has drained off." While reassurance, monitoring, and audience were the most demanding tasks, a considerable amount of outright manipulation was called for either to avoid emotional outburst or to overcome it. Thus, when a new baby arrives, a parent should carefully make sure the existing sibling gets some new toys and clearly demarcated space of his or her own; grandparents as well as parents must remember to offer all siblings some gifts whenever an individual birthday rolled around. The child is fearful? First, obviously, a parent should work to eliminate as many sources of fear as possible, so the emotion need not be exercised. But if it crops up anyway, one should plan to provide bribes and treats to help a child overcome the agony. Thus, one might put some candy at the edge of the shadow when a child fears a darkened room, and then move it farther in with each repetition; and of course parents should also take advantage of modernity by providing a night light.

Bedtime rituals almost certainly increased, for children who now slept alone and for parents who now realized their responsibilities in pushing back fears. As Dr. Spock recommended, "Don't be in a hurry to sneak away before he is asleep. . . . The campaign [against a recurrence of nocturnal fear] may take weeks, but it should work in the end." Many parents definitively began to delay toilet training—again, at clear cost of personal nuisance—in order to avoid potential emotional damage. The pleas for greater demonstrations of affection surely won response as well, presumably at less cost. As Dr. Spock again suggested, in describing a minor childish upset, "This is a time for extra hugs and comforting reminders that you love him very much and will always protect him."

A clear result of the new expectations—directly encouraged by various schools of psychiatry—was the growing belief that adult problems could be traced back to misdeeds by one's own parents. This was the flip side of the emotional maturity standards. With varying degrees of seriousness, recollections of parental lapses in one's childhood became a common pastime as well as a vital component of therapy. Here, too, the vague anticipation that one's actions as a parent could be rebuked later on could add to the new levels of stress that the addition of emotional expectations entailed.

Some of the most urgent pressure on parents may, to be sure, have eased later in the 20th century. Sibling rivalry, for example, no longer generates the anxiety level that it did fifty years ago. Parents, after all, are now accustomed to the basic notion that children's emotions need active attention, so the dire warning approach is less necessary; and some commonsense modifications—we know that siblings are not in fact automatically at each other's throats—goes into the mix as well. But the basic notion that children are emotionally fragile, and that good parents bear responsibility for active protection and guidance, remains alive and well. Popular child-rearing manuals, like the much-edited and updated Dr. Spock, keep the pressure on: "whether children will grow up to be lifelong optimists or pessimists, warmly loving or distant, trustful or suspicious will depend to a considerable extent . . . on the attitudes of the individuals who had the responsibility for a major portion of their care in the first two years." As a popular 2001 bumper sticker urged, "children need encouragement every day." Recent worries about emotional damage from teacher criticism, or the revived attention to the scars left by bullying, provide lively cases in point of the continued felt need to protect and guide children emotionally. The same applies to apparent expansion of definitions for conditions like autism, whose rates began increasing by the early 21st century in part because adults increased the rigor of their definitions of emotional normalcy in children. More broadly, key aspects of contemporary helicopter parenting—on which more follows—build precisely on the assumptions of parental responsibility for emotional development—and sometimes for emotions themselves. A helicoptered young college student, sitting in his advisor's office, asks if he can call his mother on his cell phone and, after permission is reluctantly granted, hands the phone over to the advisor with relief: "There, my mother will tell you how I feel." The emotional umbilical cord, in modern childhood, at least American style, stretches a fair distance. It's hard for parents, given the stakes now widely accepted, to feel entirely comfortable with this component of their modern assignment.

WANTING HAPPY CHILDREN

Caring for children's emotions and emotional development constitutes the tense side of the expansion of expectations for childhood in modernity. It's far more pleasant, at least on the surface, to chart the other main expansion: a growing commitment to children's happiness, at least in principle, and to the belief that childhood should be a particularly happy state. But there's a darker side here too: it's not necessarily sensible to take on responsibilities for making childhood happy, for arguably it's not an inherently happy time. Modern commitments to providing happiness are well intended, but they add to the list of what good parents are supposed to achieve, and they don't necessarily succeed in their proximate goal: modern children are not clearly happier than their traditional counterparts. Indeed, while the push for children's happiness was a somewhat belated response to the larger modern thrust toward happiness in general, it's had the same ambivalent outcome and, by making parenthood more complicated, contributes directly to the gap between modernity gains and perceived satisfactions in and around childhood.

Prior to modernity, most societies did not think of childhood as a particularly happy state. This was partly because of the realistic and pervasive association with high death rates. It also reflected the dominant emphasis, in agricultural economies, on children as workers, where they would play inferior roles and obviously, at least until later childhood, would demonstrate less competence than adults. Autobiographies rarely mentioned childhood or at most referred in passing to the sternness of fathers. Indeed, the whole notion (particularly in the Western cultural context of original sin) that childhood was a time for discipline and correction discouraged any generalized sense that this was a stage of life associated with pleasure or delight. This does not mean that many children did not have happy times—their play opportunities may have been less fettered than would be the case with modernity—or that parents did not take pleasure in seeing their children enjoy themselves. The point is that a conceptual commitment to happiness-in-principle would have made little sense. The goal was, of course, to grow up, and children who displayed early maturity might be particularly valued.

Even in the 19th century, when many ideas about children were changing, explicit commitments to happiness had yet to emerge. True, the growing belief in childish innocence furthered attention to childhood as an interesting stage of life that might be recalled with pleasure. But the literature that specifically addressed child rearing largely avoided the subject of happiness or subsumed it in a larger category of moral advancement. Thus a famous manual by Catharine Beecher urged that "children can be very early taught, that their happiness both now and hereafter, depends on the formation of habits of submission, self-denial and benevolence."

Not surprisingly, signs of change emerged at exactly the point, early in the 20th century, when so many aspects of childhood were moving away from traditional functions and values. Initial comments from the ubiquitous child-rearing authors were somewhat hesitant. New commentary first centered in the United States, though there were some precedents at least in Britain a bit earlier on. From 1903: "Don't forget to be indulgent; do your best to make a pleasure possible, and enter heartily into it. Yet bear in mind that your very readiness to bring happiness into your children's lives should in return command their absolute respect, courtesy, and obedience as your right." Happiness here is a genuinely new component of the parent-child relationship, but it's a tactic in favor of other, more traditional attributes. More energy was actually poured into cheerfulness than happiness per se, reflecting a belated realization that if this was a desirable adult characteristic (the notion launched a century and a half earlier), children might have to be involved as well. "The disposition of a man or woman is fixed by the prevailing mood of his childhood. Whatever influences him toward cheerfulness builds up his store of energy and courage . . . whatever saddens him lowers his vitality." But if cheery children were desirable, it was possible to slide over into a larger redefinition of childhood: "Parents . . . must deliberately, conscientiously be cheerful if they are to have children grow up with the light-heartedness youth should know." An old-modern idea—the desirability of having cheerful people around—was now translated into a new-modern notion of what children should be like, and of what parents had to do toward this end.

New-style education experts got into the act as well. The idea was that happy children learned better, and that education should be fun, clearly associated with play. Here, too, happiness was a tactic, though here devoted to a modern goal, to transform the dreariness of the customary rote classroom into a different learning atmosphere.

From about 1915 on, what had been a sprout bloomed into a full plant: virtually every parenting manual began to cite happiness as a central purpose of childhood and a core obligation for parents.[9] The only question, and it was vitally important, was whether children were naturally happy, so that all parents had to do was avoid messing up, or whether a more active, parentally mediated creation was needed (as would later be seen with self-esteem). "Happiness is as essential as food if a child is to develop into normal manhood or womanhood." From 1927 an interesting pair of quotations, in obvious tension: first, "they are children; they are not as old as you; they simply cannot be grave and sedate; they must be jolly" (obviously implying childhood as a naturally happy contrast with adulthood); and second, an accompanying reference to "young beings whom it is our duty to make happy and strong in life," along with the remark, "*The purpose of bringing-up in all its phases should be to make the child as happy as possible*" (italicized in the original, for emphasis).

Historians love to find the origins of new notions, particularly when they contrast so strikingly with previous conventions. In a sense it's surprising that it took so long to move from Enlightenment invocations of happiness in general to a specific focus on children. But in fact this simply reflected the strength of even older beliefs that childhood was not a happiness category and that inculcation of obedient morality must still take pride of place. It took a century for the connection to break through this older view, pushed by the new understanding of how important early childhood was to adult characteristics. "Make a child happy now and you will make him happy twenty years from now in the memory of it. And happiness is a great thing. . . . It contributes to the making of a normal childhood, which is in turn the foundation of normal manhood and womanhood." Small wonder that making kids happy became a fundamental new parental obligation, a challenge that was almost impossible to refute because it was stated from so many different vantage points and with virtually unshakable confidence. Surprisingly quickly, the innovation became ubiquitous, in the child-rearing literature but also in social and family rituals.

But there was a tension within the new happiness push and its reception. To the extent that children were naturally happy, as well as innocent, the redefinition of childhood might simply be enjoyed. But this was precisely the time when small armies of experts were talking about children's fears and insecurities, so it was no surprise that a larger body of comment urged the need for strenuous adult effort. "To begin early enough in the education of our children for a happy, useful life we must begin at least six months before their first cry" (a statement that suggested that the author had never interacted with an actual baby, but one that certainly created a dramatic obligation). "Avoid unpleasant incidents as you would the plague. They shake the fabric of happiness to its foundations." Manipulation might be called for, in trying to convince the child to seem happy whatever the real mood: "Always see that the child goes to sleep happy. . . . 'Darling we are quite happy now, aren't we? Look up and smile at mother. . . . You know she loves you so much and wants you to be always the very happiest little boy in all the world.'" Inconsistencies abounded, as in the following two passages from the same page of one 1920s manual: first, "childhood is meant to be a joyous time. In the opinion of most adults it is actually the most joyous time of life"; but then, twenty lines down, "Nevertheless it is the province and duty of parents to make the childhood of their progeny a joyous time." Was the parent simply to enjoy his or her spontaneously happy offspring, or was it necessary to be a cheerleader (an interesting pastime, introduced in the same period) or even an active entertainer? To this set of alternatives the advice literature seemed to answer, "Yes!"

At the very least—and as we will see, many parents would add in a lot more—the new goal of childhood happiness required parents themselves to be as cheerful as possible. Chastisement, it was widely urged, should give way in the face of the happiness aspiration—an obvious sign of how traditional childhood, at least in principle, was being stood on its head. For the parental obligation was unmistakable. As the rather severe behaviorist John Watson urged, "Failure to bring up a happy child . . . falls upon the parents' shoulders." Dr. Spock, a few years later, offered a little flexibility, but only a bit: "Another part of loving is finding ways to share happiness . . . children don't need to have these experiences all day long. But they do need some shared moments of happiness every day."

The happiness push was not a matter of advice alone. It also fostered important new family rituals that became part of a standard parental toolkit. Thanks in part to purely technical improvements that reduced posing time, but also reflecting the new goals for children, the early decades of the 20th century saw a massive effort to get young children to smile at a strange box—a box kids would later learn was called a camera. The importance of happy self-presentations in photographs, in contrast to dour 19th-century poses, was a key artifact of the age, with interesting ramifications for children and adults alike. During the Depression years the happy child was further symbolized by the endlessly smiling Sunshine Girl, Shirley Temple.

This was also the point at which the song "Happy Birthday" became a cherished part of childhood rituals. The tune was written in 1893, initially (and revealingly) for the schoolroom, with lyrics about "good morning to you . . . good morning dear children." The new words "happy birthday" emerged in the 1920s (though they were copyrighted only in 1935, after some disputes)—exactly the time when the larger addition to the goals of modern childhood was being confirmed. Initially used for shows and singing telegrams, the song reached more general usage as the Depression took hold and as the overall consumerism directed at children intensified. By 1940 the song's ubiquity testified to the wide assumption that children deserved a particularly happy recognition for an anniversary that, just a century before, had normally passed unnoticed. The modern reduction of the birth rate, directing more attention to the individual child, underlay this kind of new symbolism. It was similarly revealing that midcentury White House conferences on children turned from a focus on health to discussions of children's happiness.

Finally, there was the drumbeat of consumerism, as a growing force among children and amid parent-child relations. To be sure, some of the happiness advice disavowed consumerist links; as one uplifting child-rearing manual put it, "Happiness is a result of a beautiful life well and nobly lived. It does not dwell in riches, parties, wonderful clothes, jewels, or travel." But this was not the dominant message of the first half of the 20th century (or since), and it was not the message most parents and children bought into. Companies that sold to children directly, like the comic book producers, obviously did so on the basis of providing pleasure of some sort. Parents who now began to surround even infants with store-bought goods like teddy bears assumed that they were increasing comfort and happiness. A growing number of child-oriented companies began to emerge based on the dual appeals to pleasure-seeking kids and to parents who saw the provision of treats as a means of fulfilling their new happiness obligations. Disney, to take the most obvious example from the interwar decades, cut its teeth on the childhood-as-happiness theme. And to the extent that school regimes and urban settings reduced children's opportunity for purely spontaneous play, parents (and commercial purveyors) may also have dimly realized that some new provisions were essential, if not for greater happiness, then simply as compensations for older opportunities for children's expression that were now being lost.

The redefinition of childhood as happy was a truly significant change, even though its causes are, in combination, not obscure at all. Figuring out what resulted from the redefinition, for parents, other adult agents, and children alike, is at once more important and more challenging. Obviously families reacted diversely to the new goals, depending not only on material circumstance but also on personality or religious orientation—the potential variables are considerable. But the conversion to at least a periodic sense that children should be happy was considerable as well, and it had serious consequences—consequences that describe a good bit of parental activity and concern over the past sixty years.

In the first place—and this response helped confirm the happiness commitment—Americans became increasingly accustomed to assessing childhoods—their own and others'—in terms of perceived happiness. Most obviously, snap judgments about other people—"he had an unhappy childhood"—became commonplace, on the assumption that this was an unfortunate anomaly that might in turn explain other adult issues. Psychiatrists and advice literature alike increasingly encouraged adults to look back at their own childhoods in terms of what their parents had done to provide happiness, and parents were aware that this would be part of their retrospective evaluation. And children themselves could easily become aware that parents were supposed to keep them happy and entertained. By the later 20th century a child's complaint about being bored could be seen, by child and parent alike, as a legitimate call to action.

More measurably, and this was the second consequence, a growing number of institutions and parental strategies designed for children were created or adjusted along happiness lines. Cheerfulness was one of twelve characteristics enshrined in Boy Scout Law, and the Campfire Girls, in the 1920s, went them one better by insisting on happiness directly. In 1926 the YMCA, seeking to reinvolve fathers more fully with their children, stressed the provision of pleasure over more traditional paternal roles. The group "Indian Princesses," with its motto "friends forever," was (and remains) organized around games, treats, and other activities that would win childish favor for their male parents through the provision of fun. And indeed American fathers did begin to think of shared games and sports as a parental staple, far more pervasively than their counterparts in places like Sweden who maintained a more traditional approach based on discipline and role modeling. Divorced fathers could indeed become almost frenzied in their quest for one pleasurable thing after another to provide for their kids during visitation periods. More institutionally, many innovations in American schools involved attempts to make learning fun, including efforts to pack textbooks with entertaining asides or field trips and other activities designed to leaven routine with entertainment. The various programs designed to emphasize positive motivations and rewards over older disciplinary tactics in the classroom, including of course the self-esteem movements and grade inflation that began in the 1960s, owe much of their impetus to efforts to reduce the tensions between schooling and happy childhoods.

The primary vehicle for addressing the new happiness goals was enhanced consumerism itself, which became an effect as well as a cause of the redefinition of childhood. Efforts to provide child-oriented vacations multiplied, and served as the basis for huge institutions like Disneyland and what amounted to obligatory family pilgrimages. Buying things and paying for recreation seemed the best way to discharge happiness obligations, particularly on the assumption that children could not find sufficient pleasure on their own and needed adult provision. The push toward happiness helps explain why so many concerned parents really could not bring themselves to censor children's fare on radio or television, or bought video games that they disapproved of: if the stuff made kids happy, or at least reduced a parental sense of happiness inadequacy, it was hard to oppose. Buying for kids became a prime preoccupation at Christmastime, building on precedents launched in the 19th century but now greatly magnified. Earlier concerns about spoiling children, though not absent, declined precipitously, given the new goals. Not only Disney but also McDonald's and other commercial outlets shamelessly invoked claims about the provision of happiness as a central lure for parents.

American internalization of the new happiness thrust, and certainly its consumerist manifestations, was particularly intense, for the whole theme played into earlier cultural acknowledgements to children; but the movement was not American alone. American influence radiated widely, and many of the prompts for childhood happiness developed in other modern societies. (Indeed, in cases like Japan, where schooling was a more serious business than it was in the United States at least prior to college, a concern for fun might have additional functions as compensation.) "Happy Birthday" has been translated into every major language, as has the idea of urging children (and others) to smile when being photographed. Venues for childish entertainment, like Disney parks, have demonstrated wide appeal, creating obligations for middle-class Latin American parents to make the trek to Orlando that are almost as pressing as those for their United States counterparts. The United States was not the only source of a pleasure- and emotion-focused toy industry, and Japan led the way in distracting electronic games. New interests in gestures toward children's happiness, and related modifications of the standards for parental adequacy, became a key part of globalization in the later decades of the 20th century.

The whole modern commitment, American and global alike, changed patterns of parenting considerably, adding potential pleasures but heightening anxieties as well; and it directly altered childhood in ways that affected all parties involved. The result noticeably expanded the larger redefinitions wrapped up in modernity.

For children—one hopes, at least—the more explicit commitment to happiness could be quite pleasant, providing new opportunities for enjoyment and meaningful contacts with parents. In one sense the situation was less novel than the language implied: children used to work alongside their parents, and bonded in this fashion; this was far less feasible in modern circumstances, but shared play, including shared learning through hobbies or sports, could serve much the same function. Still, the idea of shared enjoyments and leisure skills could translate positively for all concerned. Clever kids also learned how to use the happiness commitment to manipulate their parents, not only claiming boredom but also emphasizing school burdens to elicit additional adult response.

The clearest down side for childhood in the happiness focus, mirroring the larger American dilemma, might also redound on parents: it became more difficult for children to seem sad. The measurable increase in rates of childhood depression, in all modern societies, owes something to changes in diagnosis—based in part on the new assumption that cheerfulness should be the normal state. Increasing rates of depression reflect family disruptions and school pressures as well as other disturbances, but they also reflect the relentless, well-intentioned insistence on seeming happy, at a stage of life that is not necessarily consistent with these expectations. A sad child generated new guilts, most obviously among parents and other responsible adults, but often for the child him- or herself, which could help move normal sadness into real despair. Other modern childhood ailments, such as anorexia, also express tensions some children experience when things are out of whack but with parents seemingly so loving, so committed to happiness that outright rebellion is inconceivable. Happiness demands can prove almost impossible to live up to.

Other down sides were more trivial, and for most parents surely more than balanced by children's pleasure and affection. There was the pressure, given the new assumptions about special entertainment fare for children, to endure some briefly appalling cultural productions. Some commercial fare, obviously, seeks to offer solace to adults even while capturing children's pleasure—Disney efforts point in that direction, though one can debate degrees of success. There are even opportunities for parents or grandparents to use the happiness obligation to enjoy performances that might otherwise seem childish (circuses are a case in point). But there is also a fair amount of agonizing drivel that must be endured for the sake of happy togetherness. Not a massive cost, but a new one in modern parenting.

More important, given the priority of trying to keep children happy, was the potential time commitment, whether sharing childish fare or striking out more independently. The idea of taking the kids on vacation began to develop, first in the upper middle class, in the 19th century, when mothers would frequently repair to some rural or woodsy retreat, with fathers/husbands joining on weekends. The arrival of the automobile and a more formal concept of vacations increased the sense of family obligation. Careful provisions of weekend entertainments might be even more challenging than acceptable vacations, for children otherwise secluded in suburbia and for parents who heeded expert implications that kids might not be able to find happiness on their own. As with the exposure to commercial notions of childish taste, real mutual pleasure could result from shared activities despite the time involved. But for parents with other obligations, a fair degree of competition for attention was almost inescapable.

Happiness goals could distort parental effort in other ways. It might seem so tempting to work to make kids happy that other parental requirements, potentially more stressful—like emotion management or preparation for successful schooling—might get shorter shrift. Modern parents who satisfied their sense of commitment with bursts of entertainment were an unfortunate byproduct of the larger emphasis—and this included many fathers who now gained family standing through provision of fun and little else. (It was revealing, in the United States, that after World War II mothers began to replace fathers as chief sources of discipline, while children began to rate fathers more highly not for substance, but for pleasure giving.) Other temptations might surface for parents more generally. Surely, amid the press of many other adult commitments, but with a genuine desire to see children at least superficially happy, the practice of plopping kids in front of the television, spiced with an occasional movie, might seem to reconcile conflicting pressures: the kids were entertained (and one might assume they were happy as a result) and there was adult time for other stuff. The same surely applied, for many parents, in the provision of comfort foods: if there wasn't a lot of time to organize more elaborate schemes for children's pleasure, at least one could give them an abundance of sugared or salted foods and sodas—knowing at least for the moment that one had produced a happiness response. The happiness goal, in sum, might encourage shortcuts and simplifications that seemed to excuse inattention to other aspects of parenting.

But the most telling pressure of the new goal, at least for more conscientious parents, was the concern that one's children might not be happy enough, that despite best efforts there was something missing. Even aside from outright depression, periods of sadness might call parental adequacy into serious question. The teenage years were particularly challenging, when parents often lost any ability to organize relevant entertainments—which might be troubling or frustrating even when the adolescents gave every appearance of being normally happy. Adolescence is a challenging time in almost any society, given the strains of sexual maturation and continued dependency. Arguably the stage becomes even more difficult—and more clearly identifiable—in modern circumstances when schooling, rather than advancement toward greater maturity in work, becomes the dominant commitment. But the fuller conversion to a mixture of peers and commercial sources for pleasure now raised an added challenge. Parents who became an embarrassment in accompanying their teenaged offspring to movies or other entertainments, or who found their heirs grumpily reluctant to continue a pattern of family vacations, had yet another reason to wonder how to define relevant goals.

A Work in Progress

The ingredients of modern childhood began to assemble fully less than a hundred years ago, and of course they must combine with other developments. It is not surprising—to repeat a key theme—that important adjustments continue, given unexpected complexities and sheer novelty. Growing reliance on day care, for example, represents a more recent effort at adaptation. It responded to new patterns of women's work, but it also provided new opportunities for emotional socialization and new pressures on many parents to provide active enjoyment when they were together with their offspring. It remained interesting that European parents seemed to take to the new institution more readily than their American counterparts, who were less willing to turn their children over to others and more eager to preserve at least an illusion of greater parental control.

More recently still, many American parents innovated in other directions, seeking to invest in better ways to meet basic modern obligations but often in an atmosphere of fearfulness that could distort some of the new efforts.

The new negatives were the first to emerge. Worries about children blossomed beyond any prior precedent from the 1980s onward, in the United States. Modern beliefs in children's vulnerability persisted, along with the almost agonizing desire to eliminate risks: but these two urges were now combined with novel beliefs in the many dangers of the social environment, amid growing media exaggeration.

Several specific developments heralded the emergence of the new mood, and provide some revealing signposts. Fears of children being kidnapped began to accelerate, bolstered by abundant media coverage that highlighted tragic dramas and could make it seem as though a distant crime had occurred in a neighbor's back yard. A milk carton campaign, picturing lost children, began in 1979, triggered by the disappearance of an appealing New York boy (he was never found): this also heightened a daily sense that children were in danger. Soon, well-meaning campaigns were claiming that fifty thousand abductions by strangers occurred each year (the actual figure was two to three hundred), and many parents bought into the scary, if wildly inaccurate, estimates. Similar exaggerations occurred on the subject of sexual predation, with hugely inflated claims about pedophile rings. Airlines (and not just American ones) began to issue bizarre new regulations prohibiting unaccompanied children from sitting next to adult men, as if a molester lurked under any gray flannel suit. Definitions of sexual offenses expanded, to include older teenagers convicted of having sex with a minor, and this in turn inflated news about released offenders relocating in various cities. One mother noted that she and her suburban friends had "to watch for dangers that lurked in every shadow." For parents protective of their children, newly precious in the best modern fashion, and eager to eliminate risk, the warning flags were ominous.

Revealing changes occurred in the traditional celebration of Halloween, long a time when children had been allowed to do a bit of mischief while collecting candy from neighbors. In 1982, reports spread widely about trick-or-treating children who had received candy laced with cyanide and apples with concealed razor blades. In fact, no verification of poisoning ever occurred. In one Long Island incident three apples were discovered with pins in them, but the razor blade stories were totally false. But accuracy was not an issue, now, where children seemed threatened. Many city governments began to limit the hours for children to be on the streets at Halloween, and concerned (though often very bored) parents now trod the streets with their offspring to make sure that nothing untoward occurred and to guarantee that no food would be touched until a careful screening occurred back home. One of the few remaining opportunities for children to range on their own was removed in this process, along with a measurable escalation of parental fears and obligations. This was the period, more generally, when most parents began to cut back hugely on their offsprings' freedom to travel alone around cities, and when summer camps began to surround children with new precautions, including stricter rules about swimming or unsupervised games.

While the symptoms of change in mood are clear, explanations are not easy to pin down. New fears built on the earlier modern ideas of children's cherished value but also their vulnerability, but new elements were essential to turn watchfulness into potential obsessiveness. The role of media reports, and related scorn for accuracy, is obvious, with vivid visual scenes of parents breaking down in grief when something had gone amiss. The liberal mood of the 1960s was yielding to greater conservatism, which provided some context for the new anxiousness; some baby boomers may, in their parenting, have been trying to compensate for their own youthful indiscretions. Growing concerns about the impact of divorce on children (after a period in which, self-servingly, the adults involved were led to believe that children could rebound rather readily), and uncertainties and guilts about the results of mothers working outside the home, may have conditioned a greater sense of anxiety. In urban centers, new patterns of immigration and greater diversity in the schools may have prompted a greater sense of insecurity that could not, given political correctness, be overtly stated but that might gain expression in worries about children. Growing distrust of key institutions, including government, obviously made many families feel new obligations to fend for their own, and this sense of separateness—famously captured in the phrase "bowling alone"—now extended to distrust of neighbors as well. Whatever the mix of factors, the impact on many parents was powerful.

And the mood continued, translating into family threats some of the most notable setbacks on the national scene. One of the striking features of collected memories about reactions to the terrorist attacks of September 11, 2001, was how quickly they turned to a sense of children in danger, in places thousands of miles away from disasters that had not, in the main, directly targeted families. Mothers, particularly, frequently recalled how their first move, on hearing the news, was to gather their children up and hold them close. Many rushed to schools to pull their kids out. A Texas mother found it important to emphasize to her six-year-old son the enormity of the lives lost and the new sense of insecurity that he should remember as he grew up. Many adults expressed their ongoing worries about driving their children across bridges or venturing downtown, lest disaster strike. In one large collection of reminiscences, fearful family references crop up in 21% of all accounts, dwarfing for example the 6% of comments evoking national or patriotic concerns. Granting the magnitude of the 9/11 shock, it remains valid to note the surprising ease with which Americans now perceived direct threats to their family—one reason, no doubt, why sales of burglar alarms and handguns soared late in 2001, despite their arguable irrelevance to actual terrorist strategies. Even in the presidential elections of 2004, a group of self-identified concerned mothers, once called "soccer moms," became "security moms," eager to support a president who seemed to be focused on protecting family safety: "I have recently become a soccer mom," one parent noted, "and I'm a security mom too. When I tuck my daughter in at night, I want to know that my president is watching my back and keeping me safe."

The new trends had some obvious drawbacks. Observers worried that the most conscientious parents were taking too much autonomy away from children: many former children needed a period in their twenties to develop the greater sense of self-reliance that previously had formed during adolescence itself. Overorganization and stress for many children were other possible dangers, as so much out-of-school time was now folded under a broader educational agenda. Modern trends of reducing free play and emotion management were being pressed to new levels. For parents themselves, the trends expressed a further intensification of responsibility, and the sheer time commitments could be an obvious challenge. This was the context in which, as one report claimed, soccer moms were the drivers most likely to be caught running a red light, in their frantic effort to stay on top of their kids' schedules and their own self-imposed parenting demands. Parenting was becoming more important, to adults and children alike, but not clearly more pleasant.

On the other hand, greater parental involvement seemed to increase the friendliness between parents and children, even in the dreaded later adolescence. It did reduce television-watching time for kids, and possibly guarded against even worse threats. While it led some parents, in extremes, to undue efforts to represent their children in school or college settings, battling for better grades or less discipline on grounds that their precious charges could not be less than stellar, it also did heighten attention to the importance of the schooling process. The hovering parents, dubbed "helicopters" for obvious reason, certainly contrasted favorably with the many parents of various social groups, including the middle classes themselves, who remained less involved and whose children sometimes careened out of control.

The new trends certainly reflected the ongoing process of fine-tuning childhood modernity and the parental stakes attached. Parents continued to refine their reactions to the central function of schooling and the added responsibilities of emotion management and happiness provision, experimenting with packages that would work for themselves and their children alike. Culturally specific anxieties might add complexities, but the basic challenge was dealing with modernity itself. The search for adjustments was not over.

Modernity improved childhood and parenting in many ways. Yet it also left widespread feelings of strain and inadequacy. Trumpets that blared potential progress a hundred years ago have largely been muted. Just as death raised new and sometimes unexpected issues at the end of life, despite modernity gains, so a gap between hopes and fulfillment opened for life's earliest stages, and for those who oversaw these stages. Basic dilemmas are by now familiar enough; it was hard to remember modernity's gains, as the past receded in memory. Gains themselves were real but generated some problems and lacunae of their own. Above all, however, the huge changes both in childhood and death encouraged rampant new expectations that almost automatically frustrated full achievement.

The new expectations were demanding, almost impossible to fulfill completely, and to a degree mutually contradictory. The sheer number and range of goals began to multiply. Placing responsibility for education, emotional guidance, physical health, and happiness on parents and schools—all while carefully keeping up with the latest expert advice through books and websites—created some difficult balancing acts. New parental divisions opened as a result, even aside from the growing minority of deliberately childless couples. Some parents were discouraged from trying very hard; others, particularly in the United States, relied on children's medications to get them through tasks like emotion management and school compliance. The same challenges generated almost frenzied oversight and participation by other parents. Either way, the satisfactions found in parenting might be compromised. Risks to children might be overestimated, childish capacity and resilience given too little credit, with resultant burdens on children and parents alike. Real problems (some of them new) along with laudable but ambitious expectations continued to bedevil modern childhoods. Even as conscientious parents kept experimenting, comfortable adjustment proved elusive.

For, even more than with death, whose complexities are inherent, childhood and parenting in modernity unexpectedly replicate the larger gap between modern gains and modern happiness. Again, the polls tell the story, at least superficially. Two polls, one in 1957 and the next in 1976, revealed massive increases in the numbers of parents who reported problems and feelings of inadequacy, and by 1979 twice as many parents claimed that children were less happy than in the past as argued for the reverse.[10] More recent data, though diverse, largely confirm a sense of parental uncertainty and, often, active dissatisfaction. Rural parents, revealingly, are noticeably happier than urban, but of course the latter are now in massive majority. A 2006 study showed childless couples with higher levels of marital satisfaction than their parental counterparts, and while a 2008 poll found mothers with one child a bit (20%) happier than their childless counterparts, fathers were more neutral; and second and third children did not contribute to satisfaction at all and even worsened it for mothers. More general polls found women putting child rearing rather low on the lists of contributors to life satisfaction, below eating, exercising, and watching television, though slightly above working and commuting. Quite generally, even for parents reporting happiness, parenthood is perceived as more stressful than it was twenty to thirty years ago. Modern gains in childhood remain very real, but they are clearly overshadowed by the equally real problems and complex expectations that modernity has also delivered. To an extent unimaginable in traditional societies, where children were a much-desired focus in life and where few alternatives could be contemplated, parenthood in modernity has eroded on the happiness scale, even when it has not become an outright negative.

Further Reading

Excellent studies of modern childhood include Viviana Zelizer, *Pricing the Priceless Child* (New York: Basic Books, 1985); Peter N. Stearns, *Anxious Parents: A History of Modern American Childrearing* (New York: New York University Press, 2003); Joan Jacobs Brumberg, *The Body Project: An Intimate History of American Girls* (New York: Random House, 1998); Merry White, *The Material Child: Coming of Age in Japan and America* (Berkeley: University of California Press, 1994); Collin Heywood, *A History of Childhood: Children and Childhood in the West from Medieval to Modern Times* (Cambridge: Cambridge University Press, 2001); Howard P. Chudacoff, *Children at Play: An American History* (New York: New York University Press, 2007); and Steven Mintz, *Huck's Raft: A History of American Childhood* (Cambridge, MA: Harvard University Press, 2006). Gary Cross offers two good surveys, *Kids' Stuff: Toys and the Chang-*

ing *World of American Childhood* (Cambridge, MA: Harvard University Press, 1997); and *The Cute and the Cool: Wondrous Innocence and Modern American Children's Culture* (New York: Oxford University Press, 2004). See also Ellen Key, *Century of the Child* (New York: Putnam's, 1909); and Christopher Lasch, *Haven in a Heartless World* (New York: Basic Books, 1977). On helicopter parenting and its origins, see Margaret K. Nelson, *Parenting out of Control: Anxious Parents in Uncertain Times* (New York: New York University Press, 2010).

For a more global approach, A. R. Colon, *A History of Children: A Socio-Cultural Survey across Millennia* (Westport, CT: Greenwood, 2001); Peter N. Stearns, *Childhood in World History*, 2nd ed. (New York: Routledge, 2011); and Paula Fass, *Children of a New World: Society, Culture, and Globalization* (New York: New York University Press, 2007).

Born to Shop

Consumerism as the Modern Panacea

Consumerism—no surprise here—has become a fundamental aspect of modern societies. It accumulates the most obvious bundle of steadily rising expectations, seemingly boundless in some instances. Increasing commitments by individuals, families, and societies at large to amass goods not needed for basic survival—the growing importance attributed to the process of acquiring and then admiring such goods and services—form a basic part of the human story over the past two centuries. Consumerism, though not so labeled, was a part of the Enlightenment vision of progress, focused on growing material comforts. But it's pretty obvious that as modernity has actually unfolded, consumerism has blossomed well beyond any Enlightenment hopes and has assumed a larger role in modernity than any Enlightenment materialist would have expected or desired.

Since its inception, modern consumerism has faced a host of critics. It's been variously blasted as: bad for health, particularly through overindulgence in rich foods, a concern in the 18th and early 19th century that contributed, along with concomitant concerns about sexual stimulation, to healthy products like corn flakes and Graham crackers. (Interestingly, contemporary commentary on obesity rarely invokes consumerism in general, as if attacks on such a firm modern commitment overall now seem hopeless.) As dangerously secular, distracting people from proper religious and spiritual concerns (though ultimately most mainstream American churches, and now most of the evangelicals as well, came to terms with consumerism as one of God's gifts). As bad for the class structure: modern consumerism has long involved some groups of people adopting patterns of dress, or styles of cars, or flashy leisure pursuits that seem above their station, challenging class (and sometimes race) boundaries and leading to accusations (by more affluent consumerists, often) that their wild spending is jeopardizing the security of their families, as well as challenging proper social order. As playing on women's frivolity: leading to manipulation by greedy advertisers or salesmen and producers of shoddy and wasteful products. As simply a sign of bad taste (often linked to the derogatory comments about the masses and their inability to appreciate higher values): this one covers a vast territory, including dislike of Hollywood fare or television as corrupting purer, preconsumerist folk pastimes. As foreign: from its early stages onward modern consumerism might be attacked as an import—from Britain or France, or obviously more recently the United States—that undermines appropriate national values. And most recently, as being bad for the environment: probably the most telling contemporary vantage point for attack in modern societies.

But modern consumerism cannot be easily dismissed. Its rise and evolution are vastly significant developments, involving truly fundamental changes in the way people live and think. Nor can the subject be disposed of simply through the accumulation of critiques—though these do merit serious attention and have an interesting history of their own.

Any pattern of behavior engaged in by literally hundreds of millions of people, and expanding now over a considerable period of time, must inevitably be regarded as meaningful. There is, to be sure, the argument that vast publics are simply duped by commercial manipulators (and new forms of manipulation did emerge, along with modern consumerism itself, in the 18th century). But while it is necessary to grant a role, sometimes a troubling role, for manipulation, there simply has to be a lot more to the widespread commitments that no snooty dismissals of debased taste or gullibility should be able to override.

In fact, modern consumerism arose out of very real human needs, some of them peculiar to emerging modernity. It retains vitality because of its continuing ability to respond to needs as well—including its contributions to coping with many of the down sides and frustrations of modernity itself. Indeed, consumerism has been asked to accomplish too much, to repair too many deficiencies that need to be addressed more directly in the gaps between modernity and satisfaction.

For we know one troubling thing about modern consumerism already: its advent makes people happier than their immediate forebears had been, but then the impact quickly plateaus. More consumerism usually continues to emerge—and its response to needs, as well as undeniable manipulation, explains why—but it does not add further happiness with escalation. It becomes too consuming, used to address an impossibly large basket of needs, not only disappointing but becoming a problem in its own right. Here, too, the broader context of ongoing modernity helps explore this dilemma.

Consumerism and Human Nature

We begin with an undeniable conundrum, not fully resolvable. Is consumerism an innate human impulse, such that its modern activation can be explained very simply by the increase in average income? If it's inherent, whether for good or ill, there would be no complexity to the historical explanation. Consumerism was held back in traditional societies by the fact most people had few resources above subsistence (though subsistence might be more or less bare-bones). Once per capita wealth began to increase, consumerism was an absolutely preordained outgrowth. No fancy formulas about responding to modernity need apply.

At the opposite pole from the human nature approach, one historian of the subject, Michael Miller, has persuasively argued that the emergence of consumerism is actually one of the most unexpected developments in modern social history.[1] The famous industrial revolution, he contends, was a snap compared to the conversion to consumerist aspirations. Far from being part of human nature, then, modern consumerism depended on a set of spurs that were both strong and unexpected.

There's certainly something to be said for the inherent-in-human-nature argument, quite apart from the fact that it takes us off the hook from having to explain a complex phenomenon or apologize for its onset (i.e., sorry, but we couldn't help ourselves, once earnings began to improve). Evidence from burial sites for hunter-gatherer groups reveals early interests in jewelry, well before the advent of agriculture. The desire for aids to personal beauty that also serve as emblems of status and relative prosperity goes back a long way, and both impulses are still clearly involved in modern consumerism. Upper classes in all agricultural civilizations clearly indulged in consumerism, if not always through personal quests for distinctive acquisitions, at least through badges of position. Thus both men and women in imperial Rome took delight in embellishing their togas with silk ribbons from China.

Once observers from the then-backward West began traveling, by the 11th and 12th centuries, they often reported on the splendors of upper-class luxury. This is what the crusaders discovered in the Arab Middle East, as they began to realize the sophisticated consumerism that came with established urban prosperity. Marco Polo eagerly reported the same from China, in the 14th century, claiming that whole cities were devoted to enjoyment, "intent upon nothing but bodily pleasure and the delights of society." Not only aristocrats but merchants often deliberately developed a high consumer profile. A 17th-century Chinese merchant, An Lutsun, planted orchids all over his home, bought gold foils and released them from a tower just to watch them float, and later purchased a series of dolls that he sailed in a local stream. One friend put mechanically controlled nude statues in one home, while a competitor designed a huge bronze urinal container, five feet tall, which he climbed every night in order to relieve himself. Premodern shades of Texas oilmen! Specifics varied depending on product availability and individual whim, but a strong case can be made that wherever incomes permitted, clear consumerism followed.

Against the idea that consumerism is so natural that it requires no further explanation, two major points count strongly. First, premodern societies featured a number of constraints on consumption, even for somewhat affluent groups: while examples of consumerism unquestionably exist, they were normally kept in considerable check by a combination of concerns. Many societies held back consumerism in favor of religious or civic expenditures—they had money to spare, but deliberately prioritized collective agendas over personal spending, in some cases additionally with spiritual goals rather than mere display in mind. Second, most traditional societies set class boundaries over individual exhibitions of wealth. It was not regarded as personal advancement for an aristocrat to sport certain fashions and lifestyles, even with a few individual twists, but for a wealthy merchant or even worse an outright commoner to venture the same was widely discouraged. Obviously, consumer-type motives and satisfactions might lurk behind aristocratic spending, but officially the goal was illustration of established status, not personal expression.

Finally, and this is the most important point to be made against assumptions of innate consumerism, within many groups themselves (particularly below the aristocracy, but where there was money above sheer subsistence), strong pressures sought to prevent much deviation from group norms, in terms of levels of display and styles alike. Merchant and craft guilds often sought to make sure that no one member had access to such high profit levels that a distinctive style of life could form.

Many groups organized display costumes that expressed margins above subsistence, collectively, but with a uniformity that inhibited demonstrations of individual success or individual taste. The goal was to fit in with the group, to show a group identity but to avoid not only individualism but also faddish changes in style. This impulse, along with a desire to protect class lines and, sometimes, a religious priority as well, led many societies to issue sumptuary laws that banned consumerist displays outright. In China and elsewhere, many individual consumers—the very types who did periodically kick up their heels and pursue affluent whimsies—were not only chastised but executed outright for violating community norms. Here was a context in which consumerism could seem very unnatural indeed; here was the context that makes the emergence of more open and extensive—more modern—consumerism in the 17th and 18th centuries such a striking development, cutting it loose from most historical precedents.

The First Wave

There is a straight line between the emergence of a new kind of mass consumerism in Enlightenment Western Europe and the phenomenon today, so again we enhance contemporary understanding by a brief look at what the initial surge in this facet of modernity was all about. The unfolding of modern consumerism's first wave, and the larger project of progress and pleasure that gained ground simultaneously, provided an initial set of mutual reinforcements that would link consumerism ever more steadily with happiness itself.

A variety of new markers appeared, initially in various parts of Western Europe. As early as the 17th century a novel passion for tulips burst forth in the Netherlands (tulips had been first encountered in trade with the Ottoman Empire): there was an obsession with buying more bulbs and more varieties, and when the growing season was over, cheap paintings of tulips lured customers as well. The whole episode has been touted as one of the first manifestations of faddish consumer frenzy in world history. More systematically, the 18th century saw a growing interest in (relatively) stylish and colorful clothing, on the part of fairly ordinary folks. Not only did purchases go up; a lively second-hand market developed and thefts of desirable apparel, even from clotheslines, took off as well. Again, passionate intensity was involved: people just had to have some of this new stuff. Growing interest in the consumption of tea and coffee anchored household purchases of porcelain tea settings (it was in the 17th century that imports became so common that the word "china" entered common usage); new attachment to more elaborate family mealtimes justified other kinds of serving items and tableware. Wills began to reflect consumer delight: people would carefully bequeath this coffee pot or that end table to a cherished relative, clearly in the belief that the consumer value would convey emotional attachment across generations.

Equally important, the interests were increasingly widely shared, granting that some sectors of the population were too poor to afford participation (save occasionally by theft). Rural manufacturing workers began dressing in more urban styles, casting aside traditional and often somber village costumes. Household items first caught on in the urban middle classes, but during the 18th century their popularity spread out to some artisans and also better-off rural families.

Here, then, by the later 18th century, were all the essential ingredients of modern consumerism, with shared interests and styles across social classes. Granting that different income levels could afford different versions of major items and different levels of acquisition, and that a large lower class was not yet in the game at all, a mass base for consumerism was beginning to emerge. As a revealing if backhanded confirmation, conservatives began to lament (with great exaggeration) the extent to which poor people were beginning to ape the styles of their betters, blurring class lines. Intensity grew: obviously, there were now some things that had clear emotional meaning beyond any rational purpose, and in related fashion the process of shopping for certain goods gained new appeal. Finally, a commitment to frequent changes in style assured that earlier reliance on group standards and considerable continuity were now under siege: modern consumerism would involve a consistent appetite for novelty and therefore, as means permitted, a steady spiral of acquisition. Add it all up: a growing number of people considered the purchase of goods not needed for subsistence, and not directly related to traditional group status, as an important, meaningful slice of life.

The whole phenomenon responded to three layers of explanation. First, thanks to an advantageous position in world trade and growing internal specialization and exchange, a significant number of West Europeans were gaining incomes above poverty levels. More, as well, were earning money by the sale of goods or labor on the market. There can be no consumerism without the monetary ability to afford nonessentials. This is a condition, however, and not a full explanation; consumerism is not an inevitable, knee-jerk response to improvements in household earnings.

Complementing higher income, and helping to bridge between potential and consumer actuality, was the availability of attractive new goods, initially provided mainly through the new levels of world trade. By 1700 many Europeans, again well down the social scale though above poverty, were increasingly hooked on some combination of sugar, tea, coffee, and tobacco—all goods of which their ancestors had largely been unaware just a couple of centuries before and all goods that came from other parts of the world. Obviously, Europeans were not alone in their propensities— Chinese and other Asians had already depended on imports of tea, Arabs (borrowing the product from Africa) had pioneered in commercial coffee use, and sugar had been popular in various places for a long time. But Europeans were now in a position to put the package together, into a set of mass consumer items that became increasingly important parts of daily life, and also to add the kinds of accoutrements that would turn product use into wider consumerism—the tea services, the smoking gear, and so on. Thus an explanation of consumerism that does not simply depend on innate human propensity might simply run: new incomes (the indispensable precondition) combined with the lure of new items that could be expanded into still-wider tastes. Case closed. No reason for more high-sounding invocations of other social or psychic needs.

But there is, without question, at least a second strand, another indispensable aspect of explaining consumerism in any modern situation and certainly for 18th-century Europe. Shopkeepers and kindred folk like manufacturers began to experiment with new ways to attract customers and manipulate wants, from the mid-18th century onward (and the sheer numbers of shops expanded, even into some villages, an inevitable concomitant of rising levels of consumerism). Product displays gained new attention, making it inviting simply to go window shopping. Stores began to offer loss leaders, products sold well under cost to draw customers into the premises where they would often buy other things at full price or beyond. A British comment in 1747 noted, "A custom has prevailed among Grocers to sell Sugars for the Prime Cost, and they are out of Pocket by the Sale," but purchases of "other commodities" for which customers paid "extravagant prices" more than made up for the loss. Consumer credit expanded as well, another means of helping people buy things they did not need. Alert manufacturers set up branch sales operations that would allow them to market-test new designs, and they were prepared to accelerate production of the items that found favor and to ship them quickly across the country; this was a pioneering stratagem of the British china maker Josiah Wedgwood: "we can make new vases like lightning" when test sales indicated "we can do so with safety." Huckster tricks abounded simply to attract attention. A former dentist who sold medicine rode "a white pony which he sometimes painted all purple and sometimes with spots," to advertise himself and his wares. Again in 1747 another salesman dressed as a high fashion lady to call attention to the gingerbread he was selling.

More important was the rise of explicit advertising, profiting not only from more elaborate store signage, now including printed posters, but also from the newly introduced weekly newspapers and handbills. Fashion prints and magazines sprang up, first in France but soon more widely. Pictures of the latest hats or dresses were inserted into pocketbooks and almanacs. Newspapers featured paragraph-length ads, looking just like news, with vivid claims spicing what was still just prose. A British newspaper in 1783 thus proclaimed a new bed:

> In the celestial bed no feather is employed . . . springy hair mattresses are used . . . in order that I might have the strongest and most springy hair, I procured at vast expense the tails of English stallions, which . . . is elastic to the highest degree. . . . It is impossible, in the nature of things, but that strong, beautiful, brilliant, nay double-distilled children . . . must infallibly be begotten.

Obviously, the word use is not contemporary, and it's fascinating that the mattresses were touted not for sleep (the present-day need) but for peerless offspring, but otherwise this sounds like the height of recognizable commercial drivel, complete with implications of modern science. Testimonials from the rich and famous (mainly presumably needy but blue-blooded aristocrats, at this stage) added to the frenzy, for products as humble as the razor strop ("acknowledged to be worth its weight in gold").

Now we have even more abundant explanation for the surge in modern consumerism: customers with some money in their pockets, with new products to help allay any disarming prudence, surrounded by a host of clever commercial attractions that might make the need to spend almost irresistible.

Most interested historians, granting all this, would add however that a third layer of causation remains essential, that all the shopkeepers and advertisements in the world can't work unless there are people newly convinced that they had vital reasons for novel acquisitions. This third layer can't be absolutely proved, and it certainly must be evaluated in combination with the other factors. Yet its recognition as at least highly probable is essential not just to explain new behaviors in the 18th century but to show that consumerism, for all its ultimate frivolity and ugliness, has always initially met real, historically conditioned, new human needs.

Two broader changes set the context for new interests in consumerism, beneath the surface of shopkeepers' clever manipulations. First, a variety of forces prompted new emotional investments in forming and maintaining families, and key aspects of the new consumerism expressed and furthered these investments. Protestantism had implicitly encouraged greater attention to family life, now that celibacy was not regarded as a condition for the holiest state. By the 17th century, Protestant writings were carrying the implications further, urging the importance of marital happiness and family warmth. One way to implement these impulses was through familial piety—fathers reading Bible passages to the group; but over a longer haul family-related consumerism could also serve relevant ends. Growing interests in comfort, another key innovation that was part of the broader current of change, benefited from and at the same time encouraged family consumerism—from the availability of tea in attractive serving vessels on a cold day to the greater variety of home furnishings. By the 18th century, new opportunities in courtship and the growing cultural valuation of romantic love provided another spur, particularly linked to the mounting concern for expressive and attractive clothing. Growing numbers of rural manufacturing workers, with new contacts with urban sales agents for their products, also had greater chances to meet different potential sexual partners through their wider commercial contacts—one of the preconditions for the 18th-century sexual revolution. Again, selective consumerism could be an element in this new romantic equation. Scholars like Colin Campbell have argued, even more broadly, that the same romantic impulses forged a greater sense of self and a related need for material expression.[2] New levels of attention to children, by the end of the 18th century, also spurred family-related consumerism. Middle-class parents began to be open to educational preparation pleas: ads for children's books at the end of the 18th century talked of "a Play-book for children to allow them to read as soon as possible" or, more crudely, illustrated material "to decoy children into reading." A package of new romantic and family values thus set one stage for a sense of new consumer needs: to express family harmony and comfort, to serve as an element in courtship, and to symbolize awareness of the new goals of childhood and parenting.

The second stimulus—perfectly compatible with the family focus, but coming from a different set of changes—involved needs for compensatory signs of social achievement. As the industrial revolution began to take initial shape, economic opportunities emerged, but there was also a host of challenges to more traditional economic callings. New competitive surges and rapid population growth joined forces here, quite widely in Western Europe. Details are not needed for this argument, but here were some of the big items: artisan masters—the people who ran craft shops—began to expand their operations a bit and in the process made it harder for craft workers to rise to master status. This was the beginning of a long trend in which craft workers, or journeymen, were increasingly converted to employee status, rather than seeing themselves as collaborators and ultimate heirs. Partly in response, many journeymen and masters increased efforts to make sure women could not gain access to most crafts. Women had lots of opportunities in home manufacturing work, but fewer chances—and they had never had equal chances—in higher-status activities. Urban economic and status systems thus encountered serious disruption, as more competitive and commercial motives took hold. In the countryside, where again there were opportunities in home-based manufacturing—of the sort that produced the new clothing and some other consumer items—the big news was population pressure. As European populations in some cases doubled in the second half of the 18th century, the possibility of providing relevant offspring with inheritance in land obviously declined: many families could cover the oldest son, maybe a dowry or two, but that was it. Many people had to contemplate a future, as they grew up, in which the classic badge of rural success would be unavailable. Some were impoverished as a result, some fled to cities, some took advantage of rural manufacturing. But all had to adjust their expectations.

The overall result was a large number of people, rural and urban alike, who might not be destitute but who were in unfamiliar and unexpected economic circumstances and, even when earning money above subsistence levels, might desperately need forms of identity and achievement that were different from full participation in a craft guild or inheritance of land—the more traditional stamps that were now increasingly unavailable. Consumerism, here, fit like a glove, offering alternative ways to express a modest degree of prosperity and to provide, through shared styles and acquisitive tastes, a sense of belonging.

The first stages of modern consumerism, in other words, met a real need—which is why first embraces of consumerism do lead to greater happiness. They concretely expressed new family ideals and they demonstrated clearly that even people shut off from traditional emblems of economic maturity were not failures if they could afford these new types of display. Meaningful consumerism thus appealed particularly to certain groups. Young people were disproportionately interested in joining the consumerist bandwagon. They often now fell into the category of people with some spending money (if, for example, they were doing home-based manufacturing) but whose parents could not arrange traditional opportunities; they also, obviously, saw connections between consumerism and courtship. They could also use consumerism directly to thumb a nose at parental stuffiness, to demonstrate flare and independence by pioneering in some of the new tastes. Women were another key consumerist group. They were not necessarily more interested than men, but they could certainly use consumerism both to highlight personal beauty (a desirable courtship attribute in a rapidly changing society) and as a means of enhancing status within the family. Using new furnishings and table ware as props, for example, women now exercised new familial authority as arrangers and regulators of family mealtimes. Here, then, is a final angle on consumerism serving real needs: it could help groups not in the formal community or familial power structure to control some separate space and find opportunities for independent expression. This service— and it's not an exaggeration to call it a liberating service—applied in 18th-century Western Europe and it would apply to the spread of consumerism to other societies later on.

Consumerism was not, then, simply a knee-jerk human response to greater prosperity or a product of manipulation by greedy petty capitalists. It gained ground because it helped people address problems and see new personal opportunities.

This first wave of modern consumerism was, however, limited in several ways, quite apart from considerable ongoing poverty. Even as the initial phases of modern consumerism gained ground, many people were swept away by new religious enthusiasms, such as Methodism, that had little truck with standard-of-living frivolities. Most interesting in revealing the tentativeness of this first round of consumerism was the reaction of many factory workers experiencing the early phases of industrialization, in the late 18th and early 19th centuries. It was a common experience

in industrializing nations, given the harsh conditions of much early factory work, for workers who began to earn wages above subsistence to use
their margin taking time off the job rather than maximizing consumer
possibilities. They simply didn't show up, or they changed jobs while
taking a few weeks off in the interim, sacrificing most consumer possibilities in the meantime. This happened in Britain early on and again in
France and Germany by the 1830s when their industrialization process
got going. Having some free time, absent the pressures of the industrial
work regime, was more important than new goods. The choice was not
surprising, in context, but it differs considerably from what many more
contemporary consumerists would opt for. Again, this was an early phase
of a complex evolution.

Phase 2: Additional Options and Additional Needs

From its base in the later 18th century, the forms and motives of modern
Western consumerism were available for later intensification. The patterns gained ground steadily in some respects, with virtually every decade
seeing some new expression. But major leaps (forward? backward?)
occurred less frequently. By the later 19th century, and into the early 20th,
modern consumerism was poised to make another major stride, in terms
of the types of people involved, the apparatus now in place, and above
all the meaning and significance of consumer behavior for participants.
Several factors combined to push beyond previous levels: familiarity with
the basic phenomenon, in combination with new products and resources;
new promotional apparatus, including now professional advertising and
the wondrous department stores; but also new needs, particularly generated by key changes in the modern work experience. What was unclear,
from these causes, was whether new levels generated any corresponding
increases in satisfaction.

Part of the process of acceleration—evident by the mid-19th century, but
still operating today—involved the redefinition of necessity. One decade's
consumer gain might become part of standard expectations, no longer
really expressing consumer aspirations at all. For example, around 1830
ordinary French workers began buying forks for the first time, something
that an imaginative historian of the era dubbed the real revolution of 1830
(for in truth the political rising of that year turned out to be pretty tame
stuff). Presumably, acquiring a new and obviously useful eating utensil

must have seemed a real consumer triumph to those who could finally manage to afford something long confined to the upper classes. But who, by 1870, would have seen the purchase of a fork as a sign of success? Many kinds of consumer gains had to escalate steadily to provide any sense of achievement or personal expression.

Sheer passage of time also helped more individuals and groups accustom themselves to the existing phases of consumerism and move from disapproval or skepticism to active acceptance, which in turn would facilitate a new phase in society at large. Mainstream American Protestant leaders, for example, argued against consumerism into the 1850s, shocked, as one put it, "by the parade of luxury, in eating, drinking and dressing, and almost every indulgence of the flesh." "Man should aspire to more durable riches than those this world can offer." By the 1870s, however, the tone began to shift with greater habituation, though certain concerns persisted. The *Presbyterian Banner*, to take one example, began to criticize women who lacked a fashion sense: "If a woman has no natural taste in dress, she must be a little deficient in her appreciation of the beautiful. . . . Indifferences, and consequent inattention to dress, often shows pedantry, self-righteousness, or indolence, and . . . may frequently be noted as a defect." Enjoyment of consumer bounty now demonstrated a true religious spirit, as against "the accumulated mould of sourness." "When the angels have enlarged and purified your own heart . . . they will thus secure to you the full unabridged edition of happiness in this world, as well as in world no. 2."

Part of this process also led to a reevaluation of envy, at least by the early 20th century. Moralists had long condemned envy as a petty, selfish emotion, and in the context of consumerism it also might reflect excessive materialism, as in yearning for the fashions or possessions of others. People should, as one Christian magazine put it in 1890, "be content with what they have." As consumerism became further normalized, however, envy began to be seen as a positive motivation to improve one's lot in life, including one's appearance. It still might involve some vanity, but most of this was "innocent . . . wholesale ambition to look one's best, to achieve beauty and distinction, to assert good taste and cultivated selection in clothes." Not surprisingly, advertisers by this point began to appeal overtly to envy as a reason to buy stuff: "The Envied Girl . . . are you one? Or are you still seeking the secret of charm?" (This turned out to rest in a particular brand of soap.) Cultural barriers to consumerism hardly disappeared, but many of them eroded as familiarity increased.

Other factors, however, further fueled the consumer mechanisms more explicitly, toward the middle of the 19th century and beyond. In the first place—though this was less an accelerator than a significant expansion of context—elements of modern consumerism began to spread beyond Western Europe. New buying habits reached upper- and middle-class groups in Russian cities, for example, by the 1850s. They would hit Japan by the end of the century. Consumerist dissemination included the lure of foreign, usually Western, example—though this also drew brickbats from nationalists and conservatives who loudly proclaimed the evils of seductive materialism. They also drew on many of the same needs that had prompted the Western phenomenon in the first place: for rewards amid rapidly changing social status, for opportunities for expression by women and youth in societies that had traditionally held them inferior.

A key early convert to growing consumerism was the new United States. Its close ties with Britain, along with growing urban development along the seaboard, prompted some consumer development even in the 18th century. New tastes for French cuisine and fashions hit by the 1840s, by which time American consumerism was clearly off and running. As we all know, and this was becoming evident to the world at large by 1900, along with the first fears of American cultural subversion, American consumerism, though initially an import, quickly became a global leader: the pupil turned teacher with a vengeance. The nation had several advantages in moving toward consumerist leadership. It was increasingly prosperous, an obvious precondition. It had a huge national market, and a culturally diverse population, both of which prompted new marketing techniques and various kinds of production (including entertainment packages, with the early rise of Hollywood as world movie capital) geared to lowest common denominators. Its uprooted immigrant population might be particularly open to consumerism as a sign of inclusion in a national culture and as a demonstration that the difficult choice of moving out of the home country had been blessed by material success. The United States also downplayed forces that, even in Western Europe, might serve as brakes on consumerist expansion. The aristocratic tradition in Europe provided precedents for sneering comments about debased mass taste that Americans simply lacked. To be sure, individual commentators, whether from Boston Brahmin backgrounds or simply intellectual snootiness, blasted ordinary American consumerism, but they lacked the force of real or imagined noble refinement. By 1900, many Europeans were noting (and usually lamenting) how many new consumer pressures were now originating on the other side of the Atlantic.

Crucial to the new consumerist surge were advances in prosperity throughout the industrial world: middle-class incomes tended to rise, and the growing lower middle class of clerks and salespeople, though not dramatically well paid, added numbers to the ranks of people often earning above subsistence (and also burdened with fewer children thanks to the declining birth rate). A minority of the working class now regularly enjoyed earnings above subsistence as well. Almost as important, at this point, was a noticeable expansion in availability of leisure hours. Many middle-class people, now that the challenges of initial industrialization were easing, found a bit more time available. Blue collar workers were beginning, through negotiation and often some legislation, to drive hours down toward ten a day and in some cases even below. There was more latitude for consumerist pursuits, including not only shopping and buying goods but also purchasing commercial entertainment—and arguably more need to find new things to fill up hours not needed for work or sleep. The expansion of gas and electric lighting also began to change the contours of nighttime in the cities, another component conducive to more consumerism.

There was also, as in the first phase of modern consumerism, a growing array of attractive goods and services to buy, another indispensable element in whetting mass appetites. Expanding world markets continued to do their part, and not just because of further expansion in the availability of once-exotic goods like coffee and sugar. The mid-19th century, for example saw growing middle-class fascination with Middle Eastern rugs and lamps—no home should be without one. And the Middle East responded by upping its output, both of handmade goods and relatively cheap factory facsimiles. Japanese expansion of the silk industry, directly designed for export, brought silk stockings and other sleek products into much wider purview, well beyond elite levels.

On the whole, however, this next round of consumerism built more on novel goods and services produced in the industrial world itself than on additional taste-teasers from elsewhere. A host of new manufactured products began to appear that soon entered must-have status for certain groups. By the middle of the 19th century the piano began to be a standard item for middle-class homes, with considerable cost involved: here, arguably, was the first consumer item, other than houses themselves, requiring substantial investment. The arrival of the bicycle in the 1870s and 1880s led to a more public consumer craze. Middle-class people took to the new device mainly for leisure purposes, rather than travel to work, so the consumerist functions predominated. Bicycle clubs formed, touring wide stretches of territory and promoting new types of tourism. The vehicles became integral to courtship, as couples found they could easily outpace any chaperones. As a foretaste of more contemporary patterns, bikes also encouraged ancillary consumer purchases: racing clubs needed special uniforms and gear, and women—heavily involved in biking activities—needed whole new outfits in order to ride comfortably.

The big new consumer durable, of course, was the automobile, which clearly built both on growing consumer interests and capacities and on new patterns of commuting. Even more than the bicycle, the car generated a host of related consumer needs and activities. Car trips became an increasingly important part of family leisure, at least in the middle classes. By the 1920s, as manufacturers realized the huge consumer potential of automobiles, they deliberately staged annual model changes sought to heighten awareness of regular obsolescence, encouraging new car purchases well before strict utility would require. Growing attention to design and interiors reflected greater interest in women consumers, either solo or as part of familial purchasing decisions.

The obvious point was that industry could now come up with new products, or at least cosmetic alterations of existing products, on a virtually annual basis. When, in the 1920s, soap manufacturers worried that they had reached the limit of their normal sales, as most Americans were now bathing regularly, a host of new hygiene needs were essentially invented, backed by pseudo-science, including deodorants and household cleansers of various sorts—an impressive combination. Women's cosmetic sales similarly branched into a previously unimagined assortment of beauty products. It was hard to keep up—which was precisely the point.

Along with products now came a host of commercial leisure services, the other great entrant into the array of available consumables that helped fuel the second surge from the late 19th century onward. People increasingly devoted major parts of their growing leisure time to activities that they purchased as consumer-spectators or, more occasionally, as participants. Eager tourists, for example, could now (by midcentury) buy package arrangements from outfits like Thomas Cook, and a growing array of guidebooks also eased any unfamiliarity in travel. Spectator sports began their move toward big business, with professional teams in soccer football and baseball. The popular music hall was another important consumerist venue, originating in working-class urban sections but increasingly appealing to "slumming" middle-class audiences; and from music hall and vaudeville would come the first entertainers participating in the movie industry by the 20th century. In the United States the amusement park constituted another vital form of consumer entertainment. The Ferris wheel was invented in the 1890s, and the roller coaster soon followed.

So: growing prosperity and available time were matched by new goods and attractions, in an atmosphere already prepared for consumerist values. The changing parade of goods, both exotic imports and locally produced manufacturing wonders, was captured by another new phenomenon, the world's fair. First opened in London, with the Crystal Palace exhibition of 1851, regular world's fairs provided opportunities for thousands of locals and tourists to check up on the latest fads, in an atmosphere of deliberate variety and abundance. Ample press coverage heightened awareness of the international support for consumer titillation and choice. This was frosting on the cake, to be sure: the main point was the steady procession of product innovations. From this foundation, a new stage of consumerism was almost inevitable.

While new products pulled consumers, two striking innovations pushed them during the same decades. First was the department store, a major new addition to urban living. The phenomenon originated in Paris in the 1830s, initially really as a collection of separate small shops that together could heighten attractions to consumers and create an impression, and to some extent a reality, of overflowing consumer opportunity. The genre was quickly refined, in London, New York, and Chicago as well as Paris. And it spread widely thereafter, adding many types of goods beyond the initial focus on clothing. Department stores, obviously, greatly expanded the lures that earlier shops had developed. Consumer items were laid out in profusion, with machine-like precision, deliberately designed to tempt a buyer's appetite and to encourage impulses that might not have existed before entry into the store. Window displays became a new art form, and managers changed them frequently to maintain the necessary air of novelty. The result was what one historian has called a "dream world" of material luxury. Clerks were given careful instruction in how to make customers ready to buy, by commenting on how good this or that looked on them and by presenting a smiling face regardless of customer mood (and regardless as well of how the clerk herself might be feeling). New promotional gimmicks were avidly sought, like the Christmas appetite whetter, Macy's Thanksgiving Day Parade in New York, introduced in 1924. Mail order catalogues added somewhat similar lures for nonurbanites.

The second great change in consumer apparatus from the late 19th century onward involved the explosion of emotion-laden advertising. Ads during the first phase of modern consumerism had focused largely on prose, which gave them a news-item, descriptive quality that, by contemporary standards, would hardly stoke acquisitive fires. By the later 19th century, in contrast, printing techniques had improved to the point that illustrations and (for posters) highly colorful material could be presented; visual display increasingly predominated. Magazines offered alluring fashion poses, and even newspapers added product imagery. When words were used, they appeared in bolder typeface and were designed to seek an evocative more than a rational response. Real or invented sales prices and bargains might be what caught the eye, rather than careful discussions of what the product was all about. Texts, where they were offered, embraced more value-laden phrases, as opposed to straightforward descriptions. Silk goods presented in the 1890s, for example, still emphasized practical features like quality and durability. By 1900, however, the tone changed, and stockings were touted as "alluring," "bewitching"—"to feel young and carefree, buy our silk." And where an explicit sensual element might help sell a show or a car, advertisers increasingly realized that draping an attractive young woman in the display might help a lot. All of these developments, finally, reflected a growing polish and professionalism in advertising itself, with big companies adding advertising personnel and formal ad agencies taking shape—like the first entries in the 1870s, with the United States proving the pioneer.

Unquestionably, the power to lure and manipulate measurably increased as part of the setting for a new wave of modern consumerism from the late 19th century onward. Along with new products themselves, and higher wage and salary levels, the result made the intensification of consumerism a virtual certainty.

Almost, but not quite. The picture can only be completed if concomitant new needs for consumerism also enter in. The question is not causation alone. The second phase of modern consumerism raises issues about happiness that are not as easy to deal with as in the first installment. Manipulation was increasing; the need to move beyond established patterns had a joyless potential. Consumerism was still responding to needs, but the balance sheet was becoming more complex.

For there were many new signs of hesitation and resistance around 1900, as the second phase gained ground. This was clearly, and unsurprisingly, true in many areas where modern consumerism was just arriving:

many Japanese, for example, stayed away from the new department stores because they seemed to be full of foreign goods for which there was no clear purpose. It was better to buy more modestly, and more tradition- ally. Travelers to the United States used their commentary to attack the hollowness of consumerism, as shown by a Dutch visitor: "Your instru- ments of civilization and progress . . . only make us nostalgic for what is old and quaint, and sometimes your life does not seem worth living." And even in the United States, many people initially held back from greater commitments—even apart from the fact that many workers still had no margin above basic subsistence or, as with many immigrants, preferred to live as simply as possible in order to send money to families back home— a distinctly nonconsumerist goal set. Many observers worried about the extension of consumerism to children. "Why foster a craving for novelty and variety that life cannot satisfy?" Larger criticisms abounded, even in the United States, about undue materialism, neglect of traditional moral and religious goals, excessive influence of commercial motivations and distorted, even fraudulent messaging. In 1899, Thorstein Veblen coined the phrase "conspicuous consumption" to designate the pretension and waste of a newly rich upper class.[3] And there were lots of snobs, on both sides of the Atlantic, ready to attack women, workers, and immigrants for buying things they could not afford or heedlessly aping their social bet- ters.

Most revealing of all, in the United States, was a combination of hesita- tion and moral compensation that at least for a time either constrained the middle class or suggested unexpected anxiety about consumer indul- gence. A number of scholars have noted how the middle classes, though already consumerist to a degree, had to be attracted into additional consumerism not by blatant appeals to material gain or sensuality but through arguments that urged the acquisition of products and services on grounds that they would improve family life, health, or work capac- ity. Consumerism on its own, in other words, risked being too blatant. But a vacation that could be justified because one would return refreshed, ready to work harder than ever (and more immune to neurasthenia), was an easier sell. A purchase for oneself might seem frivolous or selfish, but if it would improve family cohesion or help a child do better in school, the sale was made.

Even Americans, in other words, were not ready to jump into consum- erist escalation without hesitation. Over time the effectiveness of adver- tising and department store lures, plus the attractive new products, might have pushed them into intensifications despite some resistance. In fact, however, it was a final set of ingredients, combined with the traditional-sounding appeals to work and family, which really did the trick. For many groups of people the ongoing evolution of modern work seemed acceptable, and in some cases endurable, only if a consumerist life off the job improved to compensate. The fact was that accelerated levels of consumerism met, or could be seen as meeting, a set of measurably new needs.

Working-class instrumentalism was a straightforward case in point, as it took shape from the middle of the 19th century onward. The printers who grudgingly agreed that they could accept new typesetting equipment, which reduced their interest on the job, in favor of new buying power were obviously more ardent consumers in the making. Gradually, many employers realized or were forced to realize that the tradeoff was a good deal for them as well, despite the need to offer higher wages, in improving worker motivation and reducing instability and strife. Thinking of work as a basis for steady gains in consumption gained ground steadily.

A lower-middle-class version of consumerism as compensation developed as well, by the final decades of the century, sharing many features with worker instrumentalism, but dressing it a bit differently. Lower-middle-class work was not in fact necessarily much more interesting than that of factory operatives. But many clerks and salespeople depended considerably on a sense that their status was or should be superior to that of manual labor. Consumerism could help here. Already, the group boasted middle-class clothing styles on the job. More generally, even with incomes not much different from blue-collar levels, clerks began to take a lead in a variety of new consumer fashions, including attendance at professional sports events or cigarette smoking, as a new source of identity and meaning amid a particular set of work-and-status challenges.

Finally, there was the middle class itself. Here too, significant changes were occurring in the work setting, which were all the more telling given the group's commitment, at least in principle, to the glories of the work ethic. The shifts were simple but potentially profoundly disconcerting. For business people, the growth of a corporate economy meant that more and more middle-class aspirants had to resign themselves to a lifetime career as managerial employees, however well paid, with dreams of being one's own boss in the best rags-to-riches fashion increasingly cast aside. There was simply less room, in the business ranks, for classic entrepreneurial individualism. Similar changes were occurring in the professional or semiprofessional ranks. Lawyers saw opportunities develop in increasingly large law firms, as members of a team rather than quintessentially independent courtroom heroes. Engineers and architects faced even greater pressure to substitute hopes for individual operation for more secure but collective corporate or office employment. In varying but similar ways, then, members of the middle class had to abandon older visions of personal creativity and independence in favor of new kinds of job security—and the result was a perceived deterioration. Here, too, there was active interest in compensation (along with a growing interest in insisting on lower hours of work than had seemed acceptable in the heyday of individual ambitions). Here, too, consumerism could fit the bill, particularly if it was embellished by references to family or work capacity.

Just as modern consumerism at the outset met the needs of changing social circumstances, so the new round of enhancement responded to important shifts in the nature and evaluation of jobs. By 1900, quite clearly, in all the modern societies, opportunities to consume, well-organized inducements to consume, and new problems or needs that a heightened level of consumerism might seem to address were combining in unprecedented fashion. Stage two of modern consumerism entered in full force.

The result easily transcended specifics like the interest in new goods and commercial leisure outlets; it was more than higher spending, more than involvements by additional social groups. The new phase of consumerism inserted consumer goals and processes more intimately into new sectors of ordinary life, increasing what consumer activities were called upon to satisfy and increasing basic dependence on consumer motivation. In the first phase of consumerism, we could point to roles that new clothing interests played in a changing pattern of courtship; this obviously continued in the new phase, but it was part of a much more intricate intertwining of the whole process of courtship and commercialized leisure. In the first phase, bequests suggested how goods might be seen as expressing emotional relationships with family and friends; in the second phase, consumerism became a basic and ongoing part of family goals. Expectations and patterns of acquisition became part of the fabric of life.

The transformation of courtship (including the substantial abandonment of that quaint term) was a revealing case in point. As early as 1855, Valentine's Day began to turn in a more commercial direction, with the introduction (initially in Britain) of store-bought cards, which increasingly replaced any effort at more spontaneous emotional expression.

Larger shifts in behavior, a few decades later, were more obviously important. During the teens and twenties, growing numbers of American youth shifted from 19th century practices to the new phenomenon called dating, or, as one historian has aptly put it, "from front porch to back seat." The shift involved several factors, including increasing participation in coeducational schooling and a growing desire to be free from parental supervision. But the immersion of dating in consumerism was a crucial aspect of the change. Instead of a home-based setting, with exchanges of food or flowers at most, heterosexual interaction now involved arrangement of consumer outings—to movies, to amusement parks, all if possible reached by car—in which successful selection of commercial entertainments, at appropriately demanding levels of expenditure, was a fundamental criterion. In turn, of course, many male consumers expected some level of romantic or sexual return on investment, making even these responses part of a consumer exchange.

Consumerism spread directly to family evaluations as well. While hardly a legal category, consumer complaints began to enter into the growing number of American divorce actions by the later 19th century, particularly in the middle class. Disgruntled spouses readily accused each other of inadequacies, men blamed for not providing enough for an appropriate consumer living standard, wives for poor shopping and spending habits. "You don't know enough to buy your own clothes," one suing husband accused in Los Angeles in 1882, while another husband ruefully noted his "inability to support my wife in the manner she desired on my salary." Overall, as family production functions virtually disappeared, the family's role as a consumer group gained growing prominence, with the marital couple engaged in combining earnings with consumption decisions as a major expression of their collective purpose. This could work quite satisfactorily, to be sure, but some new vulnerabilities clearly emerged as well.

It was revealing that efforts to establish new symbolic support for families also turned in a consumerist direction, regardless of original intent. The United States Congress enacted Mother's Day in 1914, after tireless representations by Anna Jarvis, of Philadelphia, who deeply wanted to honor her own mother and maternal contributions more generally—but also with the support of commercial florists, who knew a good thing when they saw it. Indeed, Jarvis had turned against the holiday by 1923, precisely because it had become a modest consumer extravaganza—the best way often-distracted children knew how to express real or rhetorical feelings for mom. Jarvis protested, "This is not what I intended. I wanted it to be a day of sentiment, not profit." The whole point was that consumerism increasingly conflated the two.

Extending consumerism into childhood and child rearing was a further application of the larger family reorientation, and it was clearly picking up speed around 1900. The provision of allowances had many purposes, including the possibility of instilling experience in saving and delayed gratification and expression of appreciation for household chores accomplished, but in point of fact, and increasingly over time, giving children a somewhat controlled experience in personal spending was one of the main effects. Expanding from this, and responding as well to expert advice, parents began finding it increasingly normal to deal with behavioral problems through consumerist manipulation, particularly as emotional socialization was added to the list of parental obligations. Dealing with childish fear, and aware that simply urging children to get a grip was now regarded as harsh and risky? Place a desired consumer object near the source of fear and gradually lure the child in. A toddler resents a sibling? Buy him something separate to show your love. The association of consumer goods with emotional development and guidance grew steadily stronger.

And as a happiness goal was added in, the urgency of providing kids with consumer pleasures obviously intensified still further. Christmases increasingly became periods of virtual consumer frenzy, along with regular, and regularly futile, annual laments about how the true purposes of the holiday were being lost. (Intriguingly, by the 21st century, Christmas shopping and giving were spreading to non-Christian regions like Turkey and the United Arab Emirates, a sign of the international fascination with buying now that, even in the West, it was so easily separable from religious impulse.) For many Americans, certainly, Christmas, and to a lesser extent birthdays, became a way to show through buying how much the family meant, and what intense emotions were involved that might be difficult to express more directly.

One of the most striking though backhanded testimonies to the deep new importance of this second stage of modern consumerism was the emergence of a brand-new disease, kleptomania, which began to be diagnosed on both sides of the Atlantic from the 1870s onward. Now the impulse to steal affected people who were perfectly capable of affording many goods but who wanted more, whose addiction ran to new levels. Department stores provided the new target, their displays an unintended incitement to crime and the easily available goods from their counters an apparently irresistible temptation. The typical kleptomaniac was a middle-class woman whose consumer appetite became almost insatiable. A Frenchwoman talked of going into the new emporiums in a "genuine state of joy," as if she were meeting a lover. Another noted that she got more pleasure from her thefts than "from the father of her children." A woman arrested for stealing some alpaca wool, worth relatively little, admitted that the "idea of possessing it had dominated her to the point of subjugating her will and her reason." Kleptomania was an illness, not a common condition. But it expressed, if in distorted form, the kind of passion and individual need that consumerism was coming to express quite widely. Even illness could be consumerized.

And this leads back to the main points about the second phase of modern consumerism. It built on the first phase, but went much farther in all sorts of respects—range of goods, segments of the population involved, manipulative apparatus. Above all, it went further in terms of personal commitments and meanings. More people were banking on consumerism to embellish or even define other key aspects of their lives—and the sick extension to kleptomania was merely an extreme of this process. The expansion of consumerism continued to respond to needs; it is vital not to see the phenomenon simply in terms of blind response to solicitations or frivolous greed. But the scope of needs expanded, as consumerism was brought to bear on a variety of developments at work and even in the family. Whether further consumerism could adequately compensate for some of the issues it was meant to address might raise new doubts—as the new hesitations about the whole phenomenon suggested. We lack happiness polls for this second phase in the Western world, to tell us whether people were already passing the tipping point between satisfaction gains and unresponsiveness. But as consumerism measurably expanded, the questions were certainly looming—and they would be answered definitively later in the 20th century: was consumerism being pressed too far, asked to respond to too many modern problems, squeezed too hard to generate happiness?

Consumerism and Contemporary Happiness

The contemporary phase of consumerism opened a few decades ago. The movement had survived the Great Depression surprisingly well, with many sectors, particularly in the middle classes, continuing to advance new levels and forms of spending even as the headlines were gripped by unemployment and poverty. It surged still further in the postwar decades, as the American middle class began its rapid expansion to embrace the relatively affluent majority of blue collar workers and as suburban living came to define a further commitment to consumer criteria.

It was by the 1980s, with the United States still at the forefront, that a third stage of consumerism became inescapably identifiable, pushing well beyond the boundaries of the patterns that had been achieved before World War II. All the now-familiar factors were again in play: the new stage was defined in terms of new goods available, new manipulative apparatus, but also additional needs. What was most significant about the third phase of modern consumerism was that it began to exhibit a broader range of clearly counterproductive features. Its contributions to more than fleeting happiness diminished and it began to take on many of the characteristics of a treadmill, no longer responding to needs so much as compelling compliance despite a number of discernible and often truly painful disadvantages.

Stage Three: Super-Affluence

A revealing sign of a new stage of consumerism was the increasing evidence of a multiplicity of items: having merely one would no longer suffice. By 1995, 66% of all American families had three or more television sets, and more than half of all teenagers had a set in their own room. Multicar families became common as well, partly because of work or school needs but partly to facilitate increasingly individualized consumption patterns. The family was still a consumer unit in some senses, but more and more it was a framework for individual pursuits of its members. Even the number of bathrooms per household began to increase, in some cases more rapidly than family size. Just as Americans increasingly needed sources of food near at hand, as in office buildings, so they needed abundant and private opportunities to dispose of the results.

Cross-marketing of products, particularly for children, was at once a new-level sales device and an entry into the intensification of acquisition. By the 1980s, movies and TV shows were generating toys for kids (often used as well in fast-food restaurants), and the toys in turn encouraged attendance at the showings—further enhanced when multiple movies were made around the same action character. Collecting figures could become a passion, and various items of clothing and accessories might be added to the mix. In 1987, 60% of all toys sold were based on licensed characters. Children's consumerism was now preyed upon by a vast and interconnected industry.

A variety of measurements provided garden variety evidence of intensification over time in the United States. Personal savings rates of about 9% of income in the 1970s had dropped to 2.8% by 1986. Personal spending increased by 21% in the first half of the 1980s even though income only increased by 17%; consumer debt by 1997 reached an all-time high (to that point) of $1.25 trillion, well over 10% of the total national product. On a humbler scale: per person spending on Christmas gifts at least doubled between the late 1960s and the early 21st century, due account taken of inflation. Though precise comparisons are impossible, birthday spending also seems to have soared. Low-income rural families were committing at least one hundred dollars per child by 2009, or for the whole family upwards of 5% of total disposable income. Higher on the social scale, a Chicago party invitation, for five-year olds, specified gifts worth at least thirty-five dollars, on grounds that the previous year the birthday child had received some presents with a ten-dollar price tag that did not even cover party costs. The waves of commerce rose steadily higher.[4]

Evaluations were complicated, to be sure, by changes in income distribution from the 1980s onward. A new upper class emerged, in the United States and elsewhere, larger than the robber baron cohort that had spiced the previous age of conspicuous consumption, but similar in indulgent purpose. Thus a sign of advancing consumerism in one sense, the emergence of a new passion for large houses (McMansions), was obviously not a general social symptom so much as a sign of new interest in and capacity for class differences. The impulse was fascinating nevertheless, as childless couples bought multibedroom homes—there were 3.2 million houses with four thousand square feet or more in 2003, up 11% from 2001. This was not typical, to be sure. But even average home sizes increased, despite a largely stable per-family birth level, at a 55% rate between the mid-1970s and 2001. And while the $10 million that one wealthy New Yorker spent on his thirteen-year-old daughter's birthday, including the band Aerosmith and ten-thousand-dollar gift bags, was out of reach for most, even fairly ordinary people contributed to the $600 million now being spent on children's birthday cards, gift wrapping, and party ware annually. The push of the very wealthy was increasingly an atypical extreme of what most people expected to do—and their example, along with stagnating real wages, was one reason why consumer indebtedness kept mounting as a means of closing the gap. Small wonder that the amount of money the average family felt it "needed" to survive doubled between the 1980s and 2000 (in constant dollars), reaching a figure ($102,000) that was in turn double actual average family income. While the rich did the really bizarre stuff, as had long been the case, the less-rich were determined not to be too far behind.

Increasingly consumerist approaches to pets (themselves obviously a consumer item) provided a humble measurement of intensification. The sophistication of pet foods increased, while a host of other products and services emerged, including motel-like kennels and special cemeteries as well as a variety of toys and treats. Americans were annually spending $17 billion on pet foods alone by the 21st century. Revealingly, pet interests spread to places like China (long hostile to pets under communist regulation in a resource-scarce environment) as consumerism in general gained ground.

Another illustration of consumerism's new phase, even more obviously novel, involved the conversion of once-separate types of activities into an increasingly consumerist mold. Politics and campaigning, many observers argued, was a case in point. Electoral candidates began to be packaged just like consumer products. They chose policy positions, emotional style, and clothing on the basis of careful market research. Political consultants became marketing and advertising agents, and their roles in campaigning expanded steadily. And while a few candidates objected—"the idea that you can merchandise candidates for high office like breakfast cereal . . . is the ultimate indignity to the democratic process"—most fell in line. As early as the 1950s, ad agencies that popularized brassieres were being used to generate political slogans, and by 2000 presidential candidates were choosing shirt colors that matched what pollsters told them their image should be. Not surprisingly, consumerism moved forward in the art world as well, with pop art immortalizing consumer items as humble as the soup can. More directly still, museum stores began to move into the big business category, attached to virtually every conceivable type of exhibit. For many people, visits to the stores began to eclipse the museum walk itself, the process of picking out mementoes more interesting than the encounter with the actual objects of art or history. By 2000 Americans were buying over $1.5 billion worth of souvenirs, regarding an experience as authentic only if it yielded something to buy. Interestingly, Japanese interest in souvenir acquisition rose also, but more toward buying goods for others (reflecting a gift-giving culture but also a desire to demonstrate that exciting visits had really occurred), whereas the American focus was more on self and family.

The family itself increased its service as a consumer institution. Goods for children piled up, overflowing homes and garages. Children themselves, trained to consumer signals at an early age, not only steadily expanded their expectations but could see consumerism as a basic orientation to life: as one seven-year-old girl exclaimed, in the excitement of an otherwise fairly modest shopping excursion, "I was born to shop." Marriages themselves stepped up involvements. A British study in the late 20th century, called *The Symmetrical Family*, posited middle-class couples, each with a good job, defining their mutual relationship almost entirely in terms of shopping excursions and commercialized leisure pursuits. Similarly in the United States the baby-boom phenomenon of the "yuppie," or young urban professional, featured both individuals and couples (whether formally married or not) defined mainly in terms of elaborate consumer efforts and, in off hours, endless discussions of bargains and products. In many of these new-style consumer unions, children fit only uncomfortably, distracting in terms both of resources and time— one reason why a growing number decided on childlessness, or a late and often single venture that would not disturb adult work-and-consume patterns unduly.

Causes of Acceleration

As in the previous surges of consumerism, a variety of lures helped explain new behaviors and urges. The categories involved are familiar to a point—as they should be in explaining a recurrent modern-historical phenomenon. But compared to the two previous upticks, causation seems heavier now on the apparatus side, somewhat less compelling from the standpoint of new needs. The self-generating aspect of consumerism moves into greater prominence, which helps explain as well why consumerism began to become definably more counterproductive even as it seemed to maintain its inexorable march forward.

Product development continued to create a sense of new needs, on top of all the goods that a respectable consumer already felt responsible for from the previous surges. Electronic gear probably headed the list. Spending on computers, software, iPods, and the like began multiplying exponentially from the 1980s onward, spiced by a dizzying rate of model change, such that a new investment every other year seemed virtually essential. Rapid obsolescence in light of real or imagined product development had never burned brighter than in the computer and telephonic world.

Shopping venues changed. Just as the proliferation of small shops framed the first phase of modern consumerism, and department stores the second, so now the advent of massive shopping malls set the context for new bursts of acquisition. By 1985, 78% of all Americans were visiting a large shopping mall at least once a month. Even more than with department stores, the variety of goods and outlets in the mall not only encouraged purchases but helped further the conversion of shopping into a leisure activity in its own right. Quickly backstopping the mall were new opportunities for mail catalogues and electronic options. Acting on consumerist impulses could become virtually instantaneous.

Advertising reached new heights, or depths, becoming a virtually inescapable part not just of daily but of hourly life. The full onslaught of television was obviously the big change, along with growing viewer addiction; watching presumably alluring advertising, intermittently but steadily for several hours a day, became standard fare for children and adults alike. The basic pattern became international, but American television was far less restricted in its commercial outreach than many of its counterparts elsewhere, reflecting and encouraging the nation's more ubiquitous consumer culture. Supplementing this was the insertion of advertising into further facets of daily life. The Internet provided additional opportunities for commercial bombardment, while computer systems allowed targeted use of home telephones (somewhat constrained by law, however, early in the 21st century). Deployment of naming rights spread steadily, from tee shirts to concert halls, and while some of this aimed more at corporate visibility, a great deal was directed to product familiarity. Athletes became walking commercials, and aside from some highbrow fare, virtually every event worth going to had a loudly emblazoned consumer sponsorship. Even ordinary people seemed to delight in promoting products, as witness the proud sporting of designer labels on a variety of informal clothing, and presumably this impulse would help to inspire others in the best keep-up-with-the-Joneses fashion. The capacity to stimulate consumer appetites had never been more extensive.

But what of the final ingredient: new needs? Obviously people thought they had needs—for specific products, to maintain their image to themselves and neighbors/coworkers, to gain some sense of personal expression in an increasingly organized world. We have argued consistently that consumerism must be seen in terms of reflecting real interests, and not just advertiser manipulation or some durable if shallow human greed for things. Spending on pets, for example, reflected the diminished role of child rearing in the adult life span, with pets, and the opportunity to lavish money on them, reflecting a very real antidote to loneliness.

One historian, Susan Matt, has persuasively argued that the obviously increasing American consumer fascination with large homes was a direct response, not simply to growing upper-class affluence, but to a real need to claim roots amid unusual rates of geographic mobility.[5] The fact was that Americans moved, on average, once every five years. They disrupted or inhibited social networks, as a result, and often suffered serious blows to any sense of personal identity. The otherwise-bizarre addiction to big houses stemmed from a desire to replicate real or imagined images of past homes—often, 19th-century homes—as a means of expressing place in an otherwise transient atmosphere. The homes were ridiculously large (and, many would now add, environmentally damaging), with childless or empty-nest couples delighting in four–five bedrooms and vast living space that, given work schedules, many inhabitants actually saw only rarely. In many cases, they were now planted, in full imagined New England glory, in incongruous settings in Florida, Arizona, or California. For the idea of a gabled semimansion, sometimes vine-covered and graced with white picket fences, responded to real personal aspirations. The same impulse opened people to a wide variety of advertisements, in home magazines and television productions like Martha Stewart's offerings, "country style" labels, or the revealingly named Restoration hardware stores, that explicitly touted an old-fashioned flavor (complete with the most modern kitchen, even for people who rarely cooked, and increasingly elaborate bathroom appointments for contemporary sensuality—the package was a mixed one). The basic ideals involved went far back in the nation's past—the ever-popular song, "Home Sweet Home," was composed in 1823—but the needs involved had escalated with the pace and anonymity of modern life. A market researcher put it this way: "[Baby] boomers are a bit scared of the way things have turned out. . . . There's been a negative fallout to their legacy that they don't feel comfortable with, so we're seeing a return to an interest in stability." Correspondingly, by the end of the 20th century, spending on home-related items increased by 50% a decade, doubling the rise in American consumerism in general. All ethnic groups participated in what was essentially a giant outburst of national nostalgia. However questionable, there was real meaning involved. As the editor of *House and Garden* put it, "Sure, shopping and arranging and collecting (or hoarding) are materialistic pursuits, but they are also connected to deeper passions. . . . They nurture our souls. . . . We burrow into our coziness . . . we retreat into other centuries. . . . That's materialism in the service of history, a pretty grand idea." All this, and an obvious, showy status symbol to boot.

New needs also undoubtedly helped fuel the rising enthusiasm for the various contemporary communications technologies. Increasing numbers of Americans, and particularly young adults, were living separately, and much of the contemporary consumer apparatus reinforced a sense of individual separateness as well—captured by the ubiquity of isolating headsets, tuned to an individual music repository, as people walked or traveled. The interplay between increasing separation for many adults, and the opportunity to maintain a large acquaintance base through technology, was fascinating, and not always easy to interpret. Still, even as concerns about growing isolation and loneliness persisted, the response of third-stage consumerism to new needs and circumstances was undoubtedly involved.

Boredom: Another Spur

Despite some definably new services rendered, the linkage between the general intensification of consumerism with identifiable needs was becoming less straightforward. Fairly clearly, consumerism was expanding by feeding on internal insatiabilities—a virtually addictive compulsion to buy more, simply to maintain a sense of momentum.

Nothing better captures the self-generating qualities of contemporary consumer advance than the changing contours of boredom and related forms of impatience as evolving modern qualities. Boredom itself was a modern term and a modern condition, though the precise origins of the word are not clear. Prior to the 18th century, symptoms of what we might regard as boredom were called "acedia," a dangerous form of spiritual alienation from the community—and, it's been argued, quite apart from the fact that this was designated as a sin, few premodern people had either the time or the alternatives to develop much active involvement with the condition, few occasions to muse on a dissatisfaction of this sort. By the 18th century, however, the advent of new expectations of happiness allowed a clearer identification of a contrast between active satisfaction and situations in which happiness was not being provided. The recognition of a new and unsatisfactory state in which adequate stimulation was lacking did not, however, advance quickly, precisely because it required internalization of what was truly a novel set of criteria. From

1768 onward, initially in England, people began occasionally to be designated as boring—"tiresome" or "dull"—and obviously the implication was that their personality was defective, for a properly cheerful, incipiently modern person should be more actively entertaining. It wasn't until the middle of the 19th century, however (with the publication of Charles Dickens's *Bleak House*), that the noun "boredom" first emerged in the language, to designate an undesirable condition in which a person was not being appropriately stimulated. Still, however, the main use of the term focused on undesirable personal qualities, though these now extended: children should be coached not only not to be boring but not to be bored, for both facets were unpleasant to others and ought to be remedied.

Boredom, in its first century and a half of existence, was thus a clearly modern experience, the flip side of the new commitment to happiness. Its burden, however, rested primarily on individuals who should do something about their boredom lest they annoy other people. Etiquette books drove this point home explicitly, as part of larger strictures about character development; Emily Post, for example, argued that "to be bored is a bad personal habit." And the whole issue was not directly linked to consumerism.

This all had changed, however, by the middle of the 20th century, when boredom began to be actively attached to the latest ascending consumer curve and began to be redefined in terms of a need for compensation. The transition became clear literally in the 1950s, when child-rearing manuals began to comment on the problem of bored children and the need for parents and other adults to intervene actively to correct the condition. Boredom, now, was not only bad but undeserved, and children should be raised to expect lively compensatory entertainment. The commitment to happy children translated directly into a commitment to provide distraction and fun. It was at this point that children, quick to recognize a new weapon, eagerly picked up the new norms: plaintive cries of "I'm bored" or "I have nothing to do" became direct claims on parental time and attention: a properly raised child should not have to experience this lack of stimulation. Expert discussion expanded on the theme, worrying for example about the boredom bright kids experienced in school and wondering about long-term damage. The increasing conclusion that boredom was an unfair deprivation, much more than an individual fault to be rectified, had wide-ranging consequences.

Most obviously, contemporary-style boredom encouraged new connections with consumerism, from childhood onward. Want to make sure kids aren't bored on their birthdays? Take them to one of the special emporiums catering to children's entertainment, like Chuck E Cheese. Concerned about possible boredom during a restaurant meal? Take the family to a fast food outlet (with its explicitly labeled Happy Meal) where there's not much time to be bored and where the experience is spiced further with provision of cheap toys with the kids' meals. Worried about kids with seemingly nothing to do? Let them turn on the TV; for as the *New York Times* was noting as early as 1950, "youngsters today need television for their morale as much as they need fresh air and sunshine for their health." A series of connections was becoming part of the common wisdom, under the rubric of consumer-based happiness and urged on by eager advertisers: children did not deserve to be bored, parents must be active in providing occasions for fun as the antidote to boredom, and fun and happiness were most readily gained through consumer goods and consumer-based activities. A variety of authorities noted, and usually deplored, the transition, from a boredom that once was a goad to figure out something interesting to do on one's own to a boredom that became a not-so-subtle request to be provided with entertainment. Unfortunate or not, the transition was increasingly clear.

A final connection matured as the initial skein sunk in. Kids who were raised with a certain sense of entitlement about being entertained, and a considerable expectation that consumerism would do the trick, easily turned into adults who maintained the same approach. The urgent desire to fill time, to avoid boredom, became an additional spur to consumerism, adding to the existing effects of stratagems like planned obsolescence. The third, contemporary phase of consumerism intensified because people, from childhood onward, needed more partly because it was more.

Consumerism and Compensation

Even boredom and an impatient desire to be actively entertained, along with specific prods like a nostalgia for real or imagined homes past amid change and mobility, do not fully express the needs that helped push consumerism to yet another new level or explain why so many people were ready to respond to the increasingly sophisticated apparatus that consumer providers had at their command. Consumerism gained ground as well because of the widespread if often implicit assumption that it could compensate for some of the disappointments that attached so clearly to maturing modernity. People wanted to buy more things and more services to fill in satisfaction gaps in other key aspects of life.

The link between consumerism and compensation was well established. The first phase of modern consumerism was aimed in part at compensating for the reduction of opportunities to establish identities based on older status systems. Even more widely, consumerism's second phase fed directly off a need to develop instrumental satisfactions to counterbalance reductions in the quality of work life, for manual workers and middle-class personnel alike. At the same time, redefinitions of childhood, including the huge addition of obligations in providing happiness, promoted growing use of consumerism as part of parenting, and as part of parental definitions of adequacy.

Consumerism's role in addressing the complexities of modernity escalated further by the late 20th century. Situations at work varied, to be sure, with some work categories (and particular individuals as well) seeking more intrinsic job satisfaction than others. Still, the number of workers of various sorts who found declining meaning in work, and who invested more as a result in earnings and the potential for acquisition off the job, tended to increase. Growing routinization affected a host of job categories, extending earlier trends. Polls in the later 20th century saw 10-35% of all workers claiming to find no satisfaction in their jobs at all and a still-larger number pointing to serious constraints of the sort that would make sense only with a consumerist counterpoise.

It was revealing that, on both sides of the Atlantic, advancing consumerism began to supersede not only work itself but also earlier patterns of class protest. From the late 1950s onward, with a few interruptions, both union and strike activity declined noticeably, as workers preferred to spend their time either putting in extra hours in order to afford additional consumer amenities or simply seizing the opportunity to enjoy new consumer goods. The same consumer goals helped drive more and more married women into the labor force, again from the 1950s onward. Working women had more incomes to devote to their own consumption, and they often entered the workforce initially with the goal of furthering family consumerism—providing the basis for affording an expansion of a house or a new car or additional resources for the kids.

The same intensification clearly applied to the use of consumerism in addressing some of the unexpected tensions in implementing modern childhood. Allowances increased steadily, obviously varying by economic class, and began to apply to ever-younger age groups: the notion of pleasing and training kids through consumption became a parental reflex. The work commitments of most mothers from the 1960s onward created two parents, and not just one, who sought to express their feelings for children, and their sense of guilt about unavailability, in significant measure through consumer treats. Amid debate, to be sure, more and more families also opted for consumer rewards for good school performance and other achievements, again on the assumption that the same relationship between consumerism and activity should apply to childhood as increasingly applied to adulthood: effort should have consumer reward. Departures for college provided another opportunity for a shower of consumerism. Carloads accompanying matriculating students increased steadily in size and complexity, with electronic gear, refrigerators, as well as clothing. Provision of goods for children at various life stages served to assure parents and children alike that parental obligations had been fulfilled and (often genuine) love expressed. Compensation for the real or imagined complexities of schooling, inducements for emotional development, and obviously direct contributions (it was hoped) to childhood happiness all found consumerist outlet.

Consumerism became, for many, the strand of modernity that provided the clearest path to fulfillment, if not of happiness then at least of a fair semblance thereof. It might distract from troubling thoughts of death, it provided some of the context for recreational sexuality, and it offered tangible goals in contrast to the welter of modern complexities. As the joke went, when the going got tough, the tough went shopping. It was revealing that, in the immediate aftermath of the terrorist attacks of 9/11, the only definite recommendation for a deeply troubled public was to go to the mall. The focus was striking, as against all sorts of potential community activities that might have demonstrated courage, vigor, and unity. Consumerism had become the truest test of normalcy, the highest calling an admittedly unimaginative national administration could think of in a time of crisis.

The third stage of consumerism, in sum, had become self-generating, surpassing definable needs with a vaguer but compelling sense of purpose often linked to the new quest to avoid boredom, when nothing else provided equivalent fulfillment. Its intersection with work, family, and public life sustained its momentum, with little sense of real alternative. There was genuine danger that what had started out, two centuries earlier, as an expansive vision of progress and happiness was narrowing to a largely consumerist definition of what modernity was all about.

Pushing Too Far

For the same process that prodded consumerism to new levels also revealed new fault lines. The third phase of consumerism, particularly in the United States, began not only not to add to measurable happiness (whatever ardent consumers continued to anticipate) but actually to create additional burdens on modern life. The gains that occur when consumerism is new were long gone, and now the consumer treadmill risked eliminating too many life options and creating too many new stresses in the daily routine. Whether people could jump off the treadmill was not clear, but it seemed increasingly desirable to urge them to try.

Consumerism has always drawn critics, as we have seen, and many of them have overshot the mark. Blasts at early consumerism often reflected hostility to ordinary people and particularly to efforts to cross traditional status lines, a historically understandable approach that, however, resolutely ignored the real opportunities for meaning and expression that consumerism could provide. Blasts around 1900 might raise a larger number of points that observers would find valid still today, particularly around the emptiness of conspicuous consumption at the highest levels. But here too critiques were often tainted by continuing elitism, gender bias, or other assumptions that, again, ignored the real service that consumerism could provide.

The argument that contemporary consumerism has gone too far is itself debatable, for it does assume that many consumers, perfectly worthy in other respects, do not know their own best interests—a presumptuous contention without question. The basic case rests on the differentiation between current levels and the past, on the extent to which consumerism is now called upon to provide more compensation for limitations in other aspects of life than it can possibly fulfill—on the extent to which it is now creating problems rather than satisfying needs. What had once served as an expression of interests for women or youth, or facilitated adjustment to change, has become such a driving force that it risks consuming its own participants.

Two types of judgment are involved here. The first, familiar and unquestionably important, involves macro-level characteristics and global impacts. The second, closer to the argument about the stresses of modernity, involves smaller but often more direct impacts on individual lives.

The huge concerns are environment and the global economy. The production and utilization of key consumer items, including the fashionable McMansions in the United States, take a great environmental toll. Links between advancing consumption and environmental degradation increase steadily. The disproportionate role the United States plays in atmospheric pollution relates directly to its unusually high consumer commitments, embellished with particularly heedless obsolescence and willingness to discard—habits that have become ingrained aspects of the national consumer approach.

Within individual nations and certainly in the world at large, the recent stage of consumerism has accompanied rapid increases in inequality. Globally, 20% of the people in the highest-income countries account for 86% of private consumption expenditures, with the poorest 20% accounting for scarcely over a single percent. Injustice, human suffering, and arguably existing and potential protest movements all follow from this disproportion.

The recent economic downturn has highlighted another imbalance, the global economic role of headlong American consumerism and related indebtedness as a sales source for rising production capacities in other countries, such as China. How long this imbalance can be sustained—how long other countries will support American consumer debt (direct debt or public debts incurred in part because of the rooted unwillingness of American taxpayers to reduce their consumption through taxes sufficient to pay for public services)—is open to serious question. But the apparent remedy is both challenging and ironic as well: to get Americans to cut back a bit, a result we have yet to see over any sustained period of modern time, and to induce other people, like the Chinese, to engage in levels of consumption that American experience suggests turn quickly hollow. To encourage China to consume more, as one critic has noted, the United States needs to export "a world of false needs so that others, too, will get engaged in keeping our capitalism afloat by buying the iPods and the new technologies, which for the most part are, at best, marginal improvements on traditional goods" and are "not really necessary." Debatable judgments, to be sure, but worth considering as part of confronting imbalances in contemporary consumer behavior that go beyond the poverty divide. The global issues associated with consumerism are deeply challenging.

But there is the domestic, daily side as well, less catastrophic but deeply oppressive as well—to the individuals most engaged in consumerism's contemporary phase. Here's where consumerism's evolution has opened its own gap between modern conditions and personal happiness.

Signs of distortion had accompanied the two earlier crests of modern consumerism—as in thefts of clothing in the 18th century by people who wanted entry into acquisition but lacked the means, or the arrival of kleptomania in the 19th century. Both of these symptoms continued into the 21st century: heists of cars for joyrides or attacks on youthful owners of fancy sneakers were cases in point for the former, and kleptomania rates rose as well. But now there were signs of wider-spread collapse based on seemingly irresistible consumer addictions.

Most troubling was the massive rise of consumer debt, particularly in the United States and particularly from the 1980s onward. By 2008 the average American was spending almost a fifth of post-tax income to pay off consumer and housing debts. Average annual credit card charges, similarly, reached a full quarter of average annual earnings. Nationwide, at least before the recession at the end of the decade (itself partly triggered by overextended borrowing), annual American credit card debt was piling up toward 10% of total national domestic product.

These overall figures, troubling enough, reflected a host of personal engagements. Some were caused by factors beyond consumerism alone: medical crises or loss of jobs. But a good many reflected shopping passions that raced out of control. A woman with over one hundred thousand dollars in debt, who persisted in spending several hundred dollars a month at Starbucks, put it this way: "When I shop, I do kind of get a rush. It makes me feel good . . . but afterwards, though, I get depressed. I'll buy something even if I really don't like it because I have to come out with something." Another phrased the problem in terms of lack of maturity, a childlike hope that someone would ultimately cover the bills. A single woman noted how she "sometimes worried that living free of responsibility . . . had left me a bit reluctant to grow up, to sacrifice immediate gratification for future stability, to acknowledge the simple confines of my bank account."

Others simply tried to ignore levels of indebtedness, even as bill collectors pressed their case.

> I was desperately trying to pretend that my financial plight did not bother me. Who wants to confront such colossal failure? Besides, it was the holidays. Gifts and parties and free champagne. Every day the mail brought Christmas cards with pictures of friends' babies doing adorable, uncanny things. The mail also brought bills. . . . In my apartment alone, I had fits of anxiety. Tears, clenched fists, the

works. I lay bug-eyed at 4 a.m., wondering how I was going to get out of this mess. I needed more time. I needed more work. What I needed was an ejector seat.[6]

The problems were not uniform, as many Americans managed their consumerism far more successfully. But the fact was that a large number of people flirted with personal financial disaster and suffered massive accompanying anxieties, as temptations piled up beyond actual earning capacity. Here, obviously, was one reason advancing acquisition not only failed to bring greater happiness, aside from brief thrills, but actually pushed in the other direction. And while Americans suffered disproportionately from these woes, similar trends began emerging elsewhere in the early 21st century. Credit card transactions pushed up by 20-30% a year in Latin America, India, Turkey, and many parts of Europe; in the United Kingdom they soared almost 400% in the decade after 1994.

The first personal measure of consumerism turning sour, then, involves the individual (as well as societal) financial pressures it began to generate, directly threatening well-being and countering any real satisfaction or compensation that contemporary levels of commitment might provide.

The second measure, though related, was even more strictly American: a virtual frenzy to gain longer hours of work in order to afford more consumer satisfactions in part for oneself, in part for family. Many people were deliberately extending their work on jobs they did not particularly like, or taking second or third jobs that brought no satisfaction and generated little but additional fatigue primarily for the sake of the consumerist hunt, often preventing enough time really to enjoy the additional acquisitions the earnings allowed. There was, arguably, an irrationality here— one worked ever harder to pay for consumerism one could not really enjoy, or share with a family—that reflected a process where consumerism was running off the rails.

Americans worked noticeably more hours than people in other advanced industrial, and indeed in many advancing industrial, societies by the early 21st century. Rates in Canada, Australia, Japan, and Mexico were about 5% less than the almost two thousand annual hours Americans were logging, in Brazil and Britain about 10% less, and in Germany a full 25% less. Compared to Western Europe, the rift began to open up as prosperity returned in the 1950s, following World War II. As Europeans began to use some of their earnings gains for longer vacations, Americans resolutely avoided systematic increases in leisure time. In some cases, this suggested greater commitment to the work ethic, but in other instances it directly reflected the demands of the particularly intense national consumer treadmill. The same contrast doomed American experiments to improve work quality, as promising efforts that moved forward in Europe were still-born amid American workers' needs for rising consumer capacity regardless of other cost. The troubling disproportion persisted into the 21st century: a 2003 poll showed 57% of all Americans preferring to work overtime for more money, only 27% opting in principle for more free time—another contrast with societies where workers were in general becoming increasingly adamant in resisting pressures to move beyond stipulated weekly hours. Consumerism, meant in part to compensate for some of the strains of modern work, seemed instead to be taking command, cart leading horse.

Obviously, the two main signs of disarray—growing, often pressing debt and unreasoned work commitments—were connected. American consumer passions were producing behaviors that, for many, generated significant new strains and reduced the potential for satisfaction. The blandishments of advertising; the deep sense that advancing consumerism was vital as a context for serving the family; the personal dependence on periodic splurges—whatever the combination, the process risked spinning out of control.

Inviting a Revisit

Consumerism has a more honorable and complex history than it sometimes gets credit for. It is not simply a record of human greed and banality, or of gullibility in the face of manipulation. It has made people happier. It has met needs and allowed new and meaningful expressions for particular groups. It has helped smooth over at least some of the rough spots of modernity.

Yet the limits of consumerism have become increasingly visible, particularly with its third phase of intensification and more particularly still in its American incarnation. Improvements in living standards over the past half-century have not led to overall happiness gains, and in many cases, thanks to excessive work and even more excessive debt, advancing consumerism has substantially heightened American anxieties. It has become difficult, given consumerism's treadmill qualities, to recognize gains that have been made, because there is always something else to want, some new reason to feel deprived. The process has come to produce a self-sustaining intensification that is socially and individually harmful. It is used to provide meaning or to compensate for more aspects of modern American life than it can possibly sustain. In consumerism, the separation of expectations from reality, which creates subtle anxieties or frustrations where death or child rearing are concerned, threatens a headlong race into futility. Consumerist passions need to be seriously reviewed, their contributions to the gap between happiness and modernity more carefully explored.

Is a review possible, against the record of two centuries in which attacks on consumerism were ultimately rebuffed by the combination of clever commercial ploys and spontaneous public needs, and in which recurrent surges cropped up with clockwork regularity every three to five decades? Reactions to the recession of 2008-2009, in which many people pulled back their spending because of the uncertainties of the economy, demonstrated that temporary adjustments were possible in response to crisis. A more durable rethinking was doubtful. Most people resented their slowed consumption and assumed that normalcy would return and with it full buying bliss. Even as the crisis wore on, credit-card-wielding shoppers periodically showed up for new purchases, proclaiming that they had been "good long enough," that denial of one of life's key focal points could only go so far. The process of rethinking consumerism would be harder than temporarily adjusting to downturns—and it might prove impossible save under a more durable *force majeure*. Here was one of the greatest challenges in adjusting modernity toward greater happiness.

We have seen that other modern responses have been revisited after they proved errant or counterproductive. Can the excessive levels of modern consumerism, despite its deep roots, be added to the list?

Further Reading

Many good studies, over the past two decades, have dealt with the history of consumerism. John Brewer and Roy Porter, *Consumption and the World of Goods*, rev. ed. (New York: Routledge, 1994), best captures the early stages of the modern process; but see also Colin Campbell, *The Romantic Ethic and the Spirit of Modern Consumerism* (Malden, MA: Blackwell, 1987), and T. H. Breen, *The Marketplace of Revolution: How Consumer Politics Shaped American Independence* (New York: Oxford University Press, 2004). Good studies of "phase two" include Michael B.

Miller, *The Bon Marché: Bourgeois Culture and the Department Store, 1869–1920* (London: George Allen and Unwin, 1981); Jackson Lears, *Fables of Abundance: A Cultural History of Advertising in America* (New York: Basic Books, 1995); Roland Marchand, *Advertising the American Dream: Making Way for Modernity, 1920–1940* (Berkeley: University of California Press, 1986); Rosalind Williams, *Dream Worlds: Mass Consumption in Late Nineteenth-Century France* (Berkeley: University of California Press, 1982); and Elaine S. Abelson, *When Ladies Go A-Thieving: Middle-Class Shoplifters in the Victorian Department Store* (New York: Oxford University Press, 1992).

On other developments see David Horowitz, *The Morality of Spending: Attitudes toward the Consumer Society in America, 1887–1940* (Baltimore, MD: Johns Hopkins University Press, 1985); Gary Cross, *Time and Money: The Making of Consumer Culture* (London: Routledge, 1993); Susan Matt, *Homesickness: An American History* (New York: Oxford University Press, 2011); Matthew Hilton, *Prosperity for All: Consumer Activism in an Era of Globalization* (Ithaca, NY: Cornell University Press, 2008); Liz Cohen, *Making a New Deal: Industrial Workers in Chicago* (New York: Cambridge University Press, 2008); and Peter N. Stearns, *Consumerism in World History: The Global Transformation of Desire*, 2nd ed. (New York: Routledge, 2006).

Conclusion

Shaping Modernity

It's time to adjust the adage, given what we know about the wide history of modernity. Those who do not know the past may indeed be condemned to repeat some of the past's mistakes. That is the conventional statement, still valid. More to the point, however: those who do not know the past cannot really appreciate the forces that actively shape the present. They cannot fully understand the context for their own lives. The formation of modernity is a long process, and we're still very much enmeshed in it.

Ongoing adjustments to modernity—including unraveling some first responses—run deep in contemporary societies. As more countries mount the modernity bandwagon, we can expect issues and responses to expand. It is impossible to know exactly how other societies will define their modernities—some common basic directions are predictable, even in areas as personal as gender or sexuality, but great variety will persist. But the theme of modernity reactions is becoming increasingly global, and while the United States is farther along in the process than some, it's still arguably in a common pool.

The challenges are not, for the most part, headline grabbers. The news flashes and the policy crises still center in those areas where modernity has clearly worsened the global experience—as in environmental disasters or the enhancement of the ugliness of war and civil strife. Or they derive from shorter-term, though often agonizing, fluctuations within the modern framework, notably in response to periodic economic downturns (which had also occurred, though in different forms, in premodern contexts as well). Or they apply to more recent changes taking place beneath the modernity umbrella, such as the transition from the Cold War to the United States' brief monopoly of great power status to the rise of newly assertive—not necessarily hostile—powers like China and Brazil. The palpable rise of fear in American society, though a current testament to the frustrations of modernity in part, obviously also owes more to a largely contemporary concatenation of forces, including new economic challenges and terrorism, than to modernity broadly construed.

We live in a society and an age glued to change. Quite apart from current headlines, we indulge a variety of futurologists bent on showing how the present is virtually unrecognizable in terms of even the recent past, and of course how different in turn everything will be by 2050. Often, these visions are hampered by historical ignorance or exaggeration—even globalization is not as totally novel as some pundits make it out to be. But it is true: change is rapid, whether we focus on the habits of the current generation of expert texters, or the probable further shifts in technology, or the rise of India and China as against American assumptions of global predominance. There's every reason to ponder what a (somewhat) altered future will hold, and how we can prepare. This book, however, has emphasized a different slice of the present: its deep and ongoing links to a profound and continuing process of modern change. It has argued that our future will depend—along with the new technologies and generational styles—on how well we cope with this inescapable process of adjusting to modernity, from definable drawbacks to false starts to excessive expectations.

For beneath the headlines and the eye-catching forecasts, there's much to ponder about our links to the transformations of modernity, even though we've been grappling as a society for many decades, and a good bit still to revise. The measurable benefits of modernity must not be forgotten, including their partial relationship to reported happiness. But the magnitude of change itself has inevitably provoked confusions and defensive reactions, and these have not yet entirely dissipated. The challenge of interpreting the modern work experience remains intriguing, and even though some improvements can be registered after initial deterioration with industrialization, a number of clear issues persist, including the ongoing difficulty of really focusing on meanings in work as opposed to external compensations. And there are plenty of other problem areas. While illustrations can be multiplied, the cases we have explored show how easy it has been—not just through general overoptimism but around specific new trends in childhood or death—to complicate modern achievements with new expectations and a sense that results still lag measurably behind what a fully modern society ought to achieve.

The desirability of focusing also on modifying initial responses—particularly where cultural standards or disputes suggest a gap between proclaimed values and actual trends, whether in sexuality or later age—adds to the picture. Here, of course, key patterns show the need for continuing adjustment, but also the fact that adjustment can occur. We've come a long way in accommodating our assumptions about gender to modernity's reduction of objective gender distinctions. Even in old age, while images of decrepitude have not fully caught up with the reality of a vigorous period—what the French call "green" old age—and while confusions about retirement will surely get worse before they get better, older people themselves have helped pull the discussion away from the extreme denigration that predominated just a century ago. Change is possible, even in far-reaching initial responses to modernity, which is why it's worth discussing additional targets.

A number of recent observers have commented on the counterproductive qualities of the excessive prods toward happiness and cheerfulness that have so long accompanied modernity, particularly in the United States. Barbara Ehrenreich, fresh from a battle with cancer, writes witheringly about the relentlessly upbeat qualities of the cancer establishment, unwilling to admit the possibility either of failure or of fear or sadness in their insistence that the whole experience will make a spunkier individual. An obvious result is a widespread need to conceal feelings that, quietly, make the whole emotional situation worse and inhibit the ability to face reality with any objectivity. While Ehrenreich correctly blames the steady rise of "positive" thinking over recent decades, we have seen that the problem goes back in time. Confrontations with modern work have, for an even longer period, faced the insistence on avoiding complaint and presenting a cheerful demeanor. Here is another challenge to reassessment, and not an easy one. Almost certainly, at least by the 20th century, key spokespeople for modernity, at the personal level, have been deepening the effects of sadness by pretending sadness should not exist.

The desirability of rethinking consumerism cuts deeply into ways that compensations for the down sides of modernity have evolved over recent decades. It's not an American problem alone. Many observers comment on the hold of consumerist goals as reactions both to the rapid ascent of modernity but also to the ideological collapse of communism in places like China. Consumerism, for lots of people, has taken on too many meanings. It need not be entirely reversed, but surely it should be cut back in favor of a richer palette of personal goals.

The evaluation of modernity does not, I admit, provide precise pre-scriptions for remediation, as opposed to identifying targets for thought-ful reconsideration. This has not been a how-to book. Nevertheless, an understanding of how modernity has evolved and how disruptive and complex it continues to be ought to provoke, and to an extent guide, new responses and even experiments toward more fully successful engage-ment. Modernity is not a process that erases informed human agency. Recent history itself demonstrates that not all current modern structures are inevitable or unchangeable. More thoughtful understanding should promote greater flexibility about aspects of modernity, including over-reaching expectations or excessive cheerfulness, that don't work well, and perhaps can never be made to work well. And while most of the issues modernity creates at the personal level are not matters for govern-ment action—with a few obvious exceptions, like adjusting some of the assumptions behind retirement—reviewing modernity, and discussing the results, ought also to promote a more collective approach to some of the problems we grapple with. Too often, and probably particularly in the United States, people have been urged to face modernity through individual decisions—about how to handle work, or death, or even eat-ing choices—rather than with community involvement and support. This is one reason why excessive consumerism, that uniquely individual recourse, has sometimes seemed so appealing.

The assumption, and hope, is that deeper grasp of how we have moved from early modernity to present levels, with some remarkably persistent problems in the process, provides a basis for more construc-tive response—even without the comfort of self-help formulas or twelve definable steps to greater happiness.

In the excitement of the various comparative happiness studies that emerged in the first decade of the 21st century, a number of observers anticipated that some national governments would begin to use happi-ness polls to help determine policy success, instead of conventional mea-sures such as GNP growth. It's an interesting concept, though fraught with difficulty given the inherent imprecision of the polls and the huge differences in cultural frameworks that condition responses. Apparently, and understandably, the whole project is now on hold given the global economic downturn, which has left so many people unhappy. Only the nation of Bhutan pressed ahead, grappling with the early stages of moder-nity and testing happiness against efforts at economic development. But whether there is a more general return to the idea of formal benchmarks or not, it is important to insist that we learn to refine our happiness inquiries, beyond adjustments for culture, to make sure we try to ask people about their responses to quality of work (and not just rewards) or (and this will sound jarring in modern culture) their adjustment to the prospect of death of self or others, or more obviously their experience as parents. We know, in other words, that modernity has produced some important pressure points in the human experience, where we can take more meaningful temperatures than overall happiness polls normally generate. And in trying to measure, we can help remind people that their own criteria should go beyond consumerism or the external prodding to appear cheerful. A social, as well as personal, commitment to become more intentional about responses to modernity would be a great step forward.

The issues involved are global, as more and more societies reach a measurable level of modernity—and without forgetting the deep problems and needs of the societies that have not, at least as yet, made the turn. A key potential benefit of greater global communication involves the opportunity to share awareness of problems and look at different, initially culturally conditioned, responses. This study has not, of course, been rigorously comparative. It has however suggested that some societies do better at certain aspects of contemporary modernity than others do. Many Americans seem to have a particularly high level of anxiety about child rearing, within a recognizable overall modern context. American consumerist commitments seem unusually excessive, and there are definitely models from other societies—consumerist, but more willing to save or more committed to use some surplus to expand leisure rather than purchasing—that merit consideration. On the other hand, the United States surged ahead in more flexible policies toward retirement and in modifying previous assumptions about older workers in the process. Mutual learning still comes hard in the global community, where it remains so tempting to stick to a purely national approach, but modernity is increasingly a global experience, and there are opportunities here.

It would be splendid to rekindle more measured optimism about the prospects of adjusting to modernity. The separation between ongoing modern trends and insistence on personal cheerfulness, on the one hand, and the decline of a larger (and more social) sense of progress on the other, during the 20th century, has been understandable but not entirely healthy. No one would wish for a return to the excessive and misleading visions of a Ben Franklin or a Condorcet. No one can ignore the huge barriers to progress that modernity throws up, for example concerning the environment. But modernity has brought many real gains. Most explicitly antimodern movements have not only ultimately failed, but have characteristically exhibited a host of unattractive features—there is no realistic or desirable option here. We can shape a modestly progressive vision around a more thoughtful acceptance of modernity. The ongoing process of adjustment must be evaluated, it should in some respects be revised, but it is still abundantly redeemable.

Further Reading

Two recent books are relevant and thought provoking. Barbara Ehrenreich, *Bright-Sided: How the Relentless Promotion of Positive Thinking Has Undermined America* (New York: Holt, 2009), argues persuasively (after a personal bout with serious disease) that our culture of cheerfulness is making it harder to gain real satisfaction. Hugh Gusterson and Catherine Besteman, eds., *The Insecure American: How We Got Here and What We Should Do about It* (Berkeley: University of California Press, 2009), is one of several important studies of the levels of (often needless) anxiety in the contemporary United States.

For a preview of the future, see Joel Kotkin, *The Next Hundred Million: America in 2050* (New York: Penguin, 2010); Immanuel Wallerstein, *The End of the World As We Know It: Social Science for the Twenty-First Century* (Minneapolis: University of Minnesota Press, 2001); and Allen Hammond, *Which World? Scenarios for the 21st Century: Global Destinies, Regional Choices* (Washington, DC: Island Press, 2000).

Notes

INTRODUCTION

1. Antoine-Nicholas Condorcet, *Outlines of an Historical View of the Progress of the Human Mind* (1795); reprint of the first English-language translation (Chicago: G. Langer, 2009).

CHAPTER 2

1. Jan Delhey, "From Materialist to Postmaterialist Happiness?" *World Values Research* 2, no. 2 (2009): 31-55, http://www.worldvaluessurvey.org; Paul Taylor, Cary Funk, Peyton Craighill (2006), "Are We Happy Yet?" Pew Research Center Social Trends Report, http://pewresearch.org/pubs/301/are-we-happy-yet.

2. Readers will note that American responses in 2003 might have been depressed by the echoes of the 2001 terrorist attacks. But pre-2001 international polls offered very similar rankings, with the United States doing well but not at the top of the charts, so the post-9/11 factor can probably be discounted. Survey data came from the Pew group, one of the most experienced and globally sensitive polling organizations.

3. Angus Deaton (2008), "Worldwide, Residents of Richer Nations More Satisfied," *Gallup World Poll Data*, http://www.gallup.com/poll/104608/Worldwide-Residents-Richer-Nations-More-Satisfied.aspx; Steve Crabtree (2008), "The Economics of Happiness," *Gallup Management Journal*, http://gmj.gallup.com/content/103549/economics-happiness.aspx.

4. Ronald Engelhart, et al., ed., *Human Beliefs and Values: A Cross-Cultural Sourcebook Based on the 1999–2002 Values Surveys*, 2nd ed. (Bilbao, Spain: Fundacion BBVA, 2004).

5. http://www.worldvaluessurvey.org/happinesstrends; Jaime Díez Medrano, *Map of Happiness*, http://www.jdsurvey.net/jds/jdsurveyMaps.jsp?Idioma=I&SeccionTexto=0404&NOID=103.

6. Arthur Kleinman and Byron Good, *Culture and Depression* (Berkeley: University of California Press, 1985).

7. *Diagnostic and Statistical Manual of Mental Disorders*, 3rd ed. (Arlington, VA: American Psychiatric Association, 1981).

8. Peter M. Lewisohn, et al., "The Symptomatic Expression of Major Depressive Disorder in Adolescents and Young Adults," *Journal of Abnormal Psychology* 112, no. 2 (2003): 244–52; Steven C. Marcus and Mark Olfson, "National Trends in the Treatment for Depression from 1998 to 2007," *Archives of General Psychiatry* 67, no. 12 (2010): 1265–73; Albert C. Gaw, *Concise Guide to Cross-Cultural Psychiatry* (Arlington, VA: American Psychiatric Publishing, 2001); "Statistics by Country for

Depression," http://www.cureresearch.com/d/depression/stats-country_printer.htm;
"Prevalence, Severity, and Unmet Need for Treatment of Mental Disorders in the
World Health Organization World Mental Health Surveys," *Journal of the American
Medical Association* 291, no. 21 (June 2, 2004): 2581–90.

9. Randolph M. Nesse (2004), "Natural Selection and the Elusiveness of Happiness,"
The Royal Society, August 31, http://www.ncbi.nlm.nih.gov/pmc/articles/PMC1693419/
pdf/15347525.pdf.

10. http://www.who.int/mental_health/prevention/suicide/suiciderates/en/;
"Mental Health in OECD Countries," *Policy Brief* (Paris: Organisation for Economic
Co-Operation and Development, November 2008).

CHAPTER 3

1. Major sources for quotations in this section are Alexander Pope, *The Works of
Alexander Pope*, vol. 1 (London: H. Lintot, J. and R. Tonson, and S. Draper, 1853); Rich-
ard Parkinson and John Byrom, *The Private Journal and Literary Remains of John Byrom*,
various volumes (Charleston, SC: Nabu Press, 2010). See also Darrin McMahon,
Happiness: A History (New York: Grove/Atlantic, 2005); and Christina Kotchemidova,
"From Good Cheer to 'Drive By Smiling': A Social History of Cheerfulness," *Journal of
Social History* 39 (2005): 5-38, which provides a cornucopia of quotations on smiling.

2. William Cobbett, *A Year's Residence in the United States of America*, 2nd ed.
(London: Sherwood, Neely, and Jones, 1819); Harriett Martineau, *Society in America,
in Three Volumes*, 2nd ed. (London: Saunders and Otley, 1837).

CHAPTER 4

1. Gregg Easterbrook, *The Progress Paradox: How Life Gets Better While People Feel
Worse* (New York: Random House, 2003).

2. Richard Morin, "America's Four Middle Classes," in *Social and Demographic
Trends* (Washington, DC: Pew Research Center Publications, 2008).

CHAPTER 5

1. "Victorian Sexuality," *Sexuality and Modernity*, 1996, http://www.isis.aust.com/
stephan/writings/sexuality/vict.htm; "The Sexual Revolution of the Sixties," *Sexuality
and Modernity*, 1996, http://www.isis.aust.com/stephan/writings/sexuality/revo.htm;
Lisa Adkins, *Revisions: Gender and Sexuality in Late Modernity* (Philadelphia: Open
University Press, 2002).

2. Marie Stopes and Ross McKibbin, *Married Love* (Oxford: Oxford University
Press, 2004).

3. U.S. Census Bureau, May 1995, Economics and Statistics Administrations, U.S.
Department of Commerce, retrieved July 2009 from http://www.census.gov/popula-
tion/socdemo/statbriefs/agebrief.html; United Nations, Department of Economic and
Social Affairs, Population Division, retrieved June 2009 from http://www.un.org/esa/
population/unpop.htm.

CHAPTER 6

1. John H. Goldthorpe, et al., *The Affluent Worker in the Class Structure* (Cambridge: Cambridge University Press, 1969).
2. Lydia Saad (2008), "U.S. Workers' Job Satisfaction Is Relatively High," August 21, retrieved from http://www.gallup.com/poll/109738/us-workers-job-satisfaction-relatively-high.aspx; John Gibbons (2010), "I Can't Get No . . . Job Satisfaction, That Is," in *The Conference Board*, January, retrieved from http://www.conference-board.org/publications/publicationdetail.cfm?publicationid=1727; Tom W. Smith, "Job Satisfaction in America," in *National Opinion Research Center Report* (Chicago: University of Chicago, April 2007).
3. Studs Terkel, *Working* (New York: Avon Books, 1972).

CHAPTER 7

1. Michael Haines (2008), "Fertility and Mortality in the United States," *EH.Net Encyclopedia*, March 19, http://eh.net/encyclopedia/article/haines.demography; Herbert Klein, *A Population History of the United States* (New York: Cambridge University Press, 2004); Malcolm Fraser, "New Zealand—Infant Mortality Rates and Still Births," in *Journal of the Royal Statistical Society* 92, no. 3 (1929): 428-44.

CHAPTER 8

1. Daniel Gilbert, *Stumbling on Happiness* (New York: Vintage Books, 2007); Fred B. Bryant and Joseph Veroff, *Savoring: A New Model of Positive Experience* (London: Psychology Press, 2006); Joseph Veroff, *The Inner American: A Self-Portrait from 1957 to 1976* (New York: Book Sales, 1981); Daniel Yankelovich, *New Rules: Searching for Self-Fulfillment in a World Turned Upside Down* (New York: Bantam Books, 1981).
2. Jeffrey J. Wood, "Parental Intrusiveness and Children's Separation Anxiety in a Clinical Example," *Child Psychiatry and Human Development* 37, no. 12 (2006): 89–102; Claire Smith, "Letting Go," retrieved from http://www.phenomenologyonline.com/sources/textorium/smith-claire-letting-go/.
3. Marvin B. Sussman, Suzanne K. Steinmetz, Gary W. Peterson, *Handbook of Marriage and the Family*, 2nd ed. (New York: Plenum Press, 1999); Lynn White and David Brinkerhoff, "Children's Work in the Family: Its Significance and Meaning," *Journal of Marriage and the Family* (1981): 789-98; Frances Cogle and Grace Tasker, "Children and Housework," *Family Relations* (July 1982): 395-99; and Sampson Blair, "Children's Participation in Household Labor," *Journal of Youth and Adolescence* 21 (1992): 241-58.
4. "Dramatic Increase in Methylphenidate Consumption in U.S.: Marketing Methods Questioned," *United Nations' Warnings on Ritalin, INCB Annual Report* 1995, 28 February 1996.
5. Kenneth A. Kiewra, et al., "What Parents, Researchers, and the Popular Press Have to Say about Homework," *scholarlypartnershipsedu*, Vol. 4, Issue 1, Article 7, retrieved from http://opus.ipfw.edu/spe/vol4/iss1/7.
6. Stanley Coopersmith, *Antecedents of Self-Esteem* (Mountain View, CA: Consulting Psychologists Press, 1981).

7. Key sources on the turn to parental emotion management include Douglas Armour Thom, *Child Management* (Washington, DC: Government Printing Office, 1925); Ernest R. and Gladys Groves, *Wholesome Childhood* (New York: Houghton, 1924); Winnifred de Kok, *Guiding Your Child through the Formative Years from Birth to the Age of Five* (New York: Emerson Books, 1935); Sidonie Gruenberg, ed., *Encyclopedia of Child Care and Guidance* (New York: Doubleday, 1959); Benjamin Spock, *Common Sense Book of Baby and Child Care* (New York: Duell, Sloan, and Pearce, 1960); Dorothy Baruch, *New Ways in Discipline* (New York: McGraw-Hill, 1949); Arthur Jersild et al., *Joys and Problems of Childrearing*, 1st ed. (New York: Bureau of Publications, Teachers College, Columbia University, 1949); and of course articles in *Parents' Magazine* from the 1920s onward.

8. Grace Palladino, *Teenagers: An American History* (New York: Basic Books, 1996).

9. The following manuals provide early illustrations of the turn toward happiness: Arthur Spalding, *Through Early Childhood: The Care and Education of the Child from Three to Nine* (Mountain View, CA: Pacific Press, 1930); Thomas Walton Galloway, *Parenthood and the Character Training of Children* (New York: Methodist Book Concern, 1927); Geraldine Foster, *The Best Method for Raising Children* (publisher unknown, 1924); Ray Beery, *Practical Child Training: Complete Set—16 Parts* (Pleasant Hill, OH: Parents Association, 1917); M. V. O'Shea, *The Parent's Library: Faults of Childhood and Youth* (Chicago: Drake, 1920); Benzion Liber, *The Child and the Home: Essays on the Rational Bringing-up of Children* (New York: Vanguard, 1927); F. J. Kieffer, *The Child and You* (Milwaukee: Bruce, 1941).

10. Joseph Veroff, *The Inner American: A Self-Portrait from 1957 to 1976*, 1st ed. (New York: Book Sales, 1985); see also S. McLanahan and J. Adams, "Parenthood and Psychological Well-Being," *Annual Review of Sociology* 13 (1987): 237–57; Stacy J. Rogers and Lynn K. White, "Satisfaction with Parenting: The Role of Marital Happiness, Family Structure, and Parents' Gender," *Journal of Marriage and the Family* 60 (1998): 293-308.

CHAPTER 9

1. Michael B. Miller, *The Bon Marché: Bourgeois Culture and the Department Store, 1869–1920* (London: Allen and Unwin, 1981).

2. Colin Campbell, *The Romantic Ethic and the Spirit of Modern Consumerism*, 3rd ed. (Alcuin Academics, 2005).

3. Thorstein Veblen, *The Theory of the Leisure Class* (New York: Macmillan, 1899).

4. Hoffman, Brinker, and Roberts, *Credit Card Debt Statistics*, 2009, retrieved from http://www.hoffmanbrinker.com/credit-card-debt-statistics.html; P. Tufane, "Consumer Finance," *Annual Review of Financial Economics* 1 (2009): 227-47, retrieved from http://www.annualreviews.org/doi/pdf/10.1146/annurev.financial.050808.114457.

5. Susan Matt, "You Can't Go Home Again: Homesickness and Nostalgia in U.S. History," *Journal of American History* 94, no. 2 (September 2007): 469-97.

6. Akweli Parker, "Easy Ways to Eliminate Credit Card Debt," December 8, 2009, retrieved from http://www.womenshealthmag.com/life/avoid-credit-card-debt; see also "Women, Debt, and the Recession," 2009, http://www.careonedebtinsights.com/wp-content/uploads/2011/01/Women-Debt-and-the-Recession-Report.pdf.

Index

abortion, 83
abstinence, 86
accidents, 147–51, 181
Acedia, 243
adolescence, 204–5
advertising, 220, 230, 241
African Americans, 26, 38, 144
Age Discrimination in Employment Act, 97
agriculture, 6, 100, 175, 196
Alger, Horatio, 115–16, 117
alienation, 114, 228, 124
allowances, 182, 235, 246
American Association of Retired Persons, 95
American Cancer Society, 146
amusement parks, 229
anger, 191, 193
anorexia nervosa, 101, 203
Ariès, Philippe, 129
art, 44, 239
Asia, 16, 17, 90
Attention Deficit Disorder, 185
Australia, 107, 108, 156, 251
automobile, 148–49, 181, 204, 228, 237

baby boom, 178, 187, 207, 242
Bangladesh, 18
Baruch, Dorothy, 193
Bhutan, 258
bicycle helmets, 145–51
bicycles, 227–28
birth rates, 38–39, 71–78, 170, 178–79, 183, 199, 227
birthdays, 199, 202, 238, 245
biting, 31, 34, 35
boredom, 9, 124, 201, 203, 243–45

Boy Scouts, 48
Brazil, 85, 201, 251, 256
Britain: boredom, 244; consumerism, 219–20, 251; environment, 64; as modernizer, 19; nutrition, 100; Victorian era, 82; workers, 111, 124
bullying, 192, 195
burnout, 122

California, 52
Campbell, Colin, 222
Canada, 23, 251
Carnegie, Dale, 48, 193
Casanova, 80
Catholicism, 79
cemeteries, 43, 133–42
cheerfulness: children's, 197–206; death, 134; modernity, 7, 20, 257–58; nostalgia, 2; workers, 111–12, 119
Chicago School (sociology), 53
child abuse, 33, 62, 174
child labor, 112, 173, 175–77
childhood, 169–210; boredom, 244, 245; consumerism, 222, 231, 240, 246; death, 132, 141, 145, 150, 151–53, 166; disease, 108; food, 101; modernity, 5, 52, 255; naming, 31, work, 37–38
Children's Bureau, 179, 185
China, 107, 112, 215–17, 239, 249, 256, 257
chores, 176
Christmas, 235, 238
Churchill, Winston, 63
Civil War, 63
clothing, 33, 34, 76, 217, 221, 229, 232–33
Cobbett, William, 42
college, 177, 187, 247

College Board, 177, 187, 188
comfort, 33–35, 135, 213, 221
communes, 8, 99
community, 37, 62, 258
commuting, 36, 103, 118, 123
comparative analysis, 7, 259
computers, 36, 119–20, 240
Comstock law, 83
conception cycle, 34
Condorcet, Nicolas de, 1, 50
consumerism, 213–54; children, 182,
    199–200; happiness, 19, 24, 47, 199;
    industrialization, 33–34; old age, 95;
    standards of living, 15; youthfulness,
    34–35
contraception, 78–89
corsets, 105
Costa Rica, 17
cremation, 143, 165
crime, 53
cross-marketing, 237
crusades, 216

dating, 85, 234
day care, 171, 205
de Wendel, François, 49
death, 5, 39–40, 95, 131–67
debt, 250
Denmark, 16–19
dentistry, 43
department stores, 229, 235
Depression (1930s), 94, 102, 104, 199, 236
depression (psychological), 21–26, 139,
    203, 251
Diana, Princess, 162
dieting, 104, 106
disease, 101, 136–37, 178, 203
Disney Company, 45–46, 173, 200, 201–2,
    203
divorce, 152, 201, 207, 233
drugs, 181

Easterbrook, Gregg, 62
economists, 101
education, 15, 50–51, 75–76, 170, 173–78,

    184–87, 197
Ehrenreich, Barbara, 255
electronics, 240
embalming, 134
emotions, 189–95, 221–22
engineers, 117, 148–49, 157
Enlightenment, 1–2, 50–52; children,
    172–73, 198; consumerism, 213, 217;
    happiness, 41; longevity, 89; optimism,
    69
environment, 55, 64–65, 214, 248–49
envy, 225
Esquirol, Jean-Etienne, 22
etiquette, 239–40, 244
euthanasia, 155–56
extended families, 62–63

factories, 4, 36, 90–92, 111–16, 126
family, 71–78; childhood death, 40, 135,
    151–52; children, 40, 169; consumer-
    ism, 231, 237, 240, 246; extended,
    62–63; happiness, 19; old age, 95; war,
    63; work, 37–38, 111, 114, 117, 221
famines, 100–102
fathers, 38–39, 169–210
fear: childhood, 170, 173, 194, 235; death,
    137–38, 145–46, 165, 167; war, 65
feminism, 71, 72, 86, 98, 101
festivals, 70, 118
Fletcher, Horace, 104
food, 99–108, 100, 204
foot binding, 71
Ford, Henry, 119
forks, 224–25
France: advertising, 220; children, 184;
    consumerism, 220, 224, 236; disease,
    93, 107; happiness, 16, 19; obesity, 107;
    old age, 93, 97; vacation, 3
Franklin, Benjamin, 1, 50, 115
Freud, Sigmund, 44
Friedman, Thomas, 53, 63
Fukuyama, Frank, 53
funeral homes, 143–44

genocide, 55

Germany, 93, 185, 251
Gibson Girl, 105
global warming, 64
Graham, Billy, 45
Graham crackers, 84, 213
grandparents, 63, 180, 183, 194
Gray Panthers, 98
Greece, 90
grief, 42, 43, 131–67, 189, 193, 207

Halloween, 141, 206
happiness: children, 195–205; consumer-
    ism, 213–14, 217, 235–36, 243–44,
    247, 249–52; death, 131, 139, 159;
    disease, 106; modernity, 6, 8; obesity,
    106; work, 111–12
health, 103, 112, 178
health care reform, 108
helicopter parents, 196, 208
high school, 177, 186
hikikomari, 188
Hollywood, 226
Holocaust, 55, 161
homework, 171, 187
homosexuality, 87
hospices, 141–47, 155
hospitals, 136, 153–55
humanitarianism, 56, 101, 163
hunger strikes, 101
hygiene, 149, 180, 183, 228
hysterical paralysis, 21–22

illegitimacy, 32, 79, 85–86
immigrants, 4, 149, 175, 207, 226, 231
impatience, 9
imperialism, 54–55
India, 22
industrial psychology, 119
Industrial Revolution, 4, 37, 111, 215,
    223–24
instrumentalism, 116–28, 232
insurance, 104, 150, 154, 158
Iran, 76
Iraq war, 153
Ireland, 19, 100

Islam, 71, 79, 83

Jackson, Michael, 162
James, Alice, 21
Janus, Anna, 234–35
Japan: children, 180, 188, 202; consumer-
    ism, 226–27, 231, 239, 251; death, 142;
    environment, 64; gender, 37, 39, 74,
    76; happiness measures, 16–17, 19;
    old age, 97–98; pregnancy rates, 85;
    retirement, 94
jealousy, 183, 189–90, 192–93
Johnson, Samuel, 91
juvenile delinquency, 180, 192

Kellogg cereal, 84, 213
Kellogg-Briand pact, 54
Key, Ellen, 180
kidnapping, 205–6
kissing, 31
kleptomania, 235–36
Korea, 20, 25
Korean War, 153
Kübler-Ross, Elisabeth, 145

LaCrosse, Wisconsin, 158
Lasch, Christopher, 73, 183–84
laugh tracks, 47
leisure: consumerism, 227, 229, 251; hap-
    piness, 15; industrialization, 70; mod-
    ern work, 118; old age, 95; time, 36
Lennon, John, 160–61
lithium, 23
living wills, 145–46, 157
longevity, 51, 54, 88–89, 103–4, 132,
    135–36
Lordstown, Ohio, 126
love, 32–33, 84, 146, 221
Luddism, 114
lypemania, 22

machines, 117, 148–49, 157
malpractice, 156
Martineau, Harriet, 43
masculinity, 38–39, 71–78, 117

masturbation, 81–82, 86
Matt, Susan, 242
Mexico, 17, 19, 23, 25, 251
millennium, 52
Miller, Michael, 215
mobility, 117–18, 125
modernization, 6–7
mortality, 3, 40, 89, 131–67, 178, 183
Mosher Survey, 84
mothers, 39, 40, 71–78, 133, 149,
    164–210, 234–75
Mother's Day, 234–35
mourning. *See* grief
Mt. Auburn cemetery, 133
museums, 239

Nabisco, 102
naming, 31, 35, 172
nervous breakdown, 121–22
Nesse, Randolph, 24
Netherlands, 154, 156, 169, 217
neurasthenia, 121, 231
New Zealand, 17, 136
nostalgia, 2–3, 54, 61, 66, 242
nuclear weapons, 55, 65
nutrition, 101, 104

obedience, 174, 190, 197
obesity, 5, 70, 99–108, 136
Oklahoma City bombing, 161
old age: consumerism, 257; death, 156;
    disease, 50; life expectancy, 136; mo-
    dernity, 33–34, 35, 259; war, 63
original sin, 172, 174, 196
Oxfam, 102

Palin, Sarah, 159
parents. *See* childhood
Parents' Magazine, 179
Paris, 3, 105
pathology, 92
patriarchy, 71, 76
pediatrics, 178, 179, 183
pets, 239, 241–42
Pew survey, 261n1 ch. 2
photographs, 47, 199

piano, 227
play, 174–75, 196, 200, 208
playgrounds, 179
politics, 239
polls, 15–26, 123–25, 169, 209–10, 246
Polo, Marco, 216
Pope, Alexander, 42
pornography, 80, 82, 85
Post, Emily, 139, 244
privacy, 31, 34
progress, 49–56
prostitutes, 78
Protestantism, 42, 72, 79, 171, 221, 225
Puerto Rico, 17, 18

religion, 9, 143, 213, 223
report cards, 177
retirement, 5, 88–99, 118, 125, 259
risk, 147–51
Ritalin, 185
Roosevelt, Franklin, 47, 48
rubber, 81
Russia, 39, 48, 73–74, 116, 226

sadness, 25, 139, 203, 257
safety, 148
savings, 238
scales, 103
school: boredom, 244; children, 175,
    184–87; clock time, 36; gender, 74;
    meals, 101; parental involvement, 208;
    performance, 247
science, 51, 57, 138, 179–80
self-esteem, 180, 197, 201
self-help, 46–49
Selye, Hans, 112
senility, 92
September 11, 2001, 161–62, 207, 247
sex education, 86
sex offenses, 206
sexuality, 78–88; consumerism, 222, 233;
    modernity, 15; old age, 95; sexual
    revolution, 32–33
shopkeepers, 219
shopping malls, 241
sibling rivalry. *See* jealousy

siblings, 152, 183, 193–5, 235
smiles, 43, 46–47, 119, 134, 193
snacks, 102–3, 204
soap, 228
soccer moms, 39, 208
social class, 7–8
Social Security, 94, 95, 98
Spanish Civil War, 63
spanking, 174
Spock, Benjamin, 175, 194–95, 199
sports, 36, 175, 187, 202, 228, 232
Stewart, Martha, 3, 242
Stopes, Marie, 87
stress, 37, 120–23, 208, 251
Sudden Infant Death Syndrome, 40
suicide, 24–26, 150, 188–89
sumptuary laws, 217
swimsuits, 105

tanning, 105
telework, 39, 119
temperance, 74
Temple, Shirley, 199
Terkel, Studs, 124
terrorism, 63, 65, 161–62, 256
Thanatos, 140
time, 34–36, 113, 115
torts, 150–51
toys, 187, 194, 202, 237

unions, 93, 117, 120

vacations, 118, 201, 203–4, 251
Valentine's Day, 233
Vanderbilt, Amy, 139–40
Veblen, Thorstein, 231
Victorianism, 81, 84, 190
Vietnam War, 153
Virginia Tech, 162–63

war, 51, 54–55, 63, 65
watches, 35, 121
Watson, John, 199
Wedgwood, Josiah, 220
white collar, 117, 119, 232
wigs, 33
women, 71–78, 81–88; beauty,
    105; cheerfulness, 42; consumerism,
    214, 233, 238, 246; magazines,
    133; morality, 81–82; sexuality,
    82–88; Victorianism, 82–88; work,
    37–39
work, 35–39, 71–78, 111–27; consumer-
    ism, 232, 246, 252, 257; modernity, 19,
    91; old age, 95–96
world trade, 218–19, 249
World War I, 54
world's fairs, 229

Yalta, 48
YMCA, 202
youthfulness, 33–35, 90, 91
yuppies, 240

About the Author

PETER N. STEARNS, Provost and University Professor at George Mason University, has authored or edited over 115 books. He has published widely in modern social history, including the history of emotions, and in world history. He has also edited encyclopedias of world and social history, and since 1967 has served as editor-in-chief of *The Journal of Social History.*